D0970211

SOCIAL TRUST

SOCIAL TRUST

Toward a Cosmopolitan Society

TIMOTHY C. EARLE
and
GEORGE T. CVETKOVICH

Westport, Connecticut
London

Library of Congress Cataloging-in-Publication Data

Earle, Timothy C.
    Social trust : toward a cosmopolitan society / Timothy C. Earle
and George T. Cvetkovich.
        p.   cm.
    Includes bibliographical references and index.
    ISBN 0-275-94845-5 (alk. paper)
    1. Social psychology.   2. Trust (Psychology).   I. Cvetkovich,
George.   II. Title.
    HM251.E18   1995
    302—dc20   94-45265

British Library Cataloguing in Publication Data is available.

Library of Congress Catalog Card Number: 94-45265
ISBN: 0-275-94845-5

First published in 1995

Praeger Publishers, 88 Post Road West, Westport, CT 06881
An imprint of Greenwood Publishing Group, Inc.

Printed in the United States of America

The paper used in this book complies with the
Permanent Paper Standard issued by the National
Information Standards Organization (Z39.48–1984).

10 9 8 7 6 5 4 3 2 1

To Bo and Erin Earle

and

To Frances, Mark, and Chris Cvetkovich

As images of time were shifting and the horror of stagnation in the tomb was taking deeper root, the shore, that place of longing where the elements converge, offered the sight of the restless sea to all those who feared the miasma and sought out the foam instead.

Alain Corbin, The Lure of the Sea

I am seeking a knowledge that is finally adult, a balanced wisdom, a certain forgetfulness of death. It is not a bad thing to place oneself on the verge of my picture, where wildness begins, and where knowledge begins. Places of transition are always fecund.

Michel Serres, Literature and the Exact Sciences

Contents

Preface

Our friend and colleague, Jacques Lochard, suggested this classic case of social trust. A man walks along a seashore. He sees a disturbance among the grains of sand spread before him. The man is Robinson Crusoe, and he sees the form in the sand as the print of a human foot. A single print. Of a single foot. Since Crusoe had long thought of himself as the sole human inhabitant of "his" island, the print, though singular, was significant. It wasn't, he was certain, his own. And social trust enters here. Crusoe must decide if the footprint is a sign of good or a sign of evil. He must decide, in other words, if the footprint was made by someone like him—someone similar and friendly to him—or was made by someone different from and antagonistic to him.

Robinson Crusoe's choice was this: he could decide that the footprint was made by a friend, or he could decide that the footprint was made by an enemy. The choice was between similarity and difference. Between trust and distrust. According to Defoe, Crusoe made the latter decision. He chose distrust. He fortified his positions, and he prepared to defend himself. Why? On the evidence available to him, a simple disturbance—perhaps a human footprint—in the sand, Crusoe could as well have decided that rescue, at long last, was at hand! But no. Crusoe decided that his enemy—someone different from him, not his rescuer—had unsettled the sand.

And in choosing distrust over trust, Crusoe chose his past over his future. Crusoe's adventurous past was burdened by bad experiences with other people. His future, of course, was unknown. Crusoe chose to make his future like his past. And his past ruled his future for many years. Until he was presented with an opportunity to change his mind. And he did. He decided that Friday, escaping from his captors, was like him—that Friday was a man he could trust. From then on, Crusoe's future was free from his past—he could make of it, try to at least, what he pleased.

The story of Robinson Crusoe tells us this about social trust: it is based on cultural similarity. We trust people we take to be similar to us. And similarity is a matter of imagination, narration, and persuasion—not of evidence and argument. We create similarities when we want to move into the future; we uncover differences when we prefer to stick with the past. Like Robinson Crusoe, we can choose to move forward or backward; we can enter the future or remain in the past.

The struggle between the past and the future is a central theme of our book. It consists of three parts: Part I on the past, Part II on the present, and Part III on the future of social trust. In the course of this story, from the past to the future, we come to distinguish two forms of social trust—pluralistic and cosmopolitan. Pluralistic social trust occurs within groups and is based on existing values. Rooted in the past, pluralistic social trust tends toward singularity and stasis. Cosmopolitan social trust is an across-group phenomenon and is based on emerging values. Open to the future, cosmopolitan social trust favors multiplicity and change. Pluralistic and cosmopolitan social trust support opposing ways of life. This struggle—between past and future, singular and multiple, stasis and change, pluralistic and cosmopolitan social trust—is endless, a part of life. As Richard Rorty might say, there are connoisseurs of the past and connoisseurs of the future. In this book, we try to identify ourselves as the latter. And our story of social trust is the story of gradual movement from the pluralistic to the cosmopolitan.

We have been very fortunate in the development of our understanding of social trust to have benefited from discussions with and comments from a number of colleagues and friends. Paul Slovic, Baruch Fischhoff, Robin Gregory, Karl Dake, Tim McDaniels, Roger Kasperson, and Ray Badard were all generous with their ideas and encouragement. Our major intellectual debts are owed, on a general level, to Richard Rorty and Martha Nussbaum, who together express the brilliant multiplicity of cosmopolitanism. We gratefully acknowledge the financial support of the Decision, Risk and Management Science and Ethics and Values Studies programs of the National Science Foundation. Finally, there are two persons without whom this book could not have been written. Jacques Lochard, our model cosmopolitan, and Bo Earle, from whom one of us (T.C.E.) learned all he knows about trust. We thank them, cosmopolitans all!

Timothy C. Earle
George T. Cvetkovich
Spring, 1995

SOCIAL TRUST

Part I

SOCIAL TRUST: PAST

In "Part I, Social Trust: Past," we present an account of the ways people have, up until the present time, thought and talked about and dealt with social trust. There are three chapters. In Chapter 1, we begin by describing the recent growth of interest in social trust, particularly in the field of environmental risk management. We then outline the history of social trust, from ancient to modern times. Finally, we describe the pioneering empirical studies of trust in mid-twentieth-century America. In Chapter 2, we describe the interpretations of social trust that have traditionally dominated public discourse on the subject in America, and we show the relations of those traditional accounts to American democratic culture. In Chapter 3, we suggest an alternative interpretation of social trust as a strategy for the reduction of cognitive complexity. This description provides the context in which social trust is compared with its functional equivalents—other complexity-reducing strategies—in Part II.

1

Social Trust: An Introduction

Social trust is one of those topics, like safety, that a lot of people are interested in because its presumed opposite seems ubiquitous and troublesome. The connection is made this way. If we can only increase social trust, we can decrease social distrust; or if we can decrease risk we can increase safety. But of course nothing is this simple. Reduced risk, as Aaron Wildavsky reminds us, doesn't necessarily produce safety.[1] As for increasing social trust? Unfortunately, those who want to do this—persons, for example, who want to "make government work"—don't seem to know how to proceed. Beginning with a concern about—and working within a context dominated by—social distrust, they have been unable to produce fresh, appealing, workable ways of talking about, encouraging and enacting social trust. As a consequence, so-called trust-building schemes wind up, sadly—inevitably—where they started, in relations dominated by social distrust. In this introductory chapter, we want, first, to briefly describe how this destructive—and, we argue, unnecessary—linkage between social trust and social distrust controls public discourse in a critically important activity in contemporary America, environmental risk management. We then outline a history of social trust, from ancient to modern times, that suggests that social trust is a tool for social organization that, although always threatened by the shadow of social distrust, has evolved independently of it. Finally, we describe the first empirical studies of social trust, conducted in mid-twentieth-century America, and we indicate how those studies contributed to the coupling of social trust and social distrust in contemporary discourse.

SOCIAL TRUST IN ENVIRONMENTAL RISK MANAGEMENT

Social trust, understood in everyday terms, is the process by which individuals assign to other persons, groups, agencies, or institutions the responsibility to work on certain tasks. Within the realm of risk management, most tasks are too big and complex for individuals, regardless of technical training, to successfully complete alone.[2] As a result, for any particular risk management task most of us have either to work with or assign our responsibility to others. And since each of us is faced with more tasks than our time and abilities will enable us to tackle, even with the help of others, each of us sooner or later must confront the problem of social trust. Social trust, recognized as such or not, has served a critical social function throughout the modern era. Only very recently, however, has it attracted attention within the risk management community.

Discussion of social trust by government officials or by independent agency critics has generally followed from policy failures—failures attributed to public opposition or to an unwillingness to cooperate. The problem, the officials and critics typically say, is too much social distrust or, alternatively, too little social trust. To demonstrate the developing understanding of social trust in risk management, we outline two cases: one, dealing with the U.S. Environmental Protection Agency (EPA), is concerned with social distrust; the other, involving the U.S. Department of Energy, is centered on social trust. In both cases, however, social trust is inextricably linked with social distrust.

U.S. ENVIRONMENTAL PROTECTION AGENCY

When social trust and social distrust are linked, a judged increase in one is attributed to a decrease in the other. Unlinked, social trust and social distrust vary independently.[3] We consider both interpretations.

Distrust as Loss of Trust

One way to deal with distrust is to treat it simply as a loss of trust. In this approach, it is assumed that the normal (OK) state of affairs is based on social trust, and things go wrong when trust is "lost." This is the tack taken by Thomas McGarity (1986) who claims that, for the most part, the "risk assessment and risk management enterprise rests upon public trust in the institution or institutions charged with that enterprise . . ." (p. 10200). Thus, social trust is inherent at the beginning. But then things go wrong.[4] "In recent years the regulatory agencies have lost a large measure of the public trust that they enjoyed during the 1970s" (p. 10200). Referring primarily to the EPA, McGarity attributes the loss of trust to misdeeds by government officials and bureaucrats.

Can anything be done to pump social trust back up to its normal level? McGarity suggests "full participation" in agency decision making—by which he means "that outsiders should participate in the actual decision making process" and that members of scientific advisory committees "should be chosen with an eye toward the interest groups that will be affected by their recommendations" (p. 10204). McGarity would restore trust by restoring competition among interest groups—"pluralistic scientific policy making." He says his proposals "need not represent drastic departures from the 'interest representation' model that has dominated health and environmental decision making since the early 1970s" (p. 10202). In brief, McGarity believes that social trust and interest group representation are natural bedfellows, mutually supportive. We disagree.[5] And in this book we will, in part, present the contrary argument that "interest group representation" and other adversarial models are based on, and create, social distrust. Further, we will attempt to show that, under certain circumstances, participation based on social trust can be creative, a force for personal and social change. In contrast, participation based on distrust, as in McGarity's case, freezes positions and supports the status quo.

Distrust as Distrust

Another way to deal with social distrust is to call it by its name and work to understand what caused it and what is maintaining it. This is the approach taken by Richard Lazarus in his admirable analysis of the EPA's history as a "tragedy of distrust" (1991). In Lazarus's account, distrust was built into the EPA from the beginning—the agency being torn between environmentalists and the regulated community, between executive and legislative branches of government, between a public wanting things done and a public unwilling to change. Significantly, Lazarus does not find the locus of distrust in any one faction: dstrust is social, cultural, a strategy shared by all involved. Most important, Lazarus does not exempt the public and treat us as though we were simply innocents sinned against. Distrust, in this case, is a cultural norm, followed, consciously or not, by (almost) all.

How to escape the cycle of distrust? Lazarus offers a number of organizational reforms. But more to the point of our interest in social trust are his comments on the relations between the public and the EPA. Lazarus repeats the common observation that risk assessment depends on both technical knowledge and cultural values, the domain of the expert and the domain of the public. The two groups, Lazarus says, need to learn from each other. If the EPA "ignores the public's distinct perception of risk," he warns, "the agency's resolution of acceptable levels of risk and relative agency priorities will find little acceptance where the agency needs it most: in the public" (pp. 373-374). But risk management can't be simply a matter of pleasing the public: Neither the public nor the EPA should be allowed a pat position. To escape the cycle of distrust, all interests must be open to persuasion, to change.

Some Consequences of How We Think and Talk about Distrust

For us, the contrast between how McGarity and Lazarus discuss distrust is instructive in two ways. First, it demonstrates that how we think and talk about distrust, or any concept, can have significant effects on the conclusions we draw and the actions we take.[6] Thus, McGarity talks about distrust as a loss of social trust. But social trust is treated like a state of grace, a phantom that, when lost, is at best very difficult to find again. Consequently, McGarity's analysis leads nowhere; we are left with only nostalgic feelings for a perhaps never-existent state before the fall. Lazarus, in contrast, grounds his thinking about distrust in the battles between conflicting political interests. Distrust is a strategy of social interaction used by groups driven by self-interest and convinced that everyone else is too. The consequences of thinking about distrust in this perhaps dismal-seeming way can, in some senses, be positive. At least it hints at possible ameliorative action.

A second way in which the contrast between McGarity and Lazarus is instructive is that it suggests that it is easier for us, in our culture, to think about social distrust than about social trust. Very little has been written about social trust, and much of what has been written has been motivated by a concern not about social trust but about distrust. It seems to us that this is a needlessly negative approach to social trust, confessing neither interest in nor value placed on social trust *as such*. But one step at a time. For now—as in our second case—we approach social trust via social distrust.

U.S. DEPARTMENT OF ENERGY

Spurred by public opposition to its radioactive waste management policies, the Department of Energy (DOE) has recently developed a strenuous program aimed at "earning public trust and confidence."[7] The designers of the DOE program define their key concepts this way:

- TRUST: The belief that those with whom one interacts intend to behave in a manner that takes into account one's interests even in situations where neither partner is in a position to evaluate and/or thwart a potentially negative course of action.
- CONFIDENCE: The judgment that those with whom one interacts are competent to carry out their responsibilities and have the capacity to fulfill their commitments even in situations where considerable effort must be expended.
- TRUSTWORTHY: Meriting both the trust and confidence.

(U.S. Department of Energy, 1993, p. 14)

This set of definitions is most notable for its attempt to meld two seemingly incompatible interpretations of social trust. First, trust is said to be based on a judgment of *responsibility*—that one's interests will be "taken into account" by "those with whom one interacts."[8] Unfortunately, no explicit discussion is given on how judgments of responsibility are made. Are these judgments based on some set of universal, abstract criteria that we all agree are appropriate? Or are they based, perhaps, on some simplifying heuristic such as similarity of interests? On this latter interpretation, social trust would be strictly a within-group affair—ethnocentric, fractionating, conflict-producing—not a promising tool for the management of highly contentious, cross-group environmental problems. To be useful, this raw, untamed form of social trust would somehow have to be brought under control.

Their interpretation of responsibility aside, the DOE designers nonetheless elected to qualify *social trust* by aligning it with *confidence* in their definition of *trustworthy*. To be worthy of trust, they say, one must merit both trust *and* confidence. To be worthy of trust, that is, one must be judged to be both responsible and competent. Since trust and confidence are separate, independent judgments, the *trust* in *trust*worthy is different from, a restricted version of, trust as such. The DOE designers have tried to tame social trust by defining a range of domesticated trust judgments that are linked with judgments of competence. To be legitimate, to be *rational*, social trust should be based on judgments of both trust and confidence, responsibility and competence.

With definitions out of the way, and after discussing the importance of social trust and confidence to the operations of American government, the DOE Task Force goes on to lay out a statement of first principles. "These principles are subject to neither analytic nor empirical confirmation"; they say, "rather they represent underlying beliefs that were brought to the table or were crystallized at it. They are akin, therefore, to axioms in geometry: alter them and the conclusions may change radically" (p. 20). It is this brief statement of three principles, together with the design basis that follows from it, that best defines and delimits the DOE approach to social trust. Principle number one, for example, is this:

> *Public trust and confidence is not a luxury. DOE not only has an obligation to earn it, but it also has a compelling need to do so.*
>
> (p. 20)

The key words here are "to earn it"—social trust is interpreted as something that can be earned by behaving in appropriate—responsible and competent—ways. Judgments of social trust, in brief, are based on evidence. DOE considers no alternative, perhaps less standardly rational constructions.

Standard, technological rationality, rationality based on procedures and evidence, also dominates principle number two:

> *Public trust and confidence is not a one-way street. DOE must trust the public before it can expect the public to trust it. By the same token, the public and its representatives must be held to a standard of behavior that is itself trustworthy.*
>
> (p. 20)

It would seem that one of the basic functions of social trust is to *relieve* individuals of the responsibility of universal competence. To share the responsibility with others. To not have to worry about everything all of the time. Social trust on this construction is inherently, openly, and proudly, *one way*. But the DOE designers insist otherwise. Why? Perhaps owing to ideology. The DOE plan for social trust espouses a strong, egalitarian, participatory democracy, and this may require two-way trust. Or the DOE's desire for two-way trust—and for a public that is trustworthy—may simply be another, more acceptable way of saying that the DOE wants the public to participate on the DOE's grounds, to share the DOE's values, interests, and methods.

Principle number three in the DOE plan states that it is usually preferable to make decisions in an open forum as opposed to deliberations closed to the public. There is little to commend or object to here. More interesting to us are some of the nine "essential conditions" identified in the design basis for the DOE social trust plan. Condition number two, for example:

> *The parties must possess the competence to understand the technical and institutional problems others face and the solutions advanced to address them.*
>
> (p. 20)

In addition to the demand for universal technical competence—another version of the be-like-us argument—this condition also, contrarily, encourages parties to maintain their present positions, to interpret their current ways of doing things as somehow privileged, correct, not open to change.[9] This push toward stasis is plainly expressed in condition number five:

> *One party must not be compelled to work against the interests of any other party.*
>
> (p. 21)

Here, the existing interests of parties are enshrined: what exists is good; change is a threat to all. But change is necessary for the solving of problems—moving from a negative state to a more positive one. The current negative state is the product of conflict among existing interests. Moving to a more positive state necessarily entails changes in interests.[10] This is the central contradiction in the DOE social trust plan. Because it insists on maintaining existing interests, the DOE plan encourages *within-group social trust* and *across-group social distrust*. By failing to distinguish between within-group and across-group social trust, the DOE plan maintains the historic link between social trust and social distrust: social trust produces social distrust. This crucial distinction between forms of social trust—we call the within-group variety *pluralistic*, the across-group type *cosmopolitan*—is discussed in Part III of this book. Following that discussion, in our final chapter, we revisit the DOE social trust plan to examine some of its findings and recommendations. Toward those ends, we continue now by placing our contemporary discussion of social trust in a historical context.

SOCIAL TRUST: A BRIEF HISTORY

A simple but useful way of talking about the history of social trust can be based on two distinctions. The first is between pre-modern and modern societal systems. The internal differentiation of pre-modern societies was based on segmentation or stratification, forms of differentiation that limited societal complexity. Modern societies, in contrast, are differentiated on the basis of functional subsystems. This modern form of system building has produced increasing societal complexity.[11] Modern societies are more complex than pre-modern. The second distinction is between interpersonal trust and social trust. Interpersonal trust is based on the interaction of individuals. Through interaction, individuals can learn from and about each other. In the case of social trust, opportunities for interaction and learning are typically limited.[12] In talking of social trust, what he calls *trust in systems*, Anthony Giddens (1990) notes that it "takes the form of *faceless commitments*, in which faith is sustained in the workings of knowledge of which the lay person is largely ignorant" (p. 88). Interpersonal trust, the more basic form, was generally sufficient to the needs of relatively simple pre-modern societies. Modern societies, characterized by "extended time-space distanciation" (p. 87) and complex functional differentiation, have become more dependent on social trust.

Although in modern societies interpersonal trust and social trust often operate together,[13] the history of social trust can be interpreted as the story of its increasing relative importance as the complexity of society increased. Our brief account of this story is based, first, on a general description of the construction of trust in society. Second, we examine trust in ancient Greece. We then discuss trust in feudal society. Finally, we examine the transition of trust to the demands of the modern age.[14]

THE CONSTRUCTION OF TRUST IN SOCIETY

S. N. Eisenstadt's account of the construction of trust in society is filled with surprising delights (Eisenstadt and Roniger, 1984). One of them is that he and his co-author insist on associating ambivalence with trust. The construction of social trust entails the moving away from the simple and familiar and toward the complex and, at first at least, the strange. The force creating the tension between the old and the new is that between solidarity with one's own and prosperity in the world. The conditions that favor the maintenance of trust, Eisenstadt points out, "are inimical to the development of resources and activities needed for broader institutional complexes based on more variegated and differentiated orientations and criteria" (p. 30). The construction of social trust is always problematic, "dependent on the effective construction of broader ranges of meaning, on the extension of the symbolism of trust beyond the narrow minimal range of ascriptive primordial units, and on the connection of such trust with the organisation of broader scopes of more differentiated activities and free resources generated through the extension of instrumental and power activities" (p. 30). The benefits of trust are in the future; the costs are now. Thus, an attitude of ambivalence toward social trust is induced within society.

Another delight of Eisenstadt's discussion of trust is his unflinching[15] coupling of trust and elites, the carriers of cultural values:

> The specification of the principles of generalised exchange and of its relations with specific exchange, and the institutionalisation of those principles through the setting up of public goods and titles, are effected in all societies by institutional entrepreneurs or elites. They attempt, in collaboration or in competition, to mobilise and structure the major resources available in a society. Such undertakings are influenced by the nature of the conceptions or "visions" which inform the activities of these elites, derived above all from the major cultural orientations or code prevalent in that society. Through these, they combine the structuring of trust, provision of meaning, and regulation of power with the division of labour in society.
>
> (p. 38)

In this brief paragraph, Eisenstadt sums up much of the core argument that we present in this book: *social trust is based on cultural values that are communicated in narrative form within society by elites.*[16]

In addition to giving us a useful description of trust, Eisenstadt draws upon studies of societies, historical and contemporary, throughout the world to interpret the development of trust. In relatively simple societies with low levels of differentiation, trust tends to be tied to existing social institutions. The realm of privacy is limited, thus dampening creative initiatives in social trust.

Complex, highly differentiated societies, in contrast, provide room for privacy and thus a place for experiments in social trust. In modern societies there usually are tensions between interpersonal relations and relations with social institutions. Interpersonal relations lead to interpersonal trust and this can lead to new forms of social trust. These latter may be in opposition to established centers of society. Under normal, noncrisis conditions, however, opposition is "couched in terms of the upholding of pure interpersonal relations and values which necessarily go beyond any existing institutional order, but which on the whole accept such orders within their own realms" (p. 290). Crises tend to occur when legitimate access to the central institutions is judged to be blocked. The connection between individuals and the center is broken, social trust is withdrawn, and social order is threatened.

But the interplay of interpersonal trust and social trust depends to a large degree on societal conceptions of the individual. If the individual is talked of as independent from social groups, then social trust suffers and distrust may come to dominate society.[17] If, on the other hand, persons are described as related to social groups, then social trust in general can be enhanced: "We see thus that the construction of areas of trust through different interpersonal relations and the working out of the major tensions inherent in them is indeed very closely connected—in a dialectic fashion—with the modes of institutionalisation of trust within the social order" (p. 301). Social trust requires social individuals, and social individuals require social trust. Social trust is cultural.

TRUST IN ANCIENT GREECE

Drawing in part from the work of Eisenstadt and Roniger, Thomas Gallant (1991) has described how the ancient Greeks constructed trust as a means of coping with the dangerous uncertainties of life, particularly famine: "No household is an island unto itself" (p. 143). Gallant examines a wide range of ancient Greek writings for evidence of: (a) an ideology of social equality; (b) an ethos of reciprocity and obligation; and (c) the concept of limited resources (e.g., food). Given these elements, forms of trust can be inferred.[18] The form of trust that Gallant identifies is, from our modern perspective, a very limited one. The ancient Greek household was not isolated and self-reliant, but its spheres of support did not reach far: "At the heart of the network was the household; next came kinsmen, then friends (ritual and institutional), neighbors, quasi-associations, and finally patrons" (p. 152).

Society in ancient Greece had a relatively simple structure and relations of trust were primarily interpersonal, with vertical ties between clients and patrons, rich and poor. Even this limited form of trust declined when, in the Hellenistic period (after the death of Alexander the Great in 323 B.C.) the rich elites became stronger and, freed from the need for local legitimation, dissolved their reciprocal relations with the poor. Food was still furnished during crises, but not on the basis of trust relations. "Relief was now provided on terms and in forms which were markedly different from the previous period. The result was that in the long run the peasantry paid a much steeper premium for its subsistence insurance" (p. 196). And it was not the last time that the loss of trust proved costly.[19]

TRUST IN FEUDAL SOCIETY

As in ancient Greece and in all societies, people in feudal Europe needed to protect themselves from risks and dangers of all kinds, to establish some predictable order in their lives. Social predictability in the feudal epoch was based on what J. Douglas Canfield calls the "master trope" of the "hegemonic code," the pledged word, or "word as bond" (1989, p. xi).[20] The theme of word as bond, Canfield shows, was central to English feudal literature because it was the master trope of feudal society as a whole. According to Canfield, "The German unifying principle of *comitatus* combined with Roman contract law to produce a society based upon oaths of fealty, sanctioned first by pagan then by Christian gods. As society centralized, fealty also became centralized, attached to the person of the king" (p. xii). Was this a form of trust? Owing to the relatively simple differentiation of feudal society, only very limited, interpersonal forms of trust were possible: "[F]ealty was a personal affair, a bond between persons, modeled on the bond between fathers and sons and uttered as a word— an oath of allegiance" (p. xii). Since feudal society was patriarchal and patrilineal, "Political and sexual fidelity were essential, and they were enforced not only with swords but with words" (p. xiv).

Among the texts that Canfield interprets is the political tragedy *Macbeth*. By killing King Duncan in that play, Macbeth, as Canfield says, "has murdered trust itself" (p. 190). Macbeth lives on, a tyrannical ruler, but is destroyed in the end by the workings of distrust. For Canfield, the play "signifies the efficacy of trust, the necessity of loyalty, and the ultimate vindication of those who keep their word despite their overwhelming suffering and loss" (p. 198). It is Malcolm, Prince of Cumberland and the future King of Scotland, who expresses the values of feudal trust when he says, "What I am truly, Is thine and my poor country's to command" (4.3.131-132). In the feudal era, the central conflict in society and literature consisted of interpersonal trust based on one's word versus the breaking of that word. By the time of the Restoration, and the beginning of the bourgeois epoch, the needs of society and the content of literature had changed. And the central conflict had shifted to "the individual versus society or nature or corruption or solipsism; to Self versus Other; in short, to a master trope of Self-Reliance, where mutual trust is replaced by trust in one's god, yes, but especially in one's own will and will to power" (p. 320).

TRUST IN THE MODERN ERA

Our very brief discussion of the history of trust has been narrowly focused on two factors: (a) the degree of internal differentiation in social systems; and (b) the two primary forms of trust, interpersonal and social. We have seen that, in ancient Greek societies and in feudal Europe, low levels of differentiation based on segmentation and stratification limited the form of trust primarily to the interpersonal. The outer limit of trust in these societies, on the interpersonal/social border, occurred in client-patron relations established for protection against human and environmental uncertainties. But throughout its history and in many different kinds of societies, trust was interpreted ambivalently, as a risk itself: protection in one realm was achieved at the cost of vulnerability in another. Clients became reliant on patrons, patrons on clients. Thus, there was a permanent tension between limited interpersonal trust and the expansion of trust toward the social.

It was only in the modern era, when societal differentiation became based on functional subsystems, that a need for wide-ranging social trust developed. The beginnings of this part of the history of trust, worked out in the classic liberal texts of Locke, Hume, and Smith, have been outlined by Allan Silver (1985). Silver describes how, in the transformation from monarchy to liberal government, trust came to be understood in universal rather than exclusive terms. This had the effect of defusing trust, emotion being replaced by "the social moralities of benevolence, sympathy and prudence" (pp. 54-55).[21] In addition to becoming "calmer, more routinized and universal," trust relations in the early modern era also evolved toward a solution to the tensions between interpersonal and social trust. As the need for social trust increased, the distinction between it and interpersonal trust became more important. Thus, liberal theory, from its beginnings to today, has insisted on the separation of the private and public realms.[22]

One sector of American culture that was strongly affected by the distinction between private and public is academic psychology, the professional cadre of researchers and teachers in academic institutions. These are the people who, in the early and mid-twentieth century, created theories and agendas of research topics and methods that greatly influenced their successors. For the most part, these psychologists focused their work on the private, the individual extracted from social context. Thus, until very recently, studies of social trust, dealing with persons in social contexts making judgments about social institutions, were virtually unknown—rare and lacking influence on the profession. Studies of trust were studies of interpersonal trust. To provide a context from which to consider contemporary research on social trust, we discuss these early, "classic" studies—and their impact on what followed—in the final section of our introduction to social trust.

"CLASSIC" STUDIES OF (INTERPERSONAL) TRUST

Studies of trust by American academic psychologists have been dominated by two research programs. The first, at Yale University, was led by Carl Hovland, Irving Janis, and Harold Kelley. They published their influential book, *Communication and Persuasion: Psychological Studies of Opinion Change*, in 1953. The second program, based originally in the psychological research unit at the Bell Telephone Laboratories and later at Columbia University, was led by Morton Deutsch. Deutsch and his colleagues published many research articles and theoretical formulations beginning in the late forties. A summary statement of Deutsch's theories and research was published as *The Resolution of Conflict: Constructive and Destructive Processes* in 1973. Our comments on these programs will be based on these texts.[23] Following our assessment of these classic psychological studies, we will examine the continuing impact of these programs on contemporary studies of trust.

TRUST AT YALE: HOVLAND, JANIS, AND KELLEY

The design of the Yale Communication Research Program was based on three principles. First, its focus was on theoretical issues and basic research. Hovland and his colleagues planned to study human communication abstracted from social contexts. According to this strategy, solutions to practical social problems would follow from a solid understanding of what accepted theory identified as "the basic factors" underlying the phenomena of interest. The second principle was to derive this theoretical guidance from diverse sources, among them "learning theory," Freud and social psychology.[24] The rigorous application of laboratory experimentation, in the belief that results so generated could be generalized to significant social settings, was the third principle.

Applying these principles to the study of human communication, the Yale group developed a set of working assumptions. Among them:

> Opinions are a type of habit called "implicit verbal responses," what we say to ourselves (as opposed to externally) in response to questions.

> Opinion change is a matter of learning a new habit. A new habit replaces an old one if the incentives supporting the former are greater than those supporting the latter.

> Three main classes of stimuli act as incentives in the communication situation: the source, the setting, and the content.

The Yale group's work on trust dealt with the set of incentives associated with the source of the communication, the communicator: "An important factor influencing the effectiveness of a communication is the person or group perceived as originating the communication—and the cues provided as to the trustworthiness, intentions, and affiliations of this source" (p. 13).

Hovland and his colleagues focused their interest in source incentives on what they called "communicator credibility." As formulated, communicator credibility was learned by individual members of audiences in a variety of situations: "For example, the specific attributes of persons who are viewed as powerful or credible can be expected to differ from culture to culture. There is also likely to be some degree of variability within a given culture, particularly as different subject matters are considered" (pp. 20-21).

In their analysis of communicator credibility, the Yale group identified two components: "the extent to which a communicator is perceived to be a source of valid assertions (his 'expertness')" and "the degree of confidence in the communicator's intent to communicate the assertions he considers most valid (his 'trustworthiness')" (p. 21). But Hovland and his colleagues point out that in some cases expertness might have more to do with similarity between the communicator and the audience than with presumed special, superior qualifications: "In certain matters persons similar to the recipient of influence may be considered more expert than persons different from him. An individual is likely to feel that persons with status, values, interests, and needs similar to his own see things as he does and judge them from the same point of view" (p. 22). In the case of trustworthiness, the Yale group focused on the audience's perception of fairness (or lack of intent to persuade) as the primary indicator.

The specific aims of the Yale group in studying communicator credibility were, of course, to assess its effects on audience evaluations of message content and on any changes in audience opinions resulting from those evaluations. We will not review the results of this research program here.[25] We want instead to comment briefly on the basic structure of the program. Our argument is this: the Yale program was based on inconsistent and, in certain cases, invalid premises. Once established, however, these premises became part of an unquestioned cultural background that structured the work of succeeding generations of researchers. An elaboration of this rather intramural argument is inappropriate here. We can, however, outline the major points:

Generalization from laboratory experiments to applied settings is always problematic but especially so when the behavior required of laboratory subjects is arguably very different from that of persons in the applied settings of interest. One may learn a great deal about experimental subjects but very little about persons in context.[26]

Interpreting opinions as habits has proved not to be useful in many settings. When asked questions, instead of consulting the appropriate habit stored somewhere in their minds, people tend to construct responses from a variety of cues readily accessible in their immediate contexts.[27]

The separation of communicator and message in theory and practice seems to be different from what most people do most of the time. The communicator and her message are often interpreted as a package. And trust must be a function of the communication package, not of the isolated communicator.[28]

In their theoretical discussion, the Yale group emphasizes the likely cultural variability of judged credibility. Subsequent to that discussion, however, credibility became associated more with the communicator than with the audience, and implications of necessity replaced those of contingency.[29]

Finally, and crucial to the study of trust, the distinction between expertness and trustworthiness is slippery and inconsistent. The distinction is hard to get a hold on because, as described in the Yale theory itself, the two concepts are very similar. Expertness in most interesting cases (i.e., cases lacking universal agreement) is based on value similarity. And trustworthiness is based on fairness. Who, in most cases, will treat me fairly? Someone similar to me. In all but the most simple or artificial cases, the distinction between expertness and trustworthiness dissolves. And credibility becomes equivalent to trust. Even if we were to accept the usefulness of this distinction, its application in the Yale program is inconsistent. In the theory, it is interpreted in a relatively complex way; in the research the texture disappears.[30]

These comments on the program of Hovland, Janis, and Kelley are not meant to denigrate their pioneering work; it was an outstanding product of its time. Our remarks are aimed instead at those who uncritically followed the lead of the pioneers or who, straying from the original program, retained its crippling spirit of artificiality.[31]

With regard specifically to the study of trust, the initial framing provided by the Yale program is in place to this day, even outside the field of persuasive communication. Thus, for example, trust for most researchers is interpersonal trust, not social trust. In a recent, typically insightful article on the relations among perceived risk, trust, and democracy, Paul Slovic (1993) sometimes falls back on interpersonal metaphors when he clearly means to discuss social trust, referring, for example, to the relations between personality traits and the "fragility" of trust (p. 677). At other places in the same article, Slovic deals directly with social trust, arguing that "persons who trusted the nuclear power industry saw the events at Three Mile Island as demonstrating the soundness of the 'defense in depth' principle," while "persons who distrusted nuclear power prior to the accident [believed] that catastrophe was averted only by sheer luck (p. 679). Is trust fragile or robust, interpersonal or social? Conflation of interpersonal and social trust is one of the legacies of Hovland, Janis, and Kelley, and a primary source of conceptual confusion.

TRUST AND THE PRISONER'S DILEMMA: MORTON DEUTSCH

Although Hovland, Janis, and Kelley were very influential in subsequent studies of trust, their approach to the subject was oblique; persuasive communication was their primary interest. The case of Morton Deutsch (1973) was somewhat similar. Deutsch's main interest was conflict resolution; trust was a possible pathway toward that goal. But Deutsch paid much more serious conceptual and analytical attention to trust than did the Yale group. The result was a theory of trust (pp. 143-176).

Deutsch presented his theory in a formal manner: a list of eleven definitions followed by a list of nine psychological assumptions; followed by a list of nineteen hypotheses. This was an era when social psychology aspired to be *experimental* and *scientific*: Deutsch's theory was filled with talk of potency, power, and valences, and there was a (misplaced) aura of great precision. Since it neither survived to the present nor generated any recognizable progeny that did, we needn't concern ourselves with the details of Deutsch's theory of trust. One of Deutsch's hypotheses (number 10a) has special relevance here, however, and it conveys the general flavor of his approach:

> If an individual is promotively oriented toward himself, he will tend to be promotively oriented toward others who are perceived to have characteristics or attitudes that are promotive (e.g., through similarity) to his own characteristics or attitudes, and he will also expect such others to be promotively oriented toward him; on the other hand, such an individual will tend to be contriently oriented toward others who are perceived to have characteristics or attitudes that are contrient (e.g., dissimilar) to his own, and he will also expect such others to be contriently oriented to him.
>
> (p. 159)

In other words, people tend to trust others who are similar to them and to distrust those who are dissimilar from them. This formulation echos our reinterpretation of Hovland, Janis, and Kelley.

The impact of Deutsch's work on trust did not result from the usefulness of his theory. It derived, first, from his decision to focus on simple, two-person interpersonal trust. He intended, eventually, to expand: "There is an obvious need to investigate the development of trust in more complex social situations involving more people" (p. 214). Unfortunately for these intentions, much of Deutsch's theoretical and experimental work was ultimately limited by his research methods. These methods, centered on the well-known Prisoner's Dilemma game, were the second major source of Deutsch's impact.[32] Deutsch was the first psychologist to use the Prisoner's Dilemma. And his combination of a simple, two-person social situation and a well-defined experimental paradigm was a magnet for dozens of subsequent researchers: it seemed to offer a solution to the perennial problem of how to learn about significant social problems in a controlled, reliable way. But over the years, the Prisoner's Dilemma became a classic example of what Gerd Gigerenzer (1991) calls the "tools-to-theories heuristic." This means, in brief, that the theory follows from the tool. And when the tool is socially barren, so too will be the theory.

THE LEGACY OF THE CLASSIC STUDIES OF TRUST

For the past four decades in American social science—a period of very rapid growth in the number of practitioners if not in their cumulative societal influence—the study of social trust has been dominated by the classic studies of Hovland, Janis, and Kelley (1953) and of Deutsch (1973). Unfortunately, these studies dealt with interpersonal rather than social trust. Aspirations to scientism among subsequent social trust researchers were evidently sufficient strong, however, to overcome any reservations they may have had regarding the social content of the classic studies. Throughout the history of the study of social trust (as well as much else) there has been this struggle between competing tendencies—toward the individual and rational and toward the social and (presumably) irrational. The designers of the classic studies of trust indicated—albeit indirectly—that they believed that trust was based on social similarity. But they also apparently believed that such a conclusion would serve as an endorsement to irrationality—an admission of loss of control. So they insisted that trust have a rational basis—expertness and trustworthiness, competence and responsibility. And they confined their studies to the controlled, artificial limits of the laboratory.

Consumers of the results of the classic studies—both professionals and, through them, the public—tended to ignore the caveats attached to the original work. And they allowed the way they talked about social trust to be determined by the classic descriptions. Complex social processes were described in simple, rational terms. In practice, however, the fit between the processes and the descriptions was not always good. Attempts to "build" social trust often failed. Social trust, many observers concluded, simply does not work. Better to rely on familiar, proven processes, they argued—old standbys such as social distrust. That, in bare outline, is the story of the legacy of the classic studies of trust. Failure to critically examine the classics led to the social application of an inappropriate, limited language. And that resulted in the linkage of social trust with social distrust—the inevitable failure of the former leading to reliance on the latter.

SUMMARY

We began our introduction to social trust with a discussion of its contemporary significance in environmental risk management. In two brief case studies, we described the U.S. Environmental Protection Agency's struggle with social distrust, and we analyzed aspects of the U.S. Department of Energy's plan for increasing social trust in its management of radioactive wastes. We concluded that the DOE social trust plan was unlikely to be successful primarily because it is a force for *stasis*—that is, it is dedicated to the preservation of existing interests. Such an approach, we argued, would encourage within-group social trust at the expense of cross-group social distrust. Since it is the latter that blocks the solution of contentious social problems, the social trust plan would fail in its primary purpose. The critical error in the DOE plan, we concluded, was the failure to distinguish between *pluralistic* (within-group) social trust and *cosmopolitan* (across-group) social trust. Only the latter, described in detail in Part III, is useful in the solution of social problems.

Although social trust is inextricably linked with social distrust in many contemporary treatments such as the DOE's, we outlined a history of social trust that demonstrated its independent development. Social trust developed in tandem with complexity in society. The language of social trust supported increased societal complexity, and increasing societal complexity demanded better ways of talking about social trust. Throughout its development, social trust was based on similarity of cultural values, and this was communicated within cultural groups by narratives constructed by community leaders. Social trust was socially based. We described how mid-twentieth-century social science attempted to counter this development—attempted to bring social trust under control—by providing social trust with a rational basis. Although this program to rationalize social trust has been very influential, it is bound to fail, we argued, discrediting social trust in the process and adding to the legitimacy of social distrust. To be successful, any program to encourage social trust must accommodate the social basis of social trust in its language.

There is far from universal agreement on what we have identified thus far as the limitations of rationalized social trust. In fact, our critical position—and others in sympathy with it—are in the minority in American social science. Rationalized social trust continues to reign. The reasons for this go beyond social science, we believe. They go deep into the history and culture of America. In that context, rationalized social trust becomes *traditional social trust*. And that is the subject of our next chapter.

2

Social Trust: Traditional Interpretations

We use the term *traditional social trust* as shorthand for traditional interpretations of social trust. These are ways of thinking and talking about social trust that have been transferred across generations of American social scientists (and, through them, to the general public), handed on from one group to another as relatively unexamined beliefs. We discussed two of the proximal sources of this tradition in Chapter 1—the studies of interpersonal trust by Carl Hovland and his colleagues at Yale and by Morton Deutsch at Bell Labs. In addition to the points of theory and method already cited, the uncritical reception accorded these traditional interpretations of social-trust-as-interpersonal-trust seems due also to their being embedded in a widely shared form of American democratic culture.[1] Within that cultural context, the traditional conception simply makes too much sense to be noticed; it is too obvious to be questioned. And perhaps most significantly, traditional social trust serves a crucial function in support of American democratic culture. Any critique of traditional social trust, such as ours, might imply a critique of American democracy as well. A full-fledged cultural critique is beyond our reach here, however; we can only outline what we consider to be the key cultural aspects of social trust. First, we must describe what is meant by traditional social trust.

THE ELEMENTS OF TRADITIONAL SOCIAL TRUST

Any treatment of trust must, at minimum, provide answers to two basic questions:

- What is trust? That is, what does *trust* (or *social trust*) mean? For example, is trust a property of individuals or societies? How is trust used in a particular *theory of trust*? What are the relations of trust to other concepts in the theory?

- What is trust based on? If trust is used as a property of individuals, how does one come to trust another? If trust is interpreted as a social phenomenon, how does social trust develop?

We examined a number of recent studies of social trust to see how they dealt with these questions. In this process, we were less interested in the qualities that set the individual studies apart than in their commonalities. Our search was for some core content that was shared among them, a possible shared understanding of social trust that might be traced to the tradition. In this sense, our brief descriptions of these studies do not do them justice; individual differences are sacrificed to the identification of a shared tradition.

We begin with two widely cited studies of social trust dealing with problems outside the field of risk management. In the first study, by sociologists J. David Lewis and Andrew Weigert (1985), trust is defined as a "social reality," a property of collective social units such as dyads and groups. Within society, trust serves as a continuous, ongoing basis for social relations. Trust is social (a property of groups), not socio-psychological (a property of individuals in groups), and it is present as social relations develop over time. Lewis and Weigert rely on Talcott Parsons' discussion of trust in professionals for ideas on the conditions leading to trust.[2] After reviewing these conditions, they conclude that the generation of trust requires "an adequate symbolic representation of the competence and integrity of the professional" (p. 981). The emphasis on *symbolic representation* by Lewis and Weigert is an indication of a determinedly sociological, noncognitive interpretation of trust.

The second sociological study is by Bernard Barber (1983) who describes trust in terms of the various expectations individuals have about social interactions: "The most general is expectation of the persistence and fulfillment of the natural and the moral social orders. Second is expectation of technically competent role performance from those involved with us in social relationships and systems. And third is expectation that partners in interaction will carry out their fiduciary obligations and responsibility, that is, their duties in certain situations to place others' interests before their own" (p. 9). As with Lewis and Weigert, trust is considered an ongoing basis for social relations. And Barber is very clear on the specific bases of trust-technical competence and fiduciary responsibility. Together, these two representative studies of social trust as a general phenomenon, not referring at all to risk management, agree that trust should be defined as an ongoing basis for social relations and that it is based on competence and fiduciary responsibility.

Ortwin Renn and Debra Levine (1991) are among a number of authors who have studied social trust within the context of risk management.[3] In their analysis of the role of trust in risk communication, Renn and Levine define trust as "the generalized expectancy that a message received is true and reliable and that the communicator demonstrates competence and honesty by conveying accurate, objective, and complete information" (Renn and Levine, 1991, p. 53). In addition, definitions are given for the five attributes of trust on which this formulation is based:

- Perceived competence (degree of technical expertise assigned to a message or a source)
- Objectivity (lack of biases in information as perceived by others)
- Fairness (acknowledgment and adequate representation of all relevant points of view)
- Consistency (predictability of arguments and behavior based on past experience and previous communication efforts)
- Faith (perception of "good will" in composing information)

(p. 53)

This psychology-based analysis of trust is more detailed and wide-ranging than the sociological studies reviewed above. But the general pattern is the same: if objectivity, fairness, consistency, and faith are taken to be elements of responsibility, the familiar dual bases for trust result: competence and responsibility.

Another detailed analysis of trust within the context of risk communication is offered by Roger Kasperson, Dominic Golding and Seth Tuler (1992): "We define *social trust* as a person's expectation that other persons and institutions in a social relationship can be relied upon to act in ways that are competent, predictable, and caring" (p. 169). As with Renn and Levine, Kasperson and his colleagues identify four factors necessary to the development and maintenance of social trust:

- Commitment (based on objectivity and fairness)
- Competence
- Caring ("concern for and benefice to trusting individuals")
- Predictability ("fulfillment of expectations and faith")

(p. 170)

In this formulation, commitment, caring, and predictability can be interpreted as parallel to Renn and Levine's objectivity and fairness, faith, and consistency (though Kasperson and his colleagues rule out the need for strict consistency of behavior).

Two recent and comprehensive examinations of trust within the context of risk management are in general agreement, then, that social trust is based on competence and responsibility. Both studies also treat trust as a continuous basis (i.e., a background support) for social interaction. Kasperson, Golding and Tuler, for example, state that "trust is probably never completely or permanently attained, but rather requires continuous maintenance and reinforcement" (p. 169). A comparison of this treatment of social trust by researchers interested in risk management problems with the sociological analyses developed by authors examining social trust as a general phenomenon indicates a striking congruence in basic elements. Consistently, in these and other studies, social trust is said to be a continuous phenomenon based on competence and responsibility. This, then, is the simple heart, the value basis, of traditional social trust.[4] We are now ready to discuss the relations between traditional social trust and American democratic culture.

TRADITIONAL SOCIAL TRUST AND AMERICAN DEMOCRATIC CULTURE

We use the term *American democratic culture* to refer informally to a core set of American values that have been passed down from generation to generation since the country's beginning. It is not our purpose to attempt the difficult task of identifying and discussing all these values.[5] We want instead to briefly discuss a single issue that is centrally important to risk management: the conflict between *adversary democracy* and *participatory or unitary democracy.*[6] In the friction between these two forms of democracy, the first advocating government or management by elected representatives and the second calling for management by the people themselves, the function of traditional social trust is plainly revealed.

Participatory democracy, though distrusted by elites, nonetheless remains a core value of American culture. An ideal vision is the town meeting in which residents debate and decide their own fates (Mansbridge, 1980, pp. 39-135). The realities of life and government, of course, impose constraints on this vision: The demands of increasingly large social groups and their associated complex problems have transposed the ideal of participation (which in practice was almost always limited) more and more toward representative democracy. In many areas of life, power and authority are now voluntarily given by people to their representatives. This creates a potential problem for many Americans: How can representative democracy be reconciled with the ideal of *government of, by and for the people?*[7]

A variety of strategies are available to deal with problems of this sort; we discuss many of them in Part II. Among the most prominent, of course, are social trust and social distrust. Social trust, for example, could be used as a tool to facilitate the bridging by citizens of the gap between participative and representative democracy.[8] On the traditional interpretation, as we have described it, this trust would be based on competence and responsibility and would act as an on-going foundation for social interaction. Should the representatives prove at some time in the future to be incompetent or irresponsible, then the citizens' trust could be "lost." This way of talking about traditional social trust, as a bridge between citizens and their representative government, could be called *elitist democracy.*

Social distrust can also be used to link citizens and representatives. This strategy is traditionally associated with American populism.[9] According to this construction, social distrust, interpreted traditionally as the opposite of social trust, is the preferred relationship between people and representatives. Wisdom resides in the people. Thus, any failures in social policies and programs can be attributed by them to flaws in their representatives. Social distrust, based on the people's judgments of incompetence and irresponsibility, is therefore the rational alternative, the price the people have to pay to keep their representatives in line.[10]

This very abbreviated outline of the functions of traditional social trust and distrust in American democratic culture hints at why distrust has become such a problem for us. First, social distrust is a core value in the populist and egalitarian American traditions. Second, the concept of traditional social trust, based on competence and responsibility, tends toward ephemerality, evanescence. This is because citizens, in effect, are rewarded for "losing" it:

- Citizens presume themselves to be competent and responsible.
- When something goes wrong, blaming their representatives is a much more available and acceptable response than blaming themselves.
- Thus, social trust loses and social distrust wins.

This, then, is our deliberately simple American cultural story—the continuing struggle in public discourse between social trust and social distrust. With this basic plot established, we can now discuss in more detail the flaws in the traditional conception of social trust.

A PRELIMINARY CRITIQUE OF TRADITIONAL SOCIAL TRUST

We have described the traditional conception of social trust, and we have outlined its function in American culture. What is so wrong with it? We can summarize our analysis of the problems with traditional social trust in four points:

- Traditional social trust is part of a larger, unexamined cultural tradition.
- Traditional social trust is a political strategy that requires high levels of resources to implement.
- Traditional social trust is culture-specific.
- Traditional social trust encourages social distrust.

Our arguments in support of each of these four points follow.

Traditional Social Trust Is Part of an Unexamined Tradition

The traditional rendering of social trust, as the label implies, is an unexamined part of our cultural heritage; it's simply the way we have always understood it. One's tradition, of course, is the most valuable gift one's community can give. It can be that, however, only if one struggles against it and uses it as a basis for change. In our interpretation, and in the judgment of many Western thinkers, examining and confronting one's tradition are necessary for personal and community growth.[11] In this spirit, the task of American citizens would be to openly debate and test the usefulness of their tradition(s) as tools for coping with the problems that concern them today.[12] Though not completely absent from public debate, discussions of social trust tend to be rare and bland. This is due, of course, to the stranglehold of tradition: there is only one interpretation of social trust, the one we've always had. And within that subsystem of society responsible for "official" discussions of these matters—the social sciences—the situation is no better.

Although several empirical studies of social trust have recently been produced, none of them has explicitly addressed, in support or opposition, the traditional construction. In a study by William Freudenburg (1993), for example, survey respondents were asked, on three separate items, to indicate their level of trust in science and technology, trust in business capability, and trust in the federal government. The context of the study was public concern about a proposed low-level nuclear waste facility. The results of the survey, Freudenburg argues, show that high levels of concern are related to low levels of trust (on all three items). This is not a surprising conclusion. Unfortunately, no data and no analyses are offered to explicate this relationship. We wind up where we began. Without acknowledging it, Freudenberg embraces a realist version of traditional social trust: trust (i.e., trustworthiness) is based on competence and responsibility understood as objective attributes of institutions, not as public judgments.[13]

James Flynn and his colleagues (Flynn, Burns, Mertz and Slovic, 1992) adopted sophisticated structural modeling techniques to study the role of trust in public opposition to a high-level radioactive waste repository. One advantage of these techniques is that they force one's theoretical hand. Thus, Flynn must specify a measurement model for trust, explicitly stating the factors on which it is based. Using survey data that included public judgments of the U.S. Department of Energy's management of a proposed repository, Flynn based his concept of trust on: DOE Objectivity, DOE Disclosure of Problems, and DOE Trustworthiness. The wording of the items used to measure these factors indicates that DOE Objectivity and DOE Disclosure address, respectively, the traditional notions of competence and responsibility. Instead of using these two factors to predict DOE Trustworthiness, the latter is included with them as indicators of the latent variable, Trust in Repository Management. But Flynn and his colleagues are not interested in testing the traditional construction of social trust against alternatives. They want instead to use Trust in Repository Management to predict Opposition to the Repository. As it turned out, Trust had no direct effect on Opposition. Opposition was affected primarily by Perceived Risk, and Perceived Risk was affected by Trust. Thus, although Flynn's study is a significant advance owing to the clarity of its methods and procedures, our understanding of social trust is not much affected.[14]

Our final empirical study of social trust, conducted by Suzanne Parker and Glen Parker (1993), deals with a political context, the problem of why constituents trust their representatives. Like Flynn and his colleagues, Parker and Parker make good use of powerful structural modeling methods. In addition, perhaps owing to their familiarity with political settings, Parker and Parker have a good feeling for what's happening in social trust: "[W]e believe that trust in a legislator is predicated on the belief that the representative is serving, and will continue to serve, the best interests of his or her supporters rather than acting out of self interest" (p. 442).[15]

In the structural model that summarized the results of their survey data, Parker and Parker showed that Constituents' Trust in their U.S. Representative was predicted by System Trust and Personal Contact. In the measurement model, the two latent variables dealing with trust had five indicators; Personal Contact had four. Without going into the details of the indicator items, most of them referred, in effect, to value similarity. With regard to Personal Contact, for example, Parker and Parker say: "Our indicators of personal contact with the representative include the respondent's recall that he or she has personally met the congressman, attended a meeting where the member spoke, talked with someone from the representative's staff, or knew someone who had personal contact with the representative" (p. 445). We interpret this to mean that respondents scoring high on Personal Contact were persons who believed that the salient values of their representatives were similar to their own. The items measuring System Trust are indicators of a general trust in government. The Trust in U.S. Representative items, in contrast, indicate the value similarity between representatives and constituents. We conclude that Parker and Parker's model, showing Personal Contact and System Trust affecting Trust in U.S. Representative, can be interpreted as support for a construction of social trust based on value similarity. This is a significant break from tradition.

Such departures from the past are rare—recent additions to the still-small set of empirical studies of social trust. The flow of policy recommendations based on a naive, unexamined faith in the robust flourishing of traditional social trust continues unabated (see, for example, Mitchell, 1992).

Traditional Social Trust Has High Resource Demands

The demands of the traditional interpretation of social trust on the personal resources of individuals are very high—so high, in fact, that they run counter to generally accepted psychological principles articulated by, among many others, Herbert Simon.[16] According to the traditional rendering, a person makes a judgment of social trust based on an assessment of a number of attributes related to the competence and responsibility of a person or institution. This requires the individual, at minimum, to engage in various processes of information acquisition and integration. In addition, traditional social trust is considered to be an on-going basis for social relations. Exactly what this entails is never spelled out, but the implication is that some form of continuous functioning (or at least monitoring) is required. One can only speculate as to the cognitive, emotional, and behavioral resources this might demand. Contrary to this rather bizarre description of individuals routinely pursuing greater cognitive demands, contemporary psychology depicts individuals as normally seeking cognitive simplicity and accepting complexity only when highly motivated for some reason.[17]

This lack of synchronization between theories about how persons should behave, on the one hand, and the best scientific descriptions of how persons typically do behave, on the other, is not limited to matters of social trust, of course. The area of inquiry most richly endowed with "lack-of-realism" problems may that of ethical theory. To our great benefit, however, Owen Flanagan (1991) has analyzed these problems in a very thorough and thoughtful manner, centering his discussion on his Principle of Minimal Psychological Realism: "Make sure when constructing a moral theory or projecting a moral ideal that the character, decision processing, and behavior prescribed are possible, or are perceived to be possible, for creatures like us" (p. 32). As Flanagan demonstrates, this principle is subtle and requires some thought and effort to apply. But that is just the point: easy and final answers will never be found in philosophy or psychology or in any other discipline. The temptation to believe otherwise is a function of those individual disciplines; each needs to be tempered and made humble by the others.[18]

Another way of describing the separation of traditional social trust from everyday life as we know it is to talk of the former as a striving for a form of rationality that most of us only occasionally experience as we go about our mundane business. Rationality, according to Robert Nozick (1993), is based on reasons and reliability, reasons "for thinking the belief is true (or . . . has some other desirable cognitive virtue . . .)" and procedures that "lead to a high

percentage of true beliefs" (p. 64). In this traditional account of rational belief
we can take "cognitive virtue" and "reliability" to be congruent, respectively,
with competence and responsibility. Thus, the high-resource demands of the
traditional construction of social trust can be said to derive from its perhaps ill-
advised aspirations to rationality.

Our final, brief point on resource demands concerns the function of social
trust. Simply put, social trust evolved as a strategy to cope with increasing
societal complexity and the cognitive complexity it induced.   The
implementation of the social trust strategy, therefore, must at minimum be less
demanding than dealing with the problem in other ways. But, we have argued,
the demands of traditional social trust are greater than those of available
alternatives.

Traditional Social Trust Is Culture-Specific

Although it is presented as culture-neutral, the traditional construction of
social trust is, of course, culture-specific—a product constructed in, by, and for
Western, primarily American, social science.[19] The traditional interpretation
ignores all cultural considerations including intracultural variations. In doing
this, acting without regard to culture (i.e., uncritically within their own
culture), proponents of traditional social trust act to supply an ideological
justification for themselves and for the dominant, individualistic culture.[20]

Traditional social trust is based on competence and responsibility, values
central to traditional, individualistic American culture.[21] Advocates of the
traditional view assume that these values are central to everyone; no alternative
formulations of trust are considered. Contrary to this assumption, however,
people do vary in the values they consider most important when dealing with
other persons and institutions. And this diversity of values, as well as changing
social contexts, may provide varying, perhaps conflicting, bases for judgments
of social trust. A useful example of this diversity is provided by Girishwar
Misra and Kenneth Gergen in their contrasting lists of features characteristic of
personal functioning. Among them are, first, for the West:

- Anthropocentric and individual-centered worldview
- Belief in control over nature and humanly created order
- Autonomous and bounded self with fixed and strong boundaries
- Liberal ontological individualism and belief in freedom
- Decontextualized, contractual, and open-ended nature of relationships
- Knowledge (science) as amoral (value free) and secular

And, second, for India:

- Holistic-organic worldview
- Coherence and natural order across all life forms
- A socially constituted and embedded and relational concept of person
- Social individualism
- Contextualized relationships depending on time, place, and person
- Knowledge as moral and sacred

When listed in this way, these features seem all too familiar. And this is true for *both* lists, the Western and the Indian. To us, as ordinary Americans living our day-to-day lives, all of these features of human functioning seem to be part of, if not our own lives, the lives of people we know in various ways. But the social scientists and others who promote traditional social trust, if we take them at their word, would recognize only the first, stereotypically Western list. Our point, therefore, is not that traditional social trust can be applied only within an American context, but that it is useful within no *living* culture at all. Traditional social trust is an *abstract, lifeless* product of a Western social-scientific subculture that has lost touch with the living, changing culture around it.[22]

Aside from the pervasive professional parochialism, one of the most striking and dispiriting qualities of American social thought, at both a popular level and in the social sciences, is its ethnocentrism.[23] Of course, all societies, even the most liberally pluralistic, are ethnocentric to some extent. And some good things can be said about ethnocentrism.[24] But we are Americans commenting on *our* culture, attempting to contribute to *its* development. We are doing this within the context of other Western cultures and relative to the ideal of cultural examination outlined above. What we notice is a lack of curiosity about alternatives, an indifference to better ways of doing things and an unwillingness to learn from others.[25] This is the familiar problem of reification, treating our own contingencies as though they were states of nature (Thompson, 1988; Coligon, 1989; Warren, 1990).

Some Western researchers, social scientists and others, have been hard at work for quite some time, however, trying to crack the American cocoon of common sense, to supply to us the critical perspective on ourselves we seem so desperately to need. Harry Triandis (1990), for example, using the techniques of cross-cultural psychology, has documented the dominant individualism of American culture as opposed to more collectivist cultures elsewhere. Triandis, unfortunately, tends to talk about individual persons as individualists or collectivists, and, for reasons that we will present later, we believe that treating the self as a unitary entity is misleading in most contexts. Nonetheless

Triandis's argument that the dominant culture in America is individualist is convincing.[26]

In addition to empirical studies, there has been a proliferation of recent books and articles expressing concern about the apparent domination of American culture by individualism. These statements have come from a variety of perspectives: the right (Donohue, 1990), the left (Barber, 1984), and elsewhere (Sandel, 1982; MacIntyre, 1984). Opposition to the dominant individualism and support for various common goods have recently been spun together in an incipient American communitarian movement (Etzioni, 1989). Taken together, these empirical studies and expressions of concern indicate a growing discontent with adversarial individualism, as well as an increasing yearning for community.

Our specific area of interest is societal risk management and the role of social trust in it. In that context, it is important for us to venture beyond the boundaries of our own culture, so that we can become aware of cultural variations and possibilities. Significantly, several researchers have documented marked differences between risk management practices in America and in various European countries. Comparing the United States with Europe in general, Sheila Jasanoff (1990), for example, has noted that "if the political environment for risk regulation in the United States had to be characterized in a single word, that word would be competition" (p. 65). And in an extensive comparison between the United States and Sweden, Steven Kelman (1981) describes this anomaly: "For a country with so much consensus, America seems to have a great deal of conflict, and for a country with so much conflict, Sweden has managed to achieve a great deal of consensus" (p. 115). The key difference between Sweden and America, according to Kelman, can be found in the core values and associated institutions of the two countries: deferential values and accommodationist institutions in Sweden, self-assertive values and adversary institutions in America. In America, Kelman argues, "elements of self-assertive values and adversary institutions structurally favor those content with the status quo" (p. 230). Societal risk management based on adversarial democracy—with legitimacy granted only to self-interests and little concern for community interests—ultimately, paradoxically, leads to a giving up on democracy: surrendering to the courts, our most undemocratic institution. Clearly, institutional reform in American risk management is desperately needed. Above all, we need to create alternative dispute-management processes that are effective, efficient, and otherwise more attractive to individualist Americans than litigation. This is an improbable goal, certainly—difficult but worthy of effort. Movement away from litigation—and hyper-individualism—is not unimaginable.

Traditional Social Trust Encourages Distrust

The traditional understanding of social trust is destructive of trust and supportive of social distrust. By basing trust on competence and responsibility, qualities that are as difficult to achieve as they are to judge, proponents of the traditional interpretation seriously undermine (and underestimate) the role of social trust in daily social life. This is particularly true in American culture, where individuals are encouraged to evaluate trust negatively and its functional equivalent, distrust, positively (see, for example, Barber, 1983). Social distrust is congruent with and supportive of traditional American democratic culture, a set of values characterized by individual self-interest.[27] Social trust, on the other hand, is congruent with a social system based more on communitarian values (Bellah, Madsen, Sullivan, Swidler and Tipton, 1985). Using Jane Mansbridge's (1980) terms, social distrust is paired with adversarial democracy, social trust with unitary democracy. And, as she points out, most Americans experience democracy—even if unitary—only in its most private and selfish form—in the voting booth. Our claim, in sum, is this: that the cultural interpretation of social trust in America, based as it is on the traditional factors of competence and responsibility, is negative because it runs counter to American individualism: Competence and responsibility reside in oneself, not in one's representatives. In America, therefore, we learn to *distrust* social trust. Social distrust, in contrast, is compatible with American individualism. Accordingly, we are taught to *trust* distrust.

SUMMARY

In this chapter we described and evaluated the traditional construction of social trust. We presented a variety of rather condensed arguments depicting the traditional account of social trust as an unexamined part of our cultural heritage that demands complex cognition when it should supply simplicity, that ignores cultural variation and is itself culture-specific, and which acts to undermine trust as it generates distrust. But our critique of social trust is not entirely negative. In Part III, we present an alternative account of social trust that we believe avoids the faults of the tradition. Before we can do that, however, we must complete our preliminary work. Any useful treatment of social trust must be based on an understanding of the social contexts in which it functions. A defining characteristic of those contexts is their complexity. And social complexity is experienced by individuals as cognitive complexity. The twin problems of social and cognitive complexity—and their relations to social trust—are the subjects of our next chapter.

3

Complexity and Social Trust

One way to talk about social trust is to describe it as a tool for the reduction of cognitive complexity. *Cognitive complexity* is a term from academic psychology that refers, in general, to the complexity of a person's cognitive processes—thinking, judging, problem solving, decision making, etc. Cognitive complexity can be indicated and measured in various ways. A decision to buy a product based solely on brand, for example, would be cognitively simple compared with a decision based on the integration of several, varied types of information. Because we humans are finite, limited beings, we generally prefer cognitive simplicity over cognitive complexity. It costs less. For most people, however, neither end of this cognitive continuum is dominant over the other in all contexts nor at all times. Sometimes the benefits are worth the costs, sometimes not—and life comes to consist of swings along the length of the continuum, from complex to simple and back. An appreciation of these dynamics, we believe, can contribute to a more useful understanding social trust. We precede our description of the relations between cognitive complexity and social trust, therefore, with brief discussions of the interactions between simplicity and complexity in the broader—and perhaps more complex—contexts of science, human life in general and psychology.

SIMPLICITY AND COMPLEXITY IN SCIENCE

On the account of Paul Veyne (1988), it was the human struggle to cope with complexity—the need to reduce it—that induced the beginnings of Western thought:

Thales was the first to find the key to all things: "Everything is water. . . ."
Now, a key is not an explanation. While an explanation accounts for a phe-

nomenon, a key makes us forget the riddle. . . . An explanation is something
that is sought and proved. The key of a riddle is guessed and, once guessed,
it operates instantaneously. There is not even the possibility of an argument. The veil falls away, and our eyes are opened.

(pp. 29-30)[1]

Veyne's analysis seems to include all the right elements: Men, endowed with
limited human capacities, are troubled by the complex environments into which
they are thrown. They seek the key that will make the complex simple, that
will give meaning to the complexity—trade meaning for complexity—and thus
allow them to forget it. And Veyne stresses the crucial distinction between a
key and an *explanation*. A key *is* meaning and requires no argument, no evidence. It works because it reduces complexity, not for any matter of reason. It
is only the result—simplicity—that counts. The force of an explanation, in
contrast, depends on the quality of its supporting arguments and evidence.
Since Thales' time, science has, of course, become more rationalized, more
insistent on explanations rather than on keys. Nonetheless, the need for complexity reduction in science remains. And as we argue in Part III, keys in the
form of narratives continue to guide and give meaning to the activities of scientists even today.

SIMPLICITY AND COMPLEXITY IN HUMAN LIFE

The human struggle to cope with complexity is endless, at the bedrock
level of everyone's daily life as well as at the more abstract level of Thales'
successors. Michael Waldrop (1992) has provided a useful account of the recent activities of the latter, for whom the human struggle is understood as a
part of "nature's incessant compulsion for self-organization" (p. 125). A person, then, can be interpreted, in part, as a self-organizing psychic system that
operates to reduce its environmental complexity and to reproduce itself. In a
simplified account, dynamic systems such as a psychic system can take three
forms: order, complexity, and chaos.[2] Of these three, complexity, on the edge
between order and chaos, is the zone of life: "A system can exhibit complex,
lifelike behavior only if it has just the right balance of stability and fluidity" (p.
308). According to the new complexity theorists, lifelike behavior in a system
is characterized by the lack of central control and the emergence of structure
from the bottom up. The tendency to organize, to simplify, is inherent in life.

The emerging sciences of complexity seem to be generating powerful new
ways of talking about living systems. But these developments in systems theory
have not been limited to scientists expert in computer simulation and biology—
and some of the basic ideas may not be all that new. This is amply demonstrated in the work of two writers who have managed, in very different ways, to

integrate contemporary systems ideas within interpretations of Western tradition.

Michel Serres

Whereas simplicity in some form is unavoidable, a variety of strategies have evolved to help people cope with chaos or complexity. For Serres, therefore, simplicity is the greater, more terrifying danger. Nearing the end of his long commentary on the founding of Rome, Serres says:

> How does the multiple change into unity? Through tragedy. The tragic brings the here and the now into these dubious and uncertain places, into this moving stretch of time; it brings the thing that takes place and is represented and the proper name that will be retained. The tragic brings the *hic et nunc*, the *ecce homo*. The tragic brings the spatial, temporal, and nominal capture of the multiple. The tragic brings the concept.
>
> (pp. 279-280)

Tragedy, for each of us, is *me, here, now*—how we talk about ourselves—the singular from which we must struggle, always, to escape.

> Beneath history is tragedy. . . . But even lower, beneath tragedy itself, is the foundation of sand and straw, the peaceful multiplicities without murder or execution, under the unmoving summer sun.
>
> Here lies foundation, or, dare I say, reality.
>
> (p. 282)

The foundation of Rome is "of sand and straw"; that is, it is fluid, always changing. "Foundation is recurrent. It returns like a refrain. Rome does not cease to be founded; the act of origin or rooting continues indefinitely. To that Rome owes its long survival" (p. 263).

Now we can understand Serres's demanding metastrategy based on self-reflexivity, perpetual inquiry, and growth. Using a metaphor later appropriated by some of the complexity scientists, Serres says that, "Our chance is on the crest. Our living and inventive path follows the fringed, capricious curve where the simple beach of sand meets the noisy rolling in of the waves." This is our best metaphor for life, for risk management, for social trust: *the shore*—dynamic mixing, interpenetrating, of earth, sea, and sky. "There is only something new by the injection of chance in the rule, by the introduction of the law at the heart of disorder. An organization is born from circumstances, like Aphrodite rising from the sea" (pp. 127-128).

Niklas Luhmann

Luhmann's (1990) way is more head-on than Serres's but also more im-
bued with paradox.[3]   Luhmann uses the term *autopoietic*, borrowed from
biology, to refer to systems that are self-organizing and that reproduce themselves:

> Autopoietic systems produce their elements within temporal boundaries, de-
> pending on a beforehand and a thereafter.   Many of them, certainly
> conscious systems and social systems, consist of events only, of thoughts, for
> example, or of actions. Events happen at specific moments, and they vanish
> as soon as they appear. In this sense disorganization is a continuous and
> necessary cause of being. The system has to manage its own *creatio con-*
> *tinua.*
>
> (p. 115)

This is accomplished by complexity-reducing structures. Thus, *psychic* systems
continuously use *meaning* to reduce complexity or to create order from order
and disorder.   The contents of consciousness appear and disappear, are constructed and destroyed according to the strategies of meaning.

> The focus of actual meaningful experience cannot stay where it is, it has to
> move.   The structure of meaning based on the difference between actuality
> and potentiality relates to this problem. The function of its dual structure is
> to organize alternating attention: actuality that is certain but unstable, and
> potentiality that is uncertain but stable.   Indeed, we have to pay for our
> world either with instability or with uncertainty; we have no access to stable
> certainty.
>
> (pp. 83-84)

If one relies on existing ways of thinking and talking about the world, then
one's ability to adapt to a changing environment is impaired. But any attempt
to deal directly with a chaotic environment would, of course, leave one paralyzed by lack of direction.   Strategies of meaning, such as social trust, must
cope with both sides of this endless problem of human life.

SIMPLICITY AND COMPLEXITY IN PSYCHOLOGY

The interplay and tension between simplicity and complexity has recently
become a central concern in American academic psychology.   In the past
twenty years, for example, the general model of social cognition that has become dominant is one based on a strictly limited information processing
capacity (see, for example, Carroll and Payne, 1976).[4] These cognitive limits

encourage people to be efficient in making judgments and decisions, using, for example, simplifying heuristics and strategies (Tversky and Kahneman, 1974).[5] Cognitive limitations and cognitive efficiency are fundamental to our current understanding of social cognition, which is to say our current understanding of at least a part of what human beings are.[6] In contrast to this account of constrained human functioning, the traditional construction of social trust assumes a species capable of super-computer-like feats of information storage, retrieval, and manipulation.

Of course, the traditional account of social trust is not unique among contemporary social theories in its dependence on an outmoded and inadequate model of social cognition. Economic accounts of human behavior and decision theory, for example, have inspired numerous attacks and attempts at revision based on alleged deficiencies in descriptive validity (see, for example, Mitchell and Beach, 1990). Unfortunately, limited psychological realism has not proved to be a fatal flaw for many models of human cognition. Bernard Williams's (1988) comparison between the "standard" theory of games and newer, improved varieties provides an example of this:

> In the standard theory of games, [the knowledge necessary for cooperation] is given *a priori*, since everyone is assumed to have complete relevant information and also the capacity to apply it with complete rationality.
>
> Recent work has been more willing to weaken these assumptions. In real life there are several types of limitation, for instance:
>
> (a)   People are imperfectly informed, both about other people's preferences and about their assessment of probabilities.
> (b)   Limitation (a) itself may be imperfectly understood.
> (c)   The acquisition of such knowledge may be variously impossible, expensive, and so on. One particular difficulty is that any actual process of inquiry may itself change preferences, destroy information, raise more questions, and generally confuse the issue.
>
> (p. 4)

We take Williams's observations about the standard theory of games to indicate that he is not interested in theories that are so abstracted from real life as to preclude the presence of beings whom we would recognize as human. Similarly, we are not interested in traditional theories of social trust based on what we take to be thoroughly unrealistic interpretations of social interaction. Our interest in developing a new account of social trust derives from our belief that social trust, grounded in psychological realism, can contribute significantly to the management of social problems, particularly social risks. And psychological realism begins with an appreciation of human limitations.

SIMPLICITY AND COMPLEXITY IN SOCIAL TRUST

Every trust judgment occurs in its own social context, a context that distinguishes that particular judgment from others.   But all trust judgment contexts share the common feature of social complexity. Consider, for example, the case of individuals voting for president in the United States.   The American citizen, on one interpretation, is faced with a problem of immense complexity. The range of issue positions and other attributes on which the two (or more) candidates could be compared is (like the range of a president's duties) virtually limitless.   In contrast, the cognitive capacities of voters are decidedly limited. This, in sum, is the basic social problem of cognitive complexity: an imbalance exists between the presumed (standard or ideal) demands of the social context and the cognitive capacities of the individual.

In his useful book on American presidential elections, John Smith (1980) describes the over-matched voter: "The scope of presidential responsibility and authority is so large relative to the capacity of any single individual to observe it that it is inevitable that voters will be uninformed on a wide range of issues" (p. 121). In addition, of course, the challenges of the coming presidency are unknowable. Consequently, the relation between voter and favored candidate is one of trust, interpreted by Smith as the likelihood that the candidate's performance "will respect certain values that are important to the voter.   This broad definition is meant to imply that the general sense of trustworthiness may reflect the application of diverse sets of standards unique to individuals" (p. 121). For Smith, social trust is a simplifying strategy used by voters in dealing with complex election environments. And we note that in this particular passage (though he reverts to tradition elsewhere), Smith acknowledges the critical point that the value basis of social trust can vary, differing among both individuals and social contexts.

But voting is just a common example of a general phenomenon. Social complexity is always greater than cognitive complexity.[7] The amount of information available to an individual is always greater than the person's ability to process it. As a result, cognitive and motivational processes, such as social trust, have evolved to simplify demands on our cognitive systems. In accord with Smith's account of voting, and drawing on Luhmann's (1980) general analysis, we interpret social trust as a simplifying strategy that enables individuals to adapt to complex social environments and thereby benefit from increased social opportunities. This account of social trust differs fundamentally from the traditional interpretation that demands an on-going, complex cognitive commitment.

Social Trust and Its Functional Equivalents

Our new account of social trust centers on its function as a tool for coping with environmental complexity by reducing cognitive complexity. But social trust, of course, is not the only cognitive-complexity-reducing strategy available to people. Another necessary ingredient in our understanding of social trust, therefore, is some understanding of its rivals, its functional equivalents.[8] It is only within that context that a valid evaluation of social trust can be made. As a way of interpreting the general social context of social trust, we suggest that strategies for the reduction of cognitive complexity can be distributed along two dimensions, *social focus* and *resources required*.

Social Focus

This dimension refers to an individual's self-understanding in a given time and place. At one extreme of the dimension an individual thinks only of himself as a single, separate entity. At the other extreme, an individual thinks only of herself as a member of a community. This distinction between individuating and socially-integrating interpretations of the self is gaining prominence within contemporary American psychology (e.g., see Markus and Kitayama, 1991) and represents a break from the traditional American account that construed the individual primarily as the individuating self. Social focus is a useful tool for talking about social trust and its functional equivalents because it enables us to distinguish between strategies that narrow one's social world (and therefore diminish one's social benefits) and strategies that enlarge one's social world (and therefore increase one's social benefits).[9] An individual (or a community of individuals), when confronted with overwhelming cognitive complexity, can thus select a simplifying strategy that generates the benefits it values (along with the risks it accepts).

Resources Required

This dimension refers to the amount of resources required to implement a cognitive-complexity-reducing strategy. One end of the dimension represents high levels of many resources (e.g., time, knowledge, attention, skill). The other end represents low levels of few resources. These resources represent part of the costs (along with, for example, the diminished benefits mentioned above) of implementing a strategy. Thus, individuals with few resources and those who want to control costs can select simplifying strategies accordingly.

Classification Scheme

To simplify our task, we will divide each of our two dimensions in half: *Social Focus* into *Community* and *Individual*; and *Resources Required* into *High* and *Low*. By crossing these two dimensions, we can construct a four-part classification scheme on which we can base our discussion of social trust and its functional equivalents. Our account of these rival strategies constitutes Part II of this book.

The Risks of Complexity Reduction

By describing social trust as a tool for the reduction of cognitive complexity, we are able to evaluate that strategy relative to others serving the same function. This enables us to break the traditional link between social trust and social distrust by placing these two in a context shared by a wide variety of other activities. It also prompts us to think about social trust *as* a reducer of cognitive complexity. Complexity reduction is not a riskless activity. Taken to extreme, it can result in Michel Serres's tragic *singular*—death, literally or figuratively—the end of life or of meaningful life. But without some degree of structure, complexity becomes chaos, and life is impossible. The zone of life is the continuum of complexity between order and disorder. Social trust, therefore, regardless of what else it achieves, should not result in the elimination of complexity, in stasis.

The risk of stasis—the overreduction or elimination of complexity—is inherent in social trust, as such, regardless of what basis is claimed for it—rationalized or cultural.[10] That is, the risk of stasis is inherent in all within-group, *pluralistic* constructions of social trust. Social trust can be made into an effective tool for the solving of social problems only if the risk of stasis is minimized—only if social trust is made inherently *dynamic*, irreducibly *multiple*. This is the case in across-group, *cosmopolitan* social trust. The distinction between these two forms of social trust is discussed in detail in Part III.

SUMMARY

In this chapter, the last in Part I, we suggested that social trust can usefully be described as a tool for the reduction of cognitive complexity. After considering the dynamic relations between simplicity and complexity in science, in human life in general and in psychology, we concluded that social trust may be too powerful a tool for the reduction of cognitive complexity—that there is an inherent risk in it of singularity, of stasis. But this criticism cannot be limited to social trust. It must be applied as well to its functional equivalents—

to the other strategies we sometimes use to reduce cognitive complexity. When we use any of these strategies, we run the risk of going too far. And there are other risks—as well as benefits, of course. We discuss them all in Part II.

Part II

SOCIAL TRUST: PRESENT

In "Part II, Social Trust: Present," we describe and evaluate several of the strategies—including social trust—that people use to reduce cognitive complexity: strategies for simplicity. This survey of strategies is not meant to be comprehensive. Our purpose is simply to provide a context of comparison within which we can more usefully understand social trust. The four chapters of Part II are organized according to the resource-demand, social-focus classification scheme described in Chapter 3. We examine, first those strategies requiring high levels of resources, followed by those requiring low levels. Within each resource category, the strategies with an individual social focus precede those with a community social focus. We begin our survey, in Chapter 4, with two high-resource demand, individual-focus strategies: *social distrust* and *control*. In Chapter 5, we examine four high-resource-demand, community-focus strategies: *traditional social trust, confidence, risk assessment*, and *law and regulation*. We discuss three low-resource-demand, individual-focus strategies in Chapter 6: *hope, self-knowledge*, and *retreat*. Finally, in Chapter 7, we examine two low-resource demand, community-focus strategies: *culture* and *social trust based on cultural values*. The flow of strategies—from social distrust to social trust based on cultural values—can be considered roughly progressive, from the more negative past to the more positive future, from the destructive to the constructive.

4

Strategies for Simplicity, One, High Resource Demand, Individual Focus

The complexity-reduction strategies discussed in this chapter can be understood as those that are most suited to the stout defense of a certain specific sense of self. Persons adopting these strategies must be convinced, on some level, of the fundamental correctness of their existing ways of being. They are willing to pay very high prices for self-defense. Stasis is all; change is defeat or death. We consider two of these high-cost self-defense strategies here—*social distrust* and *control*—the former at some length, the latter only briefly.

SOCIAL DISTRUST

We began our discussion of social trust with a commentary on social distrust and the devastating effects it has had on the U.S. Environmental Protection Agency. And now we lead off our survey of the functional equivalents of social trust with more talk about social distrust. Social distrust is the heart of the matter: concern about its effects—the tremendous and varied burden of negative consequences that follow from its use—drives much of the current interest in social trust.

But what do we mean by "social distrust"?[1] It is not useful, we contend, to think of social distrust in the traditional sense as being the opposite or reciprocal of social trust. Niklas Luhmann (1979) says simply that "it would hardly be worthwhile paying particular attention to distrust if it were simply a matter of lack of trust" (p. 71). Thus, we describe social distrust as one among several functional equivalents of social trust, one of several strategies for the reduction of cognitive complexity. And, as Luhmann stresses, this complexity must be reduced: "Anyone who merely refuses to confer trust restores the original complexity of the potentialities of the situation and burdens himself with it. A surplus of complexity, however, places too many demands on the individual and makes him incapable of action. Anyone who does not trust must, therefore, turn to functionally equivalent strategies for the reduction of complexity in order to be able to define a practically meaningful situation at all" (p. 71). A person can choose from among the available strategies.

In order to make these strategic choices easier, we want to describe social distrust in ways that clearly separate it from its rivals, particularly social trust. One way to do this is to enlist Aaron Wildavsky's (1988) two-category scheme for classifying risk management strategies: *anticipatory* and *resilient*.[2] Within Wildavsky's framework, distrust would be classified as a strategy based on anticipation, that is it is a strategy that seeks safety by avoiding risks. Social trust, in contrast, is a strategy based on resilience: it seeks safety by taking risks. Distrust is risk-averse; trust is risk-accepting. Wildavsky says that "a strategy of anticipation is based on a fear of regret . . . minimizing regret is self-reinforcing: Don't allow others to act unless they can prove safety in advance . . . The fear of regret rationalizes acts of omission" (pp. 225, 226). Since any individual's knowledge of the future is inherently imperfect, distrust, which depends on that knowledge, is a very costly strategy. One is stuck where one is, paralyzed, with all energies devoted to monitoring one's fears.[3]

Social Distrust: Other Places, Other Times

Like social trust, social distrust is the specifically modern form of an age-old human-relations strategy. As society became more complexly structured in the modern era, social distrust emerged as the powerful successor to the primal form of distrust, which was limited to the interpersonal. But even in its circumscribed, primal form, distrust was (and is) a significant social force. Because of its potential for social devastation, distrust has often been interpreted, by Niklas Luhmann (1979) for example, as a wild force within us that we must learn to control: "A social system which requires, or cannot avoid, distrusting behaviour among its members for certain functions needs at the same time mechanisms which prevent distrust from gaining the upper hand, and, from being reciprocated by a process of reciprocal escalation, turned into a destructive force" (p. 75). For Luhmann, distrust is more primitive and original than trust: distrust is driven by potent negative expectations that give it what Luhmann calls its "emotionally tense and often frantic character" (p. 71). Distrust, even when serving some positive social function, has always been an untamed, unplacated fury.[4] And whereas primal distrust can destroy only oneself and families and friends and others one knows, unlimited social distrust can ruin nations and more. Thus, John Dunn (1988) describes a world darkened by a distrust that will "crush political energy and creativity in a sense of overwhelming futility," and "subvert human society more or less in its entirety" (p. 85). But if distrust is so often and so obviously a disaster to individuals and to societies,[5] how can its evident ubiquity be explained?

One account of the popularity of distrust is based on the notion that distrust is a strategy that is less freely chosen by individuals than imposed on them by society. And the part of society that does the imposing is the ruling class, the controllers of power and of knowledge. Thus, a strategy that is destructive to most members of a society is imposed from above for the benefit of the ruling few. Classic examples of this process can be seen in the history of southern Italy. Anthony Pagden (1988), for example, describes how the Spanish Habsburgs of the seventeenth century manipulated the concerns of persons at each level of society, limiting those interests to the private and familial—the socially irrelevant and the socially destructive. Diego Gambetta, tracing the rise of the Mafia, describes a similar situation in the same region in the nineteenth century, with the Mafioso "injecti[ng] . . . distrust into the market to increase the demand for the product he sells—that is, protection" (1988, p. 173). Social distrust has flourished where it has been nurtured by the powerful to benefit themselves.

Social Distrust: In America, Today

Contemporary survey data reviewed by Ronald Inglehart indicate that the levels of distrust in Sicily, Sardinia, and southern Italy remain the highest in western Europe.[6] Distrust can thus be described as a relatively stable feature of certain societies that is strongly (negatively) related to civic culture and the practice of democracy. Lack of civic culture and practical democracy, together with a growing respect for social distrust, were common complaints of critics of the Reagan-Bush era in America.[7] Can it be that Americans are regressing toward their less "industrially advanced" counterparts in southern Italy and elsewhere, abandoning the strategy of trust, adopting the strategy of distrust? Or has social distrust been a part of the American tradition all along?

Social distrust in contemporary America, as in other times and places, is a problem-solving tool, a strategy for the reduction of cognitive complexity. And it is a strategy that is learned as part of the existing dominant culture.[8] That culture, many commentators agree, is characterized by a particularly *American* brand of individualism. We argued earlier that American individualism is bolstered by the traditional conception of social trust as based on competence and responsibility. Now we can also say that, above all, traditional American culture is supported by social distrust. On this point, we appear to be in agreement with Bernard Barber (1983) who claims that, "distrust of politicians and politics has been part of American popular ideology from the beginning of the nation's history" (p. 71). But the agreement is only superficial. Barber believes that both traditional American culture and social distrust are good and that they are mutually supportive. Our argument, in contrast, advocates certain modifications to that tradition, among them a rejection of social distrust. Not surprisingly, proponents of positions congruent to Barber's, supporters of what we call "American romantic distrust," have long dominated the public discussion of distrust in America (e.g., Hart, 1978; Merelman, 1984).[9]

When we say that American individualism is supported by distrust, our argument is similar to that of the new "cultural theorists" (e.g., Dake, 1991; Thompson, 1988; Wildavsky, 1987).[10] These authors claim that people's concerns are selected (or "constructed") in order to strengthen their preferred forms of social relations. On this account, therefore, fear of regret, fear of dealing with others, fear of being made a fool of—all the varied manifestations of distrust—are selected because of the support they provide for American individualism.[11] We Americans, of course, are born with neither individualism nor distrust innate in us; we learn these attitudes, emotions, ways of knowing and being in the world as we learn our culture. And our culture is taught to us by our institutions: families, schools, jails, military, sports, politics, advertisements, governments, sciences, businesses, movies, courts, books, and so forth. As we tried to document in our chapter on traditional interpretations of social trust, the social sciences in America have contributed their bit to maintaining our twin traditions of individualism and distrust. Now, to move us toward a more useful understanding of social distrust in America, we simply note a few further instantiations of American individualism and consider some ways in which we might have learned them.

American Individualism

How is individualism expressed in America? By whom? In what circumstances? These simple questions are problematical for us because individualism, and consequently distrust, so thoroughly pervades American society that, under normal circumstances, we are simply not aware of what it is or what its effects might be. Upon reflection, however, individualism seems to pop up everywhere, to affect everyone, to dominate all aspects of our lives: our forms of personal expression, our crimes and our punishments, our ways of talking about politics.

Art, in recent years in America, has become a form of personal expression the primary medium of which is personal expression, the purest examples of which are pure personal expression. The guiding concept for artists in this mode, according to Robert Hughes (1993), is "the belief that mere expressiveness is enough; that I become an artist by showing you my warm guts and defying you to reject them. You don't like my guts? You and Jesse Helms, fella" (pp. 186-187). In this hyper-individualistic form of personal expression, concerns for values other than self-expression (such as aesthetic standards or craftsmanship) are considered elitist and anti-democratic. The art of self-expression thus becomes conflated with the politics of self-expression: all

expressions of self—sexual, racial, political, generational, national, religious—
are assumed to be equally valid and valuable, with equal claims on the attention
and respect of others, simply because they are personal expressions,
manifestations of an American individual.[12] And the American individual is
an injured, sinned-against soul: "I am a victim: how dare you impose your
aesthetic standards on me? Don't you see that you have damaged me so badly
that I need only display my wounds and call it art?" (p. 187). When art and
individualism have become one, when all that is trans-individual, social, is
wrung out of art, the cultural conversation is over. Nothing can be said. Social
distrust has won.

Crime and punishment—there no sectors of American society more
dramatically suffused with American individualism and social distrust. From
celebrity killers, excused because they had allegedly suffered abuse at the hands
of their victims, to semianonymous murderers snuffed out by the state, stories
of crime and punishment thrill and entertain millions of Americans daily. And
on each of those days, thousands of Americans are actual victims of violence
and of other criminal behavior. In his history of crime and punishment in
America, Lawrence Friedman (1993) tells this story:

> On November 16, 1991, Patricia Lexie was riding with her husband along
> the eastern edge of Washington, D.C., on the interstate highway. A car
> drew alongside. A man leaned out of the window and fired a shot, hitting
> Patricia in the head. She died almost immediately. She was twenty-nine
> years old, recently married. A few days later, the police arrested a high
> school dropout, nineteen years old, and charged him with the crime. He had
> a long record of criminal violence. But what was his motive: Patricia was a
> stranger; there was no robbery, no rape. Before the shooting, he had told
> some friends, "I feel like killing someone."
>
> (p. 440)[13]

How do we react to this story? Certainly not with surprise. Instead, we may
think, "Nineteen ninety-one? I thought that happened last week!" It all sounds
so familiar, a normal part of our lives.

But we would shake ours heads, still not quite able to grasp the notion of
murder as self-expression. Is that's how far we've come in America?[14] The
killer of Patricia Lexie was an individual, acting on his own. We condemn him
as such: a person, fully responsible for his acts. In doing so, however, we
pretend he created himself; we scramble to absolve ourselves. And in a sense
we are right: none of us is responsible for this or any other particular crime.
Criminals, of course, create themselves—but we provide the materials they use.
Like us, they are products of our culture.[15] If we, the innocent, can't accept
responsibility for the crimes of the guilty, we nonetheless can't escape
responsibility for our culture. This is Friedman's conclusion: "The siege of
crime may be the price we pay for a brash, self-loving, relatively free and open

society" (p. 464). This sounds a bit passive to us. If we don't want to be victims of criminals, we can't talk about ourselves as victims of our culture. Our culture is always changing. And anyone can volunteer to contribute to the direction and extent of those changes.

One way to participate in cultural change is simply to take more care, to be more deliberate, in the way we talk, the way we communicate with ourselves and with other people. Mary Ann Glendon has demonstrated how carelessness in political discourse, particularly on the matter of the rights of individuals, can lead to the most unfortunate consequences: "In its simple American form, the language of rights is the language of no compromise. The winner takes all and the loser has to get out of town. The conversation is over" (1991, p. 9).[16] In other words, American rights talk is the standard verbal expression of American individualism: if I claim a right, there is nothing you can say that can affect my claim: it is "absolute, individual, and independent of any necessary relation to responsibilities" (p. 12). The central irony of American rights talk, of course, is that, instead of preserving democracy, it destroys it.

Mary Ann Glendon's interpretation of American rights talk unfortunately does not appear to be the dominant one, even among critics of the standard version. Edward Sampson (1993), for example, is an advocate of what he calls *identity politics*, "A politics based on the particular life experiences of people who seek to be in control of their own identities and subjectivities and who claim that socially dominant groups have denied them this opportunity" (p. 1219). On our interpretation, the problem with identity politics, as described by Sampson and others, is that two incompatible claims are made: first, Sampson says that "identity movements are seeking a *voice* for themselves in their own terms" (p. 1223). We can support only this claim; it is through irritation and stimulation by minority voices that the majority language evolves in useful ways. Second, however, Sampson argues that modes of discourse based on existing power relationships must be modified to accommodate these new *voices*: "These people have become both more diverse and more restless. Their differences are showing and will not be silenced by appeals to ideas that continue to speak in the voice of their dominators" (p. 1228).[17]

We agree, of course, that appeals in the dominant language will not silence minorities who do not accept the terms of that language. But this is exactly the point: Sampson evidently believes that speakers of the dominant language should accept appeals in minority languages. But why? Because of rights? Sampson is silent. And it is just here that he reveals his unstated *realist* thinking; offering no argument, Sampson must assume that the voices of identity politics are in some way more *real*, more representative of the way things *really are* or *really should be*, than the alternatives. But on our account this belief in the reality of one's own world descriptions as opposed to the distorted descriptions of others, this insistence on the unconditional acceptance by others of one's own voice, can be interpreted as just another manifestation of

American individualism, another barrier against the development of dynamic, effective democracy.[18]

Learning Individualism in America

In America, our culture of individualism is taught to us by our institutions: families, schools, jails, military, sports, politics, advertisements, governments, sciences, businesses, movies, courts, books, and so on. We can only briefly describe one of these. We have chosen the *electronic media* (including but not limited to television and various personal-computer-based media) because we believe that they have become the most powerful institutions of learning in America. And their power is growing daily.[19] The power of the electronic media derives primarily from their ability to alter what Joshua Meyrowitz has called the "situational geography" of social life: by undermining our ability to discriminate among social situations, these media deprive us of the traditional bases on which certain judgments were made.

Compare, as Meyrowitz suggests, the geography of a print society with that of an electronic society. A print society is a divided society: the literate from the nonliterate; the public from the private; those who can read and use specific technical languages from those who cannot; those trained in the use of abstract, linear argument and those who are not.[20] An electronic society, if not united, is nonetheless a society with few barriers. Use of electronic media can be learned quickly and easily by almost everyone; with data recorded and available on every aspect of everyone's life, the distinction between public and private disappears; access to information can be made independent of technical training; persuasion can be based on commonly shared narrative forms. The electronic media eliminate barriers within and between people. What do we learn from that?

One thing we learn is equality. Distinctions among people lose their meaning: expert/novice; leader/supporter; supervisor/worker; doctor/patient; teacher/student; priest/parishioner; man/woman. In Alan Fiske's (1991a) terms, we move in some settings from relations based on authority ranking to relations based on equality matching.[21] We sacrifice authority for equality. Because there are no experts, no leaders, social trust becomes obsolete. We revert back to a simpler form of life; we become what Meyrowitz calls "hunters and gatherers in an information age" (1985, p. 316). But the irony of our situation is entirely modern: our inability to distinguish, for example, between useful and destructive knowledge has evolved at a time when our need for the dominance of the former over the latter is perhaps greater than ever in our history.

And there are other problems. Certain barriers between people appear to be impregnable to the assaults or the magic of the electronic media. Thus, while equality matching reigns in certain settings, Fiske's three other models dominate elsewhere. In America, of course, there are the barriers of race and class, as yet unbreached, unmarked, by the electronic offensive, seeming to grow taller and thicker each year. No equality matching here. Instead, with race we have communal sharing: identity based on ancestry. And with class we have market pricing: identity based on economic role.[22] Thus, the barriers that survive in the electronic society are the barriers that separate the rich from the poor, barriers the owners and primary users of the electronic media have no interest in lowering.

Through the electronic media, then, we learn new modes of equality in some life contexts while we maintain and strengthen our old ways of relating in other life contexts. When we examine the total pattern of relations, what is most striking is the decline of social relations that *bridge social differences.* In the case of the demise of authority and the rise of equality, we have the obliteration of differences. And in the case of continued communal and market relations, we have separate societies, solitary solidarities. In both cases, on this unfortunate account, the electronic media produce individual, self-absorbed, isolated entities among which the most genuine, heartfelt connections consist primarily of deep, dark distrust.[23] The master villain in this sad scenario is, of course, television.[24]

Though television dominates all aspects of American culture and is therefore difficult to approach afresh, several critics (e.g., Gitlin, 1986) have managed to wrest useful meaning from it. Foremost among them is Bill McKibben (1992), a naturalist and writer who came in from his beloved woods one day, sat down, and viewed twenty-four straight hours of programs (the same single day) for each channel on a large cable TV service, a total of nearly two thousand hours of video tape. As unpromising as it may sound, these thousands of hours of television (contrasted with his similar number of hours outdoors) taught McKibben a good deal. Among his conclusions:

- Television divorces us from nature.
- Television breaks down the sense of community between human beings.
- Television mocks shared values.
- Television worships the individual and teaches us to do the same.
- Television teaches a fear of humiliation.
- Television cultivates a sense of hip, ironic detachment.
- Television has trained us not to take it seriously.

Finally, McKibben argues, perhaps counter to popular assumption, that television, far from filling our heads with fluff and fantasy, instead insinuates into our compliant minds a raw, brutish form of reality: "It is anti-utopian in the extreme. We're discouraged from thinking that, except for a few new products, there might be a better way of doing things" (p. 78). In its insistence on what is, TV is both the great comforter and the great frustrater—the master of stasis.

In many ways, American television seems to be the perfect institution for bolstering American individualism, the perfect distrust-reification machine (Warren, 1990): we sit alone in half-light or dark and we absorb the message, the same message, over and over, in all its varying cultural guises, that *human beings are asocial, self-formed monads*. We are taught above all else to value self-expression, our personal opinions and ourselves. Our opinions *are* our selves, essentially, uniquely. And we learn what is really important and holy: the immutable me. In this way, we learn that social engagement and public debate are worthless. Why should we listen to a bunch of dopes who disagree with us and who want to do us in? Television teaches us to distrust.[25]

Social Distrust, Summary

In our discussion of social distrust, we argued that, as a strategy for the reduction of cognitive complexity (thereby helping one to cope with complex social environments), distrust is paralyzing, risk averse, and costly. Why, then, would anyone adopt distrust? We suggested that distrust is normally not freely chosen by individuals but instead is imposed by society as part of a dominant culture. This is done because distrust, in its effects, supports the existing structure of the society, as, for example, in southern Italy. We described the use of distrust in contemporary America to reinforce the dominant culture of individualism and its resultant social structure.[26] In America, distrust is supported by a wide variety of institutions all of which seem to be dominated by or dependent on television and other electronic media.

Still, the question seems unresolved: if social distrust has so many negative consequences, how can it survive? And the notion that distrust is imposed on us by some distant "ruling class" through the vague, amorphous workings of some "dominant culture" doesn't quite satisfy our need for concrete, street-level explanation. Our problem, perhaps, is that we have allowed our discussion of distrust to be dominated by bleak negativity when we could have chosen instead to describe the many *positive* consequences of distrust. This tactical error, if that's what it is, may be compounded by the fact that the negative results of distrust affect either "no one" (i.e., the society at large, future generations, etc.) or persons with no power.[27] Thus, who cares? The positive consequences of distrust, in contrast, accrue to the powerful people in our society, subscribers to what John Kenneth Galbraith (1992) calls the "culture of contentment." And, since distrust has benefited the American "contented class" so greatly, one would expect those persons to use their considerable influence to assure its survival. Our goal, dim and distant though it may be, is the opposite: to undermine and discredit the strategy of distrust. But no fear: social distrust is so deeply ingrained in the dominant American culture that few active measures may need to be taken in its defense—other than, of course, the usual marginalizing and trivializing of emergent critical voices.

Though on first hearing cynical sounding, we think that Charles Lindblom's (1990) typically trenchant analysis restates our argument in a useful way:

- Understanding the social world depends on communication and other interchange.
- People enter into interchanges in order to control others.
- Interchange is consequently impairing.
- Everyone—citizen and functionary alike—builds his understanding of the social world on impairing interchanges.
- A competition of ideas offers some escape from impairments.

The five steps just taken now pose the question of how rigorously ideas in fact compete. The proposed twofold answer: (1) the advantages in communication and other influences of some participants severely weaken and narrow the competition of ideas, (2) through a predominance of ideas that defend the varied advantages of the advantaged.

(pp. 78-81)

Lindblom's argument is a simpler, straight-to-the-point, American-pragmatic version of Jürgen Habermas's (1984, 1987) concerns about communication. And on this point at least we agree: Distrust is dominant because it serves the purposes of the privileged.

CONTROL

Within our individualist culture, the popularity of self-control as a strategy for the reduction of social complexity is routinely manifested in bookstores where the promise to bring the unruly in oneself under control is a common theme among the best sellers. The goal of self-control appears to be unquestioned. Instead, the primary debate among these books concerns the relative efficacy of the various techniques within their contexts of application: which technology can generate the strictest control over one's self? With minimal effort, of course.

We can escape this contemporary technological debate by invoking a historical comparison that is based on different assumptions. Moses Hadas's (1965) account of self-control in ancient Greece centers on the distinction between two realms of being, the divine and the human: "The gods behave as it behooves gods to behave, and man must behave as it behooves man to behave; he must give expression to his own humanity, not seek to assimilate himself to an ideal (which he cannot in any case know) outside humanity" (p. 110). Hadas notes that this may not have been the dominant understanding among the Greeks, but it is one that sets them apart from us. On this understanding, a key difference between humans and gods is that humans do not have control over their lives, and they should not aspire to that divine power. Instead, humans should attempt to excel *as humans.* A *hero,* for the Greeks, was a person who had lived an exemplary life and, in death, was a source of inspiration. Hadas contrasts the Greek hero with the Christian saint: "A man approaches sainthood in the degree that he suppresses the impulses of ordinary humanity and assimilates himself to a pattern outside humanity. A man becomes a hero in the degree that he emphasizes his human attributes" (pp. 111-112). Thus, as with Achilles sulking in his tent, Greek heroes were not necessarily nice and lovable all the time: on occasion, they seemed out of control. They were human.

And humans, unlike gods, must live with limitations: we will die; our loved ones will die; terrible and wonderful things will happen to us. It is when thinking about these limitations and their meaning that Martha Nussbaum (1990) reminds us of the Greek conception of *hubris*: "The failure to comprehend what sort of life one has actually got, the failure to live within its limits (which are also possibilities), the failure, being mortal, to think mortal thoughts. Correctly understood, the injunction to avoid *hubris* is not a penance or denial—it is an instruction as to where the valuable things *for us* are to be found" (p. 381). That is, in concrete, limited human life. And we should make no deadening attempts to transcend our limits by applying abstract notions of control (i.e., certain ethical theories that we may take to be the words of the gods) to ourselves. Instead, we should immerse ourselves in human social life and attend to the stories told of heroes, attend not to the theories spun about them but to the emotions in their lives and in ours.

We experience emotions; the gods don't. Self-control is a strategy to eliminate the power of emotions in our lives and make us more like gods. But a wide range of philosophers agree, Martha Nussbaum notes, that emotions "are either identical with or partly constituted by judgments of value—judgments that certain worldly items have great importance, items that the agent does not fully control" (p. 387). As *individuals,* human beings are incomplete. We are condemned to being social, dependent—our emotions in the hands of fortune. To a person striving for the devine, this is unacceptable. Thus, "A self-sufficient and complete person . . . has nothing to grieve for, nobody to love in the usual human sense, the sense in which love implies incompleteness and the absence of control" (p. 387).

Appealing to a mundane modern metaphor, the attempt by an individual to gain control of one's fate is analogous to societal attempts to achieve order through reliance on law and regulation. And the arguments against self-control are the same as those against "law and order." Self-control can work only if one limits one's life to those contexts over which one has control. The set of such contexts necessarily constitutes a   narrowly circumscribed world. And living within an extremely limited world restricts one's ability to adapt to the inevitable changes that will occur *even within that small sphere.* But assume you could control everything in your little world. Any life context that can be controlled at reasonable cost (i.e., without killing yourself) must necessarily be easily understood and, in particular, it must be socially simple. In the language of Aaron Wildavsky, self-control is the ultimate anticipatory life strategy: seeking safety by avoiding risks. Like all risks, social risks can be avoided, but not without costs. The strategy of-self control ultimately requires that one withdraw from complicating interactions with other people. The primary consequence of control, then, is becoming stuck at a low and unhappy level of social (i.e., human) development.[28]

Another way of understanding the strategy of self-control is suggested by Niklas Luhmann (1990). For Luhmann, control means *"comparison of input to memory,* to memory only; that is, comparison of the present not to the future but to the past. Control in this sense means looking backward" (p. 101). On this account, when a person adopts a self-control strategy he works to increase his ability to store information about the past. He devotes all his resources to knowing the past in the belief that it will improve his judgments of the present. But since knowledge of his limited past cannot affect future events in society, this increasing supply of old information cannot help him achieve any but the most limited goals in his life. The result, according to Luhmann, is increased disappointment: "Increased storage capacity must mean that we fall more and more into the dead hand of the past—of past facts and past fancies. . . . We may become unable to forget" (pp. 101-102).

SUMMARY: COMMITMENT TO PERSONAL CORRECTNESS

The two strategies we discussed in this chapter, distrust and control, are both backward-facing self-defense strategies. They derive their seductive appeal from their encouragement of individual vanity, hubris, the belief we all want to have that each of us is self-made, unique, and specially blessed. Control and distrust tempt us one step further by assuring us that we deserve, and promising us that we will achieve, protection, preservation, . . . immortality? But none of this can happen. Instead, control and distrust generate tragic disappointment because the future, as the product of uncontrollable social processes, cannot ever match the past. And to devote oneself solely to the past is, in any event, simply to give up on life.

5

Strategies for Simplicity, Two, High Resource Demand, Community Focus

In the previous chapter we discussed complexity-reduction strategies that functioned primarily in self-defense. The strategies we consider in this chapter are similar to those, particularly in their strong commitment to correctness. What is taken to be accurate, genuine, and authentic in the present set of strategies, however, is not one's self but one's community. Adopters of these strategies are willing to pay very high prices in defense of their communities, the sources and guarantors of their personal wisdom, goodness, and truth. We discuss four high-cost community-defense strategies here: *traditional social trust, confidence, risk assessment*, and *law and regulation*.

SOCIAL TRUST: TRADITIONAL

We have already argued in some detail, in the chapter on traditional interpretations of social trust that the treatment of social trust within American social science had until very recently been bound to a rationalist tradition that, if not universally endorsed, was certainly not effectively challenged. Traditional social trust continues to be characterized by its unexamined, assumed correctness within traditional American individualistic culture. Among the ironies attendant to traditional social trust is one generated by its empiricism. Traditional social trust is a thoroughly empirical concept, based as it is on judgments of competence and responsibility. Individuals are to make these judgments, we are told, only after extended observations of performance, data collection, and data processing. We are to act, on this model, individually, as independent, amateur scientists. And of course this is how we are expected to perform all our social judgments within traditional American culture. Empiricism and individualism go hand-in-hand:

> empiricism . . . like most individualistic views in contemporary social phi-
> losophy . . . has not been much aware of itself as individualistic and hence
> as one of the possible alternative views. It has seemed, rather, in this re-
> spect, the obviously right view.
>
> (Will, 1985, p. 122)

The irony is that American social scientists, after insisting on an empirical basis for social trust, have (with the few commendable exceptions noted earlier)
acknowledged no need or responsibility *on their part* to supply supporting evidence for *their* judgments.[1] But social scientists aren't the only proponents of
traditional social trust. Social philosophers and ethicists have also promoted
this concept in their varying ways.

Philosophy and Traditional Social Trust

We wouldn't expect philosophers to provide empirical support for their
accounts of social trust. But this deliberate distancing from data leads, unfortunately, to the great general weakness of moral philosophy—its lack of
"psychological realism."[2] A major cause of this, it seems, is the choice by
many philosophers to begin their investigations from abstract principles rather
than from human problems. And from that lofty beginning, they tend to deal
with trust as though it were something that, for humans, existed somewhere
else—a far-off place which we must struggle "to see clearly." Sissela Bok
(1979), for example, describes an essential relation between trust and truth: "If
there is no confidence in the truthfulness of others, is there any way to assess
their fairness, their intentions to help or to harm?" (p. 33). Our answer (and
the assumption on which we expect most people behave) is, "Of course there
is!" We can and do assess fairness (and justice and trustworthiness, etc.) under
all kinds of conditions, even under the assumption that almost all communication is "untruthful" or "impaired" (Lindblom, 1990).

To talk about truth and trust the way Bok does requires either a disregard
for or an ignorance of the basic human task of making inferences about people's values based on imperfect information. Imperfect information is all that
any of us will ever have in any interesting human context.[3] Of course
"truthful" information, if we can agree in some time and place what that is,
would always be preferred to "untruthful." But we say that only on the understanding that words like *true*, *fair*, *just*, and *trustworthy* are simply
compliments "paid to beliefs which we think so well justified that, for the moment, further justification is not needed" (R. Rorty, 1991a, p. 24).[4] More
bluntly, F. G. Bailey, in his rhetorical account of truth and lying, describes
these as "political words, weapons for use in competition for power" (1991, p.

128)[5] What can be done? Bailey sensibly advises, "enter the debate" (1991, p. 129). Trust, like anything human, is not perfect; it's what we make it.

The principles-first, people-last approach taken by many philosophers when dealing with trust and related concepts can lead to bizarre discussions based on an abstract essentialism that, if ever put to practice, would be just plain silly. Of course the goals of most philosophers, being normative rather than descriptive, are different from those of social scientists, and they encourage a certain detachment from life as we live it. But this separation of moral theories from human life is interpreted, by some philosophers, as a problem to be corrected. Virginia Held (1984), for example, argues that "we ought to begin with the point of view of a sincere moral agent with experience of the problems in question, not the point of view of an ideal observer removed from our actual reality. We should then develop a method for understanding and dealing with actual moral problems" (p. 3). Any attempt to construct a unified theory for all moral problems, Held contends, will fail to be practically useful. Instead, we should develop partial models of moral behavior for different domains of life. And, significantly, these theories should be developed within and tested against moral *experience*. Held does not argue for a science of ethics but simply for a higher degree of psychological realism.

Trust is described by Held primarily in interpersonal terms—as a mutual willingness to cooperate, for instance.[6] As a moral philosopher, however, Held is concerned with how social trust can be justified in various contexts. It is at this point, unfortunately, that Held seems to lose touch with psychological realism. For example, she is critical of *any* trust granted to corporations, "among the most undemocratic of all modern institutions" (p. 75). We believe that Held is twice wrong here. First, she assumes some general disunion between the interests of all corporations and the interests of all individuals. But this is untenable: each of us can think of corporations, perhaps even those for which we work, with which we share significant interests. And those interests, we contend, could provide a basis for trust. Second, she apparently supports distrust.

The universality of Held's attack on corporations is an indicator of her general approach which soon becomes bogged down in "rights talk." At that point, the conversation is pretty much finished. Held has left the realm of human problems and flown off to the land of abstract principles. She claims, for example, that disjunctions between what she calls "rights to basic necessities" and the Constitutional rights of Americans (as interpreted) are grounds for distrust of the entire system: "A more obvious basis for *mistrust* in the American social system would be hard to imagine" (p. 77).[7] What has gone wrong? Why have Held's good intentions yielded such barren results? The primary problem, it seems to us, is what might be called Held's "monoculturalism," her insistence on the correctness of a particular worldview. It is a worldview that we would identify as traditional—one that, in rights terms, demands competence and responsibility.[8]

Another philosopher who has attempted to write usefully about trust is Annette Baier (1986). Unlike Held, Baier interprets trust very broadly, using that term, for example, to refer to behavior that we would speak of as routine matters of culture: "We trust those we encounter in lonely library stacks to be searching for books, not victims. We sometimes let ourselves fall asleep on trains or planes, trusting neighboring strangers not to take advantage of our defenselessness" (p. 234). All of these cases cited by Baier are cultural norms; they are matters of certainty, not trust. No thought is given; no risk is taken. We'd be totally shocked if these norms were breached. In another part of her essay, however, Baier defines trust in a way we can recognize: "it is letting other persons (natural or artificial, such as firms, nations, etc.) take care of something the truster cares about, where such 'caring for' involves some exercise of discretionary powers" (p. 240).

Yet elsewhere, and at length, Baier advances the notion of "infant trust." Now, the concept of infant trust is not unique to Baier, even among philosophers.[9] But Baier's formulation is troublesome. First, on a side issue, she takes trust to be the inverse of distrust. This has the unfortunate effect of narrowing the range of options one considers. On the main matter, Baier effectively eliminates significant cognitive differences between infants and adults, reducing the latter to the level of the former. This, of course, runs counter to her earlier definition, which was based on the acceptance of vulnerability. Infants obviously cannot accept vulnerability: they have no choice. But Baier also claims that adults cannot trust at will—either one already does trust or one requires reasons to do so. This could only hold true, however, if *trust* and *not trust* were the only options one had. Suppose that A asks for my trust. Contrary to Baier, I could have known about A, a good deal or a little, but have had no occasion to trust her or not. The question hadn't entered my mind. Now that it has, however, I certainly *can* trust at will if I choose to do so.[10]

These considerations aside, Baier's discussion of trust is very helpful. Particularly valuable is her attack on the dominance of the trust conversation by males throughout history. Once we understand this, the traditional formulation of social trust suddenly makes sense—it's all male: *competent, responsible . . . rational, abstract, distanced from life.* And Baier correctly suggests that our thinking about trust must be broadened to include what the male theorists left out, specifically concerns, like caring, that are associated with unequal power relationships. To illustrate this point, Baier analyzes a child-care conflict to identify what behavior by the care-giving mother might lead to the sabotaging of the father's trust. "The disturbing and trust-undermining suspicion," Baier notes, "is not necessarily that she doesn't care about the children's good, or cares only about her own—it is the suspicion that what she cares about conflicts with rather than harmonizes with what he cares about and that she is willing to sacrifice his concerns to what she sees as the children's and her own" (p. 254). Trust, in other words, is not (necessarily) based on competence and responsibility. It's based on *shared values,* whatever, in any particular case, they may be.[11]

The Limits of Traditional Social Trust

The philosophical accounts of trust, interpersonal and social, that we have briefly outlined in this chapter tend to be more complex and wide-ranging than their social science counterparts. In their meanderings among varieties of trust, these accounts often vacillate between traditional and innovative constructions. On the whole, however, Bok's account is more traditional than Held's and Held's more traditional than Baier's. This developmental direction—away from the traditional—should be considered in any reconstruction of social trust.

Moving away from the traditional means, in part, a reduction in resource requirements. The high-resource demands of traditional social trust derive from its required empirical base. On the other dimension of our classification scheme, traditional social trust is community-focused. Such a focus is inherent in any concept of social trust. Whatever the specific construction, social trust refers to a relationship between individuals and some group, agency, or institution in society. Traditional social trust, however—because of its demands for competence and responsibility, molded on the model of the isolated male— turns the focus of individuals away from their communities and back toward themselves. Communities that teach traditional social trust are dominated communities. Thus, traditional social trust is designed to fail. It forces non-dominant individuals to select alternate strategies for reducing cognitive complexity. And the strategy most available to them, the preferred strategy of the dominant class, is distrust.

CONFIDENCE

The concept of confidence is often confused with or used as a surrogate for social trust, as in *The Confidence Gap* by Seymour Martin Lipset and William Schneider (1983). When the discussion of social trust is based at all on empirical data, the data often refer to confidence, not to trust (e.g., Barber, 1983; Kasperson, Golding, and Tuler, 1991). Confidence, on our understanding, is not social trust.[12] The confusion between the two concepts can be interpreted as a product of the traditional construction of social trust. As we have noted previously, traditional social trust is based on competence and responsibility. Competence refers to degree of technical expertise. Responsibility refers to "doing the right thing," where "the right thing" refers to cultural expectations.

Since traditional social trust is defined within traditional American culture, the expectations of that dominant culture are assumed—that is, being competent. Within that cultural context, then, social trust boils down to degree of technical expertise. And confidence is just that: a belief in technical expertise, competence or ability (Dasgupta, 1988; Luhmann, 1988).

Our differentiation between confidence, and social trust is based on the distinction between a familiar environment (in which one may have confidence) and a risky environment (in which one may make a judgment to trust).[13] Trust, as Luhmann (1988) says, "presupposes a situation of risk. If you do not consider alternatives . . . you are in a situation of confidence. If you choose one action in preference to others in spite of the possibility of being disappointed by the actions of others, you define the situation as one of trust" (1988, p. 97). The alternative to risk, which Luhmann associates with trust, is danger, which is linked with confidence: "[O]nly in the case of risk does decision making (that is to say contingency) play a role. One is exposed to dangers" (Luhmann, 1993, p. 23). Thus we have *a given*, familiar environment, danger, and confidence. Opposed to that we have *a choice* among different environments, risk, and trust. In a situation of confidence, one is exposed to dangers, but no thought is normally given to them because they are familiar and fall within one's realm of competence to manage. In a situation of trust, in contrast, one must decide between alternate futures, each of which may or may not turn out to be manageable.[14]

Our adaptation of Luhmann's analysis of confidence helps us to appreciate this strategy's limitations. Most significantly, confidence limits one to the familiar. We can describe this problem in two ways. First, because confidence is based on a judgment of technical expertise, a confident person (i.e., a person using that strategy) must believe in her ability to make such a judgment in the given context. Thus, a confident individual is confident in herself. But the contexts in which any person believes herself to be confident are limited. The effectiveness of confidence in reducing cognitive complexity is therefore inherently constrained. Indeed, if one has high standards for personal confidence, the benefits of confidence judgments may often be exceeded by their costs.

But, of course, that's not the way it is in practice. For us, the more significant problem in daily life is not underconfidence, it's overconfidence. Confidence, in other words, is a strategy that works too well! And overconfidence is a general problem of human judgment, often leading to seriously negative results. In a series of landmark studies by Paul Slovic, Baruch Fischhoff, and Sarah Lichtenstein (1982), for example, overconfidence was shown to be an important factor in disputes over the severity and management of environmental and technological hazards. The general workings of overconfidence have been elucidated by Lee Ross, Richard Nisbett, and their colleagues in a variety of studies over the past fifteen years (Nisbett and Ross, 1980; Ross and Nisbett, 1991). Much of this work has centered on the following problem:

- People make predictions of behavior (of others and themselves) primarily on the basis of what they believe to be valid dispositions and traits. That is, they use lay personality theories. People tend to be confident in these predictions even when the information they have is minimal and of questionable validity.
- The behavior to be predicted, in contrast, is often constrained or produced primarily by the situation in which it occurs. Because people tend to underestimate the behavior-producing power of situations, their predictions, even about themselves, are often wrong.

Nisbett and Ross have called this problem the "fundamental attribution error." Since our understanding of confidence is based on a given, familiar situation, this tendency to overconfidence would be expressed in the application of that strategy to a new, unfamiliar situation. Thus, the strategy of confidence can lead to overconfidence, and that can lead to dangerous errors.[15]

Our second way of describing how confidence limits one to the familiar is perhaps more convincing than the first. It derives from the idea of contingency. On our understanding, everything is contingent, the unnecessary products of chance: our world, the cultures, nations, and communities in it, our families, and ourselves. This is unfortunate for the strategy of confidence because contingency and confidence don't mix: contingency undermines the familiar and erodes one's confidence. Bad for confidence, but, we do not doubt, good for us. Confidence is stuck in the familiar; but we are not. Until we die. This is Michel Serres (1991), describing the founding of Rome, the founding of us: "The crowd, then, on that summer day, founded its temples not on rock or stone but on what melts. A good foundation is built on what moves. . . . [L]iquid is not liquid, it is the most solid, most resistant, most permanent of beings in the world. We must found on liquid, not on solid; we must found on time. Or on sand, the sandglass of time" (p. 275).

But we can't live without some degree of confidence, some belief in our ability to predict what is to come. At the same time, we have to be aware of the limitations of confidence. And we have to guard against our desire to be seduced by it. We have to learn to live, alert, on the edge of confidence and contingency, aware of but not paralyzed by life's arbitrariness. "Such recognition," Owen Flanagan (1991) points out, "is a good if it renders infertile the grounds for overconfidence in one's life and intolerance for alternative lives. It is more problematic, however, if it renders these grounds so infertile that nothing but ennui, despair, and cynicism can take root" (p. 196). But how can one live on the edge of confidence and contingency? The calm allure of the former's simplicity would certainly always dominate the latter's unsettling complexity. This, of course, is the context in which social trust evolved. And social trust is a solution to the problem of confidence and contingency: by taking risks and trusting others, we are able to move away from the familiar and into the new. Social trust, in brief, allows us to trade cognitive complexity for social complexity.

RISK ASSESSMENT

We use the term *risk assessment* informally here to refer to a varied set of analytical techniques that have been developed in recent years to address risk-management problems.[16] Our purpose here is not to review these techniques; instead, we want to make a brief, simple point that applies, we believe, to all of them. We take our lead from Aaron Wildavsky (1988). What all these risk-assessment techniques have in common is that they are based on *anticipation*. According to Wildavsky, strategies that are based on anticipation assume a stable or securely predictable social environment, an agreed-upon goal and the availability of adequate knowledge. But, as Wildavsky and others (notably Lindblom, 1990) abundantly demonstrate, the problems that concern us most meet none of these specifications.

The problems that arouse us most, on the contrary, are characterized by unstable or unpredictable social environments, disagreement on goals, and lack of adequate knowledge. Instead of anticipatory strategies, what we need in these difficult cases are strategies based on *resilience*. Resilience is superior to anticipation in unstable, discordant, and unfamiliar situations because it relies on social interaction, an energetic play among diverse interpretations, rather than on magisterial, removed-from-the-fray cogitation (Wildavsky, 1979; Lindblom and Cohen, 1979). Because it forces an awareness of contingency and weakens confidence, social interaction is modest in its knowledge claims. And social interaction also benefits greatly from the error-correcting effects of competition among multiple contending accounts. Cogitation, in contrast, tends to be narrowly overconfident, committing errors that are sometimes dangerous and often difficult to detect and correct.[17]

What are the consequences of dependence on an anticipatory risk assessment strategy? Anticipation is a baldly ironic expression because, in practice, it consists of looking backward. The anticipator gazes toward the past because he assumes that the future will replicate it. If not as a faithful copy, the future is certainly understood as being safely predictable from the past. The world of the anticipator, the risk assessor, is stable, socially homogeneous, and well known. The risk assessor is, therefore, deeply conservative, a defender of what was, what used to be. All of which, he fails in his restricted view to notice, was contingent, the product of chance. As of course is his future, into which he is pushed, backwards, by time, the safety of the familiar fading from view.[18]

Another, related way to talk about what's wrong with anticipatory risk assessment is to discuss its social isolation. What sets the risk assessor apart is his belief in his mastery of the facts. He knows more than we do because his techniques permit him to "glimpse the world as it really is." Unfortunately, the justification he offers for his privileged powers is convincing only to persons very similar to himself. Outside that small group, his facts are interpreted as opinions, his pronouncements as just another voice in a raucous public debate. And convinced of his correctness, the risk assessor's only interest in debate is in winning. Failing that, he withdraws, giving up on social interaction, a risk too great to take.

The struggle between proponents of cogitation and those of social interaction is ancient, but it is also basic to any contemporary discussion of social policy. Similarly, much of contemporary social philosophy in both America and Europe has revolved around criticism of "modern" Western philosophy and its search for transcendental, universal justifications of truth and morality. Many contemporary social thinkers have abandoned cogitative approaches and have come to rely more on social interaction. Wisdom and usefulness in social philosophy, and the policies based on it, are more likely to emerge through the application of resilient rather than anticipatory strategies. This criticism can be interpreted, as Richard Rorty (1979) does, as being against professional, technical philosophy, a philosophy based on inquiry, and in favor of practical philosophy based on, for example, conversation (pp. 389-394). Rorty himself, however, is often criticized for giving up on philosophy as such and for advocating a "conservative" brand of conversation, one that he insists is inevitably conditioned by Western liberal culture. Others, Jürgen Habermas (1985) and Richard Bernstein (1983), for example, want more. But it is what connects Rorty, Habermas, Bernstein, and others, not what separates them, that is most important to us now: their shared rejection of anticipatory strategies based on cogitation and their shared embracement of social interaction.

LAW AND REGULATION

These approaches to the reduction of cognitive complexity are, of course, prime exemplars of Aaron Wildavsky's (1988) anticipatory strategies: "Whether society should mainly seek to increase its ability to respond to unexpected dangers by increasing its resilience, or whether it should seek to anticipate dangers to prevent them from doing harm, is what the risk debate is about" (p. 35). Safety (i.e., the reduction of cognitive complexity) cannot effectively be legislated, according to Wildavsky, because safety is a process, a search, not a condition.[19] Search is essential because uncertainty is ever present; the safe and dangerous are inevitably intertwined; and protecting the parts of a system endangers the whole. "Trial and error works to increase the resilience that improves safety because it is the most vigorous search procedure in existence" (p. 227).

Wildavsky's critique of law and regulation is shared by many authors within risk management (e.g., Jasonoff, 1990) and in other fields (e.g., Shapiro, 1987).[20] If Wildavsky's position seems more extreme than the others, however, it's because he writes from deep within the heart of American individualism, expressing the sort of ideas that provoked Steven Kelman to remark (not necessarily with Wildavsky in mind) that "some social scientists obsessed with unintended consequences sometimes appear to go so far as to argue that there is no connection between intention and result. But this is a view that would seem both excessively ornery and inconsistent with evolutionary pressures favoring creatures better able to choose means that fit their ends" (Kelman, 1992, p. 182). In discussing future generations, for example, Wildavsky argues rather bizarrely (but in accord with many economists) that "our duty lies not in leaving them exactly the social and environmental life we think they ought to have, but rather in making it possible for them to inherit a climate of open choices—that is, in leaving behind a larger level of general, global resources to be redirected as they, not we, will see fit" (Wildavsky, 1988, p. 216). In brief, quantity is the only value that counts. Culture and the connections and interactions among cultures across space and time are irrelevant. Wildavsky is, of course, aware of these limitations (Douglas and Wildavsky, 1982), but his willingness to advance such an extreme admonition (or cultural preference) demonstrates his comfort with it.

An argument against reliance on law and regulation not raised by Wildavsky, and one which we favor, is based on the relations between a litigious society and a distrustful society. When regulation and litigation become ways of life, distrust comes to dominate social interaction. And distrust, as we have argued, is an inefficient, destructive means of reducing cognitive complexity. Thus we have adversarial legalism, arising, in Robert Kagan's account, "from a vicious circle" (1991, p. 397). It is a circle centered on a contradiction—Americans wanting both a weak government and one that delivers the goods. Government is designed to fail—to fail those without private sources of power. And those who want government to work seem condemned to watching the lawyers chase each other around the circle. We are reminded of the vexing problems besetting the Environmental Protection Agency (Landy, et al., 1990).[21] But Kagan suggests ways in which the system could be improved through the use of "public deliberation" and a "dialogic community." "The key to diminution of adversary legalism seems to be a bit of magic—in a disbelieving age, to restore faith in the competence and public-spirited nature of governmental authority" (1991, pp. 398-399). Kagan is describing social trust, trust based on the traditional values of competence and responsibility. For reasons we have outlined earlier, we do not believe that a broadly viable social trust can be based on competence and responsibility. In some limited contexts, primarily those in which the two bases could be easily assessed, traditional social trust might work. In general, however, social trust must be based on a *variety of context-specific cultural values.*

SUMMARY: COMMITMENT TO COMMUNITY CORRECTNESS

The four paths to cognitive simplicity we discussed in this chapter, *traditional social trust, confidence, risk assessment* and *law and regulation,* all passed through the land of community correctness. And they all emerged as high-cost community-defense strategies. The choice of any of these seems motivated to some degree by fear of the new and strange, the belief that what is familiar is true and beautiful and that what is different should be avoided. These strategies are formulas for insulation, for seeking comfort in what is certain not to be threatening—benign, imagined communities filled with folks just like us who simply want to stick together. Places that never were and better than any place will ever be. Places worth defending at any cost.

We have now finished talking about high-resource-demand strategies, and we turn to those that, regardless of their effectiveness, at least have the advantage of not costing much.

6

Strategies for Simplicity, Three, Low Resource Demand, Individual Focus

The strategies discussed in this chapter—*hope, self-knowledge,* and *retreat*—differ most significantly from their high-resource-demand relatives, *social distrust* and *control*, in their comparatively modest expressions of certainty. Persons who select one of the former may be less convinced of their personal correctness than those who choose one of the latter—and therefore less willing to expend large amounts of resources in self-defense. Or they may, for some reason, simply not care very much about self-defense. This doesn't mean their degrees of caring (and their concomitant commitment of resources) won't increase—in some cases to ruinous levels. But diminished concern for self-defense is also possible. *Hope, self-knowledge,* and *retreat*, therefore, are *supple* strategies, useful both when one is in a defensive, backward-facing posture *and* when one chooses to turn around and move forward.

HOPE

At the end of Voltaire's masterpiece on optimism and hope, Candide is impressed by the splendid hospitality shown him and his companions by a Turkish farmer. Candide asked the farmer if he had "an enormous and splendid property?"[1] "I have only twenty acres, replied the Turk; I cultivate them with my children, and the work keeps us from three great evils, boredom, vice, and poverty." As they walked back to their farm, Candide commented to his friends that he thought that the farmer might be on to something. But Pangloss, the philosopher of optimism, babbled uselessly on about the sad fates of kings. Candide interrupted his friend's recitation: "I know also . . . that we must cultivate our garden." Martin, the pragmatic scholar, added: "Let's work without speculating . . . it's the only way of rendering life bearable." And Candide replied, "That is very well put . . . but we must cultivate our garden."

Candide does not remain alive for us today because it is an attack on foolish optimism. We don't need Voltaire for that. *Candide* lives for us because it describes something that we have difficulty expressing for ourselves: the ambiguity of hope. Most of what has been written about hope interprets it as an undoubted good. A few contrarians have described hope in nothing but negative terms. And some writers have found it useful to distinguish between good and bad brands of hope. But very little has been written about the ambiguity of hope. To broaden our understanding of hope, we will briefly describe some of what has been said about it in the good, bad, and mixed categories. Then we will return to *Candide* and the ambiguity of hope.

Hope Is Good

Hope's greatest advocate, judged on the basis of quantity if nothing else, is Ernst Bloch, the author of the exhaustive three-volume account, *The Principle of Hope* (1986).[2] Bloch's book consists of an extensive theoretical discussion preceded and followed by meditations on every form in which he takes hope to be manifested. In the small: daydreams, fairy tales, fashion, travel, film, theater. In the large: social systems (utopias), technology, art, and architecture. Everywhere: literature, philosophy, religion. All of European culture is connected somehow to hope. "How richly people have always dreamed of this, dreamed of the better life that might be possible" (p. 3). Bloch's hope is not the passive emotion of religion. It is the active emotion of politics: the enemy is in the world; eliminate him, and the better life you dream of will be yours.

"Thinking means venturing beyond" (p. 4). Bloch's positive insistence on the future and his criticisms of Freud's negative insistence on the past, his positive talk in all its guises, is uplifting, inspiring. But in the end it is not convincing. The problem for us is not in his theoretical arguments for hope.[3] We can agree that the importance of hope in the small, psychological sense, seems self-evident. The problem is in linking that "subjective hope" with "objective hope," larger social events and a particular political utopia. For Bloch that utopia was the Soviet Union. Even before its collapse, it would have been difficult for us to agree that our everyday experiences of hope were precursors of the absolute hope that was embodied in the Soviet Union. On our account, Bloch's "objective hope" is at least as much a product of human imagination as "subjective hope," at least as fallible and subject to disastrous error.[4]

Strong advocates of hope can also be found in the social sciences. Ezra Stotland's *The Psychology of Hope* (1969) is reminiscent of Morton Deutsch's work on trust in that both authors labored within the context of an academic psychology that strove for the appearance of scientific respectability. Doggedly pursuing scientism, Stotland, a cognitive psychologist, talks neutrally of "organisms" and roots his conception of hope in "perceived probability": "An organism's motivation to achieve a goal is, in part, a positive function of its perceived probability of attaining the goal and of the perceived importance of the goal" (p. 7). Hope is strictly cognitive; affect results from the combination of hope and goal importance. Thus, in the process of making hope comfortable within scientific psychology, Stotland strips it of whatever made it comfortable within everyday human life.

Another way to talk about hope within the social sciences is to interpret it primarily as affect. Although the subtitle of Lionel Tiger's *Optimism* (1979) is *The Biology of Hope*, much of his argument is based in psychology and anthropology. Tiger, for example, defines optimism as "a mood or attitude associated with an expectation about the social or material future—one which the evaluator regards as socially desirable, to his advantage, or for his pleasure" (p. 18). Note that there is no "objective" basis for Tiger's optimism; it can be based on anything an individual desires. And, whereas, in their self-justifications, many people proclaim community concern, optimism is morally neutral. Nonetheless, Tiger claims that his individualistic optimism can work for the good of the community. In attempting to construct a pro-social account of optimism, Tiger is seduced by biological metaphors that, unfortunately, contribute little to our understanding. Optimism and hope boil down to simple positive affect about the future; and the only alternative that Tiger considers is hopelessness.[5] But we do have other options—strategies such as social trust that, in the right circumstances, can offer us both positive affect and useful cognitive content: working together toward a positive future.

A final, straightforward but disturbing defense of optimism is given in the work of Martin Seligman and his colleagues. Seligman is a clinical psychologist whose basic message is that optimism is good for your mental health (1991). He is interested, therefore, in the production of optimism. A recent empirical study, for example, examined the relations between optimism and style of religious belief (Sethi and Seligman, 1993). Three styles of religious belief were studied, ranging from fundamentalist (e.g., Orthodox Judaism) to moderate (e.g., Catholicism) to liberal (e.g., Unitarianism). A variety of data, including measures of optimism, were collected by questionnaires from members of congregations representing these three styles of belief. In addition, the contents of the sermons, prayers, and hymns used by the various congregations were analyzed for level of optimism. Sethi and Seligman's results, in brief, were these: Persons in fundamentalist congregations were more optimistic than moderates, and moderates were more optimistic than liberals. In addition, the greater optimism of the fundamentalists seemed to be the product of the contents of the religious services as well greater religious hope and involvement. The disturbing part of this study is expressed in the authors' final conclusion: "It has been a fashion for modern social science to argue that authoritarian upbringing and doctrine damage mental health.[6] In contrast, we find that the more authoritarian religions produce more hope and optimism, and we suggest that the question of mental health, authoritarianism, and religious belief be reopened" (p. 259). What is wrong with Sethi and Seligman's implied formulation: authoritarian religions > more hope and optimism > better mental health? Without going into the details of the measures and procedures used by these researchers, we can only point out the usual methodological problem of non random assignment of subjects and the fact that the authors presented no data on mental health.[7] Nonetheless, this study is troubling because, on the surface at any rate, it associates concepts that we don't want associated, and it demonstrates the moral neutrality of hope.

Hope Is Bad

Perhaps because of our traditional democratic culture and our residual religious values, all-out attacks on hope are rare in America. Hope might be understood in this context as the strategy of the dispossessed, and any criticism of it condemned as the product of mean-spirited elitists. But John Dewey (1948) was neither mean spirited nor an elitist. And possibly because of this, he restricted his censure to Panglossian optimism:

> The optimism that says that the world is already the best possible of all worlds might be regarded as the most cynical of pessimism. . . . In declaring that good is already realized in ultimate reality [optimism] tends to make us gloss over the evils that concretely exist. It becomes too readily the creed of those who live at ease, in comfort, of those who have been successful in obtaining this world's rewards. Too readily optimism makes the men who hold it callous and blind to the sufferings of the less fortunate, or ready to find the cause of troubles of others in their personal viciousness. It thus cooperates with pessimism, in benumbing sympathetic insight and intelligent effort in reform. It beckons men away from the world of relativity and change into the calm of the absolute and eternal.
>
> (pp. 178-179)

For Dewey, then, it is Panglossian optimism that is the tool of dominating elites. To attack that brand of optimism and its symbiont, social distrust, is to act in support of democracy. And Dewey, the democrat, in the spirit of Voltaire, the aristocrat, would replace optimism with meliorism, the belief (based on social trust) that life can be made better through the application of human intelligence in social interaction.[8]

For a good, solid attack on hope, we can always look back to the Greeks, to Hesiod's story of Pandora—his answer to the question, Why is life so difficult? As in our discussion of the topic, Pandora's hope can be understood in various ways. The dominant interpretation is positive, as expressed, for example, by Lionel Tiger: "When in the myth the various forces of life escaped from Pandora's box, one remained at the very bottom—hope. . . . Even if the gods and other such forces have fallen, or become slogans, what Pandora rescued maintains its claim on our attention, if only because where it is dark it is difficult to see" (1979, pp. 283, 284). But this positive interpretation appears to result from either willful or careless distortion of the original. What Hesiod (in translation)[9] calls "sad troubles," Tiger identifies as "forces of life." And Tiger claims that Pandora "rescued" hope, as if for our good. But Pandora was sent to punish us; it was Zeus who contained hope in the jar. A positive interpretation of hope and Hesiod's text seem difficult to reconcile.

Moses Hadas (1965), however, has demonstrated how easy it is to derive a negative understanding of hope from the story of Pandora. First, he asks a very sensible question: "What was hope doing in a box reserved for calamities?" (p. 115).[10] Then he supplies the obvious, if unwelcome, answer: "It must be that hope is not a good thing. To accept as a likely eventuality an outcome we have no rational grounds for expecting is not healthy, and hope is therefore a drug for sick minds" (p. 115).[11] Hadas's argument with hope is that it is not rational. He describes the struggle between Zeus and Prometheus, the rebel benefactor of man, as a contest between rationality and sentimentality, under which hope is subsumed. And the efforts of Prometheus, "like the meddling of all sentimental do-gooders . . . are not only softheaded but arrogant. Men must be allowed to work their fate out by behaving well as becomes men to behave and leave the gods to behave as becomes gods to behave" (p. 116). Hope is not good for men.[12]

Hope Can Be Good or Bad

In one of the few contemporary philosophical accounts of hope, John Patrick Day (1991) makes the not-unexpected claim that "A is justified in hoping, or being hopeful . . . if and only if (1) A's hope, or hopefulness . . . is not objectionable on moral, prudential or aesthetic grounds; and (2) A's hope, or hopefulness . . . is reasonable" (p. 80).[13] Day's account of hope is a standard, if detailed, rationalist interpretation, unconcerned in its analyses with matters of human psychology.[14] Can hopefulness be reasonable? Only, according to Day, "if it were objectively probable that everything will be all right" (p. 81). But this is a standard too difficult, in most cases, to meet. In addition, unreasonable hopefulness (i.e., that which is based on insufficient evidence) is rejected on moral and prudential grounds since it leads to disappointment and complacency. Aesthetically, all hopefulness is good because it is predominantly pleasant. Day concludes that "Wantful Hoping," in which the subjective probability of the desired outcome is a product of the desire rather than an inference from the evidence, is a poor strategy for life. But all is not lost, since a person can be "cured" of his error and returned to rationality through *education*: "For we like to think of ourselves as rational and informed beings, so that we can be shamed out of irrationality and ignorance" (p. 89). What a disappointment: Once again, it's the familiar rationalist's rallying call, stubbornly, ironically maintained against all reason and evidence.[15]

Ronald Aronson's (1991) approach to good and bad types of hope—through the work of Ernst Bloch—is very different from Day's. Although part of Aronson's criticism of Bloch derives from Bloch's apparent unwillingness to argue his case directly, Aronson does not succumb to the adverse temptation of thinking that the solution to hope lies in abstract analysis and rational argument. At the end of his essay on Bloch, Aronson considers whether, given Bloch's enormous effort and consequent failure, we should abandon hope. Reluctant to give up the positive core of the concept, Aronson suggests an alternative formulation: realistic hope, "a chastened hope, one that is humbler, more tentative, narrowed, even if just as profoundly (but now critically) connected to some of humanity's deepest longings and visions" (p. 231). As opposed to Bloch, who chained his hope to a never-to-be ideal society, Aronson grounds his in our lived-in world. But beyond his demand for realism, psychological and otherwise, Aronson offers no guidance, only caution.

Hope Is Ambiguous

Our discussion of hope has ranged from the all-encompassing, utopia-bound account by Bloch to Stotland's subjective probability estimates, from Tiger's positive affect to Hadas's reason-destroying drug. Hope is good. Hope is bad. It depends. What can we conclude from all this? We can note, first, that, based on its ubiquity in our speech and on the passion devoted to it by writers, that hope is important. Second, pointing to the diverse ways in which it has been described by writers, we suspect that hope is difficult to think about. A lot of thought has been applied to understanding an important concept, but with no fully satisfying results. This is not surprising. Hope, like most important concepts, is endlessly ambiguous, with no prospect of settled meaning. In the end, of course, as Candide learned, hope is what we make it. The problem is in knowing what we want.

Or, as Michel Serres (1989a) puts it, the problem is in knowing what we don't want: "My hope lies in the unexpected—what can I expect from the dreary execution of laws? . . . My hope does not follow the straight road, the monotonous and dreary methodology from which novelty has fled; my hope invents the cut-off trail, broken, chosen at random from the wasp, the bee, the fly" (p. 23). Richard Rorty (1989), in a different style and context from Serres, also knows what he wants hope to avoid: "We need a redescription of liberalism as the hope that culture as a whole can be 'poeticized' rather than as the Enlightenment hope that it can be 'rationalized' or 'scientized.' That is, we need to substitute the hope that chances for fulfillment of idiosyncratic fantasies will be equalized for the hope that everyone will replace 'passion' or fantasy with 'reason'" (p. 53). Both Serres and Rorty insist that hope be devoted to the unknown, the unpredictable, the new.

Richard Rorty's most sustained discussion of hope is structured on (what was at the time) a typically fresh comparison between the ideas of John Dewey and Michel Foucault.[16] Dewey and Foucault, Rorty argues, are pretty much in agreement in their criticisms of the social science tradition. "We should see Dewey and Foucault as differing not over a theoretical issue," Rorty says, "but over what we may hope" (1982, p. 204). For Dewey, liberation from traditional notions of rationality, objectivity, method, and truth means that we are free to make ourselves, to experiment with new ways of living. Dewey is hopeful. Liberation for Foucault, in contrast, means the acceptance of knowledge claims as exercises in power. Foucault is hopeless. But this is wrong because this understanding of hope is based on a notion rejected by both men: that all people are connected by some common human nature to which we must conform. On the contrary, "What Dewey suggested," Rorty points out, "was that we keep the will to truth and the optimism that goes with it, but free them from the behaviorist notion that Behaviorese is Nature's Own Language *and* from the notion of man as 'transcendental or enduring subject.' For, in Dewey's hands, the will to truth is not the urge to dominate but the urge to create, to 'attain working harmony among diverse desires'" (pp. 206, 207). Rorty urges us not to let the differences between the way Dewey talks and Foucault talks block our understanding of their common passion:

> This is the attempt to free mankind from Nietzsche's "longest lie," the notion that outside the haphazard and perilous experiments we perform there lies something (God, Science, Knowledge, Rationality, or Truth) which will, if only we perform the correct rituals, step in to save us. Although Foucault and Dewey are trying to do the same thing, Dewey seems to me to have done it better, simply because his vocabulary allows room for unjustifiable hope, and an ungroundable but vital sense of human solidarity.
>
> (Rorty, 1982, p. 208)

Hope is unjustifiable[17] because it is simply part of life,[18] of moving into the new.

SELF-KNOWLEDGE

Learning more about one's self can be a seductive route to the reduction of cognitive complexity. One's object of study, presumably, is at hand, and little persuasion is needed to convince one that the course of study will be both fascinating and profitable. The basic argument advanced by the numerous advocates of self-knowledge is simple and straight forward: If a person knows himself well, if he knows who he is and what he wants, then his judgments and decisions will be enlightened and rational, his interactions with his environment relatively friction-free.

But this self-seduction may prove disappointing. The study of one's self would seem most productive if that self were singular and stable. Thus, if one were to use self-knowledge as a means to reduce cognitive complexity, one would be drawn either toward the restriction of one's life (in a simple environment such as a monastery, with a resultant simple self) or, because the unrestrained self one needs to know is too fluid, toward failure and frustration. One must either oversimplify one's life or oversimplify one's self-description. Although the monastery is no longer a popular option, contemporary surrogate-simplifiers abound—for example, in the self-shrinking electronic media. Still, in our self-centered society, it is likely that self-doubt, resulting from failed attempts to simply know one's complex self, is the more common outcome. In any case, the direction of this often-advocated route to self-knowledge is *inward*. And we argue, to the contrary, that one can learn about one's self (and about the world) only by moving *outward*, by interacting with other people.

The fundamental flaw in the notion that inner-directed self-knowledge is a useful way to reduce cognitive complexity is this. It is based on the idea that the self is individual in two senses, singular and asocial. On this understanding, there is *a* self to be known. And that self can be known through a process of self-examination, a person studying, in what ever ways he can, his self. These are not good ideas. Based on a wide variety of studies, the consensus within contemporary cognitive psychology is that the self is best interpreted as multiple and social: "It is misleading to speak of a single representation of the self. In fact, there may be many representations that are stored independently of one another. They may also be retrieved independently, depending on the situational factors that elicit them or objectives that make one or another representation useful" (Wyer and Gordon, 1984). A person can be described, informally, as "having multiple selves," with the manifestation or generation of each dependent on the social context: "There is no single or average self-image continuously changing, but rather a collection of self-images whose relative accessibilities change" (Sherman, Judd, and Park, 1989). Although there is widespread agreement on the notion of multiple selves, the term *multiple* has been variously interpreted. Thus, to broaden our understanding of self-knowledge, we briefly describe several of the many senses of multiple selves. In each case, we compare the multiple with its singular counterpart.

Multiple Personality Disorder versus Normal, Unitary Personality

In multiple personality disorder, a person is described as having multiple selves, each of which is unaware of the others.[19] Psychologists, psychiatrists, and others frequently interpret this form of dissociation as an effort to cope with childhood trauma. Ernest Hilgard (1977), for example, describes its genesis in "a disintegration of values at the heart of the family, with violent and excessive punishment, overt sexual assaults in childhood, unbalanced parental roles, one parent occasionally sadistic, the other rather passive and aloof. In resolving the conflicts over identification and guilt, and in trying to cope in a context in which a unified strategy cannot work, the person divides" (pp. 39-40). Multiple personality disorder is, and always has been, a controversial construct. Many clinicians are convinced of its validity and usefulness.[20] Other clinicians, academic psychologists, and interested laypersons have strongly objected to the use of this construct, claiming that the disorder is iatrogenic and that its diagnosis generates more harm than good.

Our discussion of multiple selves is confined to normal psychological functioning. That is, "multiple selves" as we and most social scientists use it has nothing to do with pathology. We mention multiple personality disorder here for two reasons. First, we want to forestall confusion between it and multiple selves. Second, this dubious disorder, ironically, is the only form of multiplicity given credence by certain economics-based strong rationalists such as Jon Elster (1987) who advises that "We ought not to take the notion of 'several selves' very literally. In general, we are dealing with exactly *one* person—neither more nor less. That person may have some cognitive coordination problems, and some motivational conflicts, but it is *his* job to sort them out. They do not sort themselves out in an inner arena where several homunculi struggle to get the upper hand" (pp. 30-31).[21] Clearly, any understanding of the self that is not in some way strongly unified generates difficulties for a wide variety of theories, including those based on a unitary rational decision maker.

Eastern versus Western

By "Western" we specifically mean American, but this can be extended to all cultures based on Western European liberal individualism. And "Eastern" means non-Western. Writers who make this distinction claim, in general, that the Eastern self is multiple, the Western self singular. Their work falls into two categories: that which discusses the conceptual self and that which is devoted to the experienced self.

The Conceptual Self

A concept of the self is an idea or theory of the self that is shared by members of a culture. Richard Shweder and Edmund Bourne, for example, describe the sociocentric concept of self as an aspect of the holistic worldview in which one's attention is focused "on the context-dependent relationship of part to part and part to whole; the holist, convinced that objects and events are necessarily altered by the relations into which they enter, is theoretically primed to contextualize objects and events, and theoretically disinclined to appraise things *in vacuo*, in the abstract" (Shweder, 1991, p. 153). The self varies across social contexts. This is the Eastern concept of multiple selves. In contrast to that, Shweder and Bourne describe the egocentric-contractual concept of self, the familiar, singular Western self. Many writers, varying in the details, have described these general differences between Eastern and Western self concepts. And some have claimed that understanding these differences is critical to the success of basic social functions such as education (Pratt, 1991).

Other writers have complained that differences between Eastern and Western self concepts have been overstated. Milford Spiro (1993), for example, reasonably objects that, "a typology of the self (or of personality) that consists of only two types—a Western and a non-Western—is much too restrictive to accurately describe either, and only serves to distort both" (p. 144). One can only agree. Spiro is mistaken, however, when he describes the Western/non-Western comparison as a *typology of the self.* The purpose of the comparison in all of the cases that we have reviewed is not to accurately map the ways the self is conceptualized but simply to contrast the version dominant in social science, the Western, with a popular alternative, the non-Western. This is an important undertaking since it demonstrates the parochialism of much of social science. Once this basic point is accepted, then the matter of more finely tuned typologies will become a matter of more direct concern. A number of anthropologists, Douglas Hollan (1992) and D. W. Murray (1993), for example, being in the vanguard on this matter, are impatient for greater cultural sophistication. But most of us have a lot to learn.

The Experiential Self

This is the self that is experienced by a person in a given culture. Some anthropologists such as Douglas Hollan (1992) argue that the experiential self, based as it is on a wide variety of social contexts, can differ significantly from the simplified, idealized conceptual self. A number of psychologists, most notably Hazel Rose Markus and Shinobu Kitayama (1991), have shown that very simple matters of cultural self-construal—for example an interdependent (i.e., multiple, Eastern) self versus an independent (i.e., singular, Western) self—affect many aspects of experience.[22] Thus, the conceptual self and the experiential self may, in some cases, be more tightly tied together than Hollan, Murray, and others suspect. But, again, that is not the main point. For psychologists, the primary concern is to broaden the cultural base of their theories and data. The Eastern/Western dichotomy is obviously too simple for most applications, but it is a way of getting beyond the prevailing Western monopoly.[23] Progress in that direction is indicated in the very promising new, non-Western way of talking about the self and culture developed by Alan Page Fiske (1991a).[24]

Communitarian versus Liberal

The communitarian/liberal distinction is similar in many ways to Markus and Kitayama's (1991) contrast between interdependent and independent selves. What distinguishes the communitarian/liberal debate is its confinement primarily to Western political philosophy. Communitarian conceptions of the multiple self are based in history, tradition, and, of course, community. "I inherit from the past of my family, my city, my tribe, my nation, a variety of debts, inheritances, rightful expectations and obligations," Alasdair MacIntyre (1981) says, "These constitute the given of my life, my moral starting point. This is in part what gives my life its own moral particularity" (p. 205). Communitarians claim that a "thick," "embedded," community-constituted self concept is a necessary guide to the good, moral life. The background for these communitarian critiques is provided by a singular, shadow-thin liberal self, atomistic, egoistic, rational, and alone. Of course, this caricature liberal self is rejected by many liberal political philosophers who claim that a concept of the self, so central to communitarian arguments, is not a major concern. Michael Waltzer (1990), for example, says that "the central issue for political theory is not the constitution of the self but the connection of constituted selves, the pattern of social relations" (p. 21).[25] Communitarians tie the self and community together; liberals separate them. For Richard Rorty, the self is "a centerless bundle of contingencies . . . compatible with *any* sort of politics, *including* liberal politics" (1991c, p. 197). Individuals can engage in any sort of self-creation, but in the public realm each is constrained by others: "Societies are not quasi-persons, they are (at their liberal, social democratic best) compromises between persons. The point of a liberal society is not to invent or create anything, but simply to make it as easy as possible for people to achieve their wildly different private ends without hurting each other" (p. 196). On this interpretation, the private, liberal self, in its limitless self-creation,[26] is, in a sense, far more multifarious than the entrenched communitarian self.

Actual Full Identity versus Self-Represented Identity

"Actual full identity," a concept developed by Owen Flanagan (1991), "is constituted by the dynamic integrated system of past and present identifications, desires, commitments, aspirations, beliefs, dispositions, temperament, roles, acts, and actional patterns, as well as by whatever self-understandings (even incorrect ones) each person brings to his or her life" (p. 135). "Self-represented identity," again according to Flanagan, "is the conscious or semiconscious picture a person has of who he or she is" (p. 137). Self-represented identity is thus a part of, and much simpler than, actual full identity. Actual full identity—the inter-subjective product of many observers—is the objective self. As such, it serves the useful purpose of offering an object, a dynamic, emerging object, for self-knowledge. For Flanagan, as for many philosophers, psychologists, and others, self-representations are structured as narratives. The multiplicity question, then, turns on the number of narratives.

Multiple Self-Narratives versus the Narrative Self

Interest in multiple self-narratives has increased dramatically within the various social sciences in recent years. In anthropology, for example, Katherine Ewing (1990) and Victor De Munck (1992) have presented evidence from Pakistan and Sri Lanka demonstrating the functions of multiple, inconsistent self-narratives. We must limit ourselves here to a brief discussion of Owen Flanagan's (1992) account of the narrative self. First, Flanagan offers a set of reasons for the seemingly natural fit between narrative and our lives: "life is experienced as lived in time"; "our memories are powerful"; "we look toward the future . . . and we do so with a grasp of our present beliefs and desires and of who we are, given our past"; and "we are social beings," our lives are filled with characters (pp. 198-199). But no matter how many characters are in the narrative or how complex the plot, "oneness reigns when it come to selves" (p. 199).

Flanagan appears to be torn between the neat fictions of philosophy (the unitary self) and the messier fictions of psychology (multiple selves). On several occasions he slips into such locutions as, "This is the self that we present to ourselves (strictly, we present aspects of ourselves)" (p. 199). And, "Once formed, it, or better, different aspects of it, bubble up each day" (p. 203). On one occasion—describing himself, his two selves, familial and philosopher—he briefly uses the explicit language of multiple selves: "These two selves are, from my first-person perspective, part of an integrated and unified narrative that contains, as proper parts, both of these selves, which I sometimes display in isolation. In fact, I have many other selves (or other aspects of my self) besides these two" (pp. 203-204). Although he finds the language of multiple self-narratives almost unavoidable, Flanagan restricts his use of "multiple" to multiple personality disorder. He insists on a single, integrating narrative self.

But Flanagan's integration is weak and thin. "A dynamic integrated system," he says, "need not consist of a remotely perfect union, not need it, in all cases, be what we think of, in a normative sense, as ethically or psychologically well integrated" (1991, p. 136). Confronted by the experience of multiple self-narratives, Flanagan appeals to biological theory for support of unity. "The Darwin Machine itself favors minimal cognitive dissonance and maximal integration at the level of conscious thought and action guidance," he points out before adding, parenthetically, "harmony at the top may well belie all sorts of disagreement and competition among lower-level processors" (1992, p. 200). But the harmony at the top may be *within* multiple narrative selves, not *across* "aspects" of a single narrative self. Interpretation is simply a matter of use. Thus, in some contexts it may be useful to emphasize integration in one's talk of the narrative self; in other contexts talk of multiple narrative selves might make more sense.

Dialogical versus Monological

While the notion of multiple selves has, in varying forms, become dominant in contemporary psychology, the related concept of the dialogical self, long influential in contemporary philosophy (e.g., Taylor, 1991) is taking hold in psychology as well (e.g., Bruner, 1986, 1990, 1991). As described by Hubert Hermans and his colleagues (1992), the dialogical self is very similar, in some ways, to multiple narrative selves—with multiple 'I's" distributed in imaginal space, each with a story to tell the others. Hermans's dialogical self also includes distinguishing properties, such as strong emphases on the "embodiment" of the self, its location in particular contexts, and on the self as social. Related to the latter is the central, identifying concept of dialogue, inspired by the work of Mikhail Bakhtin (1984). "To live," Bakhtin insists, "means to participate in dialogue . . . In this dialogue a person participates wholly and throughout his whole life" (p. 293). The dialogic self, then, is a strong interpretation of multiple selves: to become monologic is to die.

The Implications of Multiple Selves for Self-Knowledge

We have briefly described several ways of talking about multiple selves. Some of these accounts of one's self may seem odd to nonspecialist Westerners, since they appear to violate our general cultural expectations. In practice, however, matters are less strange. In any manifestation, the multiple possibilities of the dialogical self, for example, must be expressed within a set of cultural constraints. In the West, and particularly in America, those constraints, in general, work to limit multiplicities and to form a relatively strong, centralized self. Across a variety of cultures, then, a range of culturally conditioned multiplicities, from wildly diverse to mildly unitary, is likely to result.

In one interpretation, the implications of multiple selves for self-knowledge are clear and simple: what one learns in one social context may not be valid in another. (And this applies also, of course, to outside observers such as psychologists and pollsters.) Our selves are dynamic, never ending construction projects, changing with social context and time.[27] Expanded social options, opportunities for growth and development, are associated, therefore, with a complex collection of loosely integrated subselves, each of which has its own form of simplicity. Simplicity is in the subself, not in the collection of subselves. It is hard to imagine a simple, master narrative self which can make all the subselves cohere, make sense of all of them. And why need this be done? On this account, a singular, unified self is fundamentally unknowable. But one can always, with awareness or not, limit one's quest for knowledge to a particular subself. In doing that, however, identifying one's self with a particular subself, one is paying for cognitive simplicity by forgoing opportunities for future development, cutting oneself off from the world.

Owen Flanagan (1992) moves beyond the problems of a too-narrow, atomistic self by insisting that self-knowledge have *actual full identity* as its object. "Actual full identity," Flanagan says, "is the self as described by the most enlightened version of the story of the self that emerges as science advances and first-person opacities and distortions are removed" (p. 209). Optical metaphors aside, we can accept actual full identity as a useful construct of the social self. It enables us to understand, for example, why self-knowledge would be difficult to generate within a community of like-minded individuals. A like-minded community is similar to a monologic self; without dialogue based on diversity there is no basis for useful self-knowledge. Such a community doesn't *delude* a person; it simply *deprives him of the tools* necessary for self-knowledge. Implicit in the notion of actual full identity (but obscured by the optical metaphors) are the limits of self-knowledge. The "most enlightened version of the story of the self" will always be vastly less than any self can be. Most of one's self, if one wants it that way, can forever remain unknowable because it is always in the future. These limits, Flanagan argues, can be liberating. One can free one's self from knowledge of the past; similarly, one can free one's future from ideal forms. Flanagan proposes that we, "abandon the idea of a single ideal type of moral personality. As fictions go, this is an especially constraining and damaging one. It keeps us from appreciating the rich diversity of persons that everywhere abounds, and it seeds the ground for intolerance, disrespect, and overconfidence in one's own life form. These are all good things to be rid of" (1991, pp. 335-336).

Self-knowledge, we conclude, can be a worthwhile activity under two conditions. First, *it must be based on diverse social interactions.* You can learn useful things about yourself only from people who differ from you. Second, *it must be future oriented.* The purpose of self-knowledge is to support the construction of a flourishing future; understanding the past is not necessary for this, and it may be counterproductive. Self-knowledge, in the spirit of John Dewey, is an experimental process: the testing of new ways of acting in life. Thus understood, self-knowledge could serve as a creative basis for social trust.

RETREAT

An increasingly popular strategy to reduce the cognitive complexity generated by the apparently uncontrollable problems of the world is to give ground, to withdraw to an environment with seemingly simpler, more manageable problems. In America, signs of decreasing public participation in the solution of public problems are everywhere. Only a minority of American citizens, for example, vote consistently. And in the 1992 national elections, having retreated by freeway an hour or so from the problems of the cities, the majority of voters lived in suburbs. Those with money in the city can hide behind barricades or in tall buildings. Those without money withdraw into alcohol and other drugs.

Retreat need not be physical, of course. One can also build a barricade of concrete-reinforced, dialogue-proof ideas. "Ideology," as Terry Eagleton (1991) has demonstrated, is a malleable term that has been interpreted in many ways. We use it here to mean "lack of reflexivity." A person is said to have retreated into ideology when she has no interest in changing her current vocabulary or way of thinking. She has given up on growth. Lacking reflexivity, she is unaware of her retreat. "The speaker 'forgets,'" Eagleton notes, "that he or she is just the function of a discursive and ideological formation, and thus comes to misrecognize herself as the author of her own discourse. . . . Language itself is infinitely productive; but this incessant productivity can be artificially arrested into 'closure'—into the sealed world of ideological stability, which repels the disruptive, decentered forces of language in the name of an imaginary unity" (pp. 196-197).

Closure isn't always negative: persons in dialogue need temporary closure in order to act on the problem they have been discussing. Then the process of growth continues. But dialogue, temporary closure, and growth are social processes and, therefore (since they involve other "freely" acting persons), risky.[28] The ideological retreater is risk-averse, uncomfortable with contingency, at home with the idea of certainty. Retreat restores simplicity, but the problems outside remain unsolved, developing, becoming more and more complex. The only way out, as Richard Rorty and many others have stressed, is to give up the hope for certainty and accept the contingencies of human social life, life in man-made communities. "Our glory," Rorty (1982) reminds us, "is in our participation in fallible and transitory human projects, not in our obedience to permanent nonhuman constraints" (p. 166). Just how such nonideological participation can be realized in any significant context remains to be demonstrated. That it is a worthy goal is undoubted.

SUMMARY: AMBIGUOUS STRATEGIES

The three low-resource-demand, individual-focus strategies discussed in this chapter—*hope, self-knowledge* and *retreat*—are all ambiguous. The ambiguity is bi-directional, forward and backward. When used in their backward sense, these strategies are tools for self-defense, for protecting what is. But in their forward sense, they make use of what is to move ahead, as platforms from which we can launch experiments into new ways of living. How can you tell when you hope, seek self-knowledge, or retreat if you are doing the right thing? If you are interacting with people who are different from you and if you are moving into something new, you may be uncomfortable, but you are probably doing the best you can. And you may be creating a new basis for social trust.

7

Strategies for Simplicity, Four, Low Resource Demand, Community Focus

The fourth and final set of strategies for simplicity, those with low resource demands and community focus, consists of only two—*culture* and *social trust based on cultural values*. These are strategies for sociality, low-cost tools for the establishment and maintenance of cooperation. On this brief description, culture and social trust based on cultural values sound like solutions—social strategies designed to dissolve problems as they emerge. We acknowledge some truth in this. But the limitations of even these low-cost, community-focused strategies can be demonstrated simply by pointing to the creation and continuing popularity of high-cost alternatives such as law and regulation. Culture and social trust based on cultural values operate *within* specific social groups. And, as in all social systems, the very factors that work to facilitate cooperation within groups act as barriers to cooperation across groups.

CULTURE

The fundamental generalization in contemporary social science is that human beings are inherently social. This understanding of human nature (banal-seeming, perhaps, but differing from some earlier accounts such as that of Freud, 1930) is best explicated in the recent work of Alan Page Fiske. Fiske argues that human sociality has evolved based on a set of four fundamental relational structures: Communal Sharing, Authority Ranking, Equality Matching, and Market Pricing (1991a).[1] People use these models to organize most domains of social thought and action; but none of them is implemented in the raw. In practice, the fundamental models are wrapped in culture, systems of symbols and meanings shared by groups of people. It is within the context of this cultural variability that we can accept Fiske's universals. The claims on human nature are minimal, biological: a capacity for sociality that can be manifested, like the capacity for language, in many different ways through culture.[2] Fiske thus describes two universal and indispensable ways in which cognitive complexity is reduced. First, through the four inherent models of social relations, with which all people are born. Second, through the cultural milieu in which the four models are implemented.

Culture has four functions, according to Fiske: constitution of social relations; establishment of the entailments of the fundamental models (needs and obligations); making sense of social reality; and coordination. Culture is a necessary and powerful reducer of cognitive complexity. But there are inevitable gaps between the skeletal forms of the elementary models and their full-bodied manifestations in culture: shore-like spaces for intermingling, mixing, and change. Thus, we have diversity among cultures—contingent, chance-generated experiments in ways of life. Culture constitutes us, but we, in turn, make culture, continually changing, adapting.[3] And this cultural diversity is whatever we make of it, a tool for future-building or an excuse for future-destroying.

To demonstrate the varied workings of culture, we briefly discuss cultural diversity in two domains: moral judgments and risk judgments. We conclude our discussion of culture with a description of a cultural form that is designed specifically for future-building, cosmopolitanism.

Moral Judgments

The traditional cognitive-developmental interpretation of moral judgments claims that judgments of actions are based on their consequences for others. These judgments are said to develop through a set series of stages as a child matures, arriving ultimately at a stage that could be called "rational."[4] For advocates of this account, such as Lawrence Kohlberg (1984), justice is an objective reality and moral judgments are either right or wrong. At the final, mature stage of development, moral guidance is provided by "universal ethical principles that all humanity should follow" (1984, p. 412). Critics of cognitive-developmentalists, cultural psychologists such as Richard Shweder (1991), and feminist-psychologists such as Carol Gilligan (1982), offer the counter claim that justice is a social (cultural) construction and that moral judgments can differ (in limited ways) according to these constructions. The argument here, in brief, is between a monistic-rationalist account versus a pluralistic-intuitionist version.[5]

A number of studies have recently generated strong support for limited pluralism in moral judgments. Jonathan Haidt and his colleagues (1993), for example, compared the moral judgments of adults and children in Brazil and in Philadelphia. These subjects were classified according to two cultural variables: *westernization* (roughly, individualism) and *socioeconomic status* (SES).

Both of these factors, Haidt's results showed, affected moral judgments. Westernized and high-SES subjects, for example, made large distinctions between stories that depicted harmful situations and those describing harmless but offensive scenes. These subjects acted in a "mature, rational way." For less westernized and low-SES subjects, "morality appears to be broader. Stories that involved disgust and disrespect were moralized, even when they were perceived to be harmless" (p. 625). These subjects, guided by their cultural preferences, veered away from the rationalist norm. Westernized, high-SES subjects (e.g., college students in *both* Brazil and Philadelphia) expressed an *individualistic*, anti-emotive morality in which "the link between harm and moral judgment is tight, and there is an effort to weaken or deny the link between affect and judgment" (p. 626). For non-Westernized and low-SES subjects, in contrast, no victim is required, and affect is a legitimate basis for moral judgment.

Risk Judgments

At times, culture works in subtle and embarrassing ways. Consider, for example, the case of the Society for Risk Analysis-Europe (SRA-Europe, the European branch of the Society for Risk Analysis). SRA-Europe is composed of risk analysts, risk managers, risk communicators, and other professionals concerned with the management of technological and natural hazards. Without doubt, it is a very sophisticated group of academics, bureaucrats, industrialists, and private consultants. As such, they decided to honor an outstanding contributor to their field, a person whom they considered to be one of their own, by bestowing on her their Distinguished Scientific Work Award. In the event, the recipient—Mary Douglas—felt less "at home" in their company than they apparently did in hers.

Mary Douglas is an anthropologist, the developer (based on work of Emile Durkheim) of the culture theory of personal preferences (see, for example, Douglas, 1975, 1982). In 1982, Douglas, together with Aaron Wildavsky (whom Douglas credits as being the "inventor of the anthropology of risk"), published the seminal work *Risk and Culture* (Douglas and Wildavsky, 1982). Before Douglas and Wildavsky, risk preferences for the most part were attributed either to the environment (objective dangers out there) or to universal psychological processes (shared perceptual distortions of what is out there). Douglas and Wildavsky argued, and their followers have shown, that risk judgments to a large extent are the products of culture or, more specifically, cultural patterns, ways of life. According to culture theory, there are five cultural patterns or worldviews: *hierarchical, individualist, egalitarian, fatalist,* and *autonomous.*[6] On this account, it is important to note, risk judgments have no necessary relation to the opinions (or "findings") of "risk experts." Instead, risk judgments are constructed to support one's preferred worldview. "In other words," Karl Dake, a leading proponent of culture theory says, "among all possible risks, those selected for worry or dismissal serve—sometimes intentionally, often not—to strengthen one of these cultures and weaken the others" (1992, p. 28).[7]

Mary Douglas and the other culture theorists countered the monistic risk-judgment theories of the technical experts and universalist psychologists with a pluralist theory based on cultural differences. But culture theory is not incompatible with these other accounts; it simply includes them as special cases. Many risk analysts, for example, prefer the hierarchical worldview within risk-management contexts. The problem for experts (as for others), of course, is in the acknowledgment of alternative worldviews, granting them legitimacy. In her speech of acceptance for the SRA-Europe award, Mary Douglas compared her awarders to priests, describing herself, in contrast, as a spokesperson for the (wayward) people:

> I must confess that I am very surprised at receiving this award. . . . I do not see evidence [in the presentations at the conference] of the sophistication that cultural theory could bring to the discussion. . . . On the matter of physical risks and probabilities of damage, your discussion is highly professional. On the cultural matter of human behavior and perception of risks, I am sure you do not want to talk like a bunch of amateurs. Yet when words such as "culture," "risk culture," and "safety culture" are bandied about, we do not hear any systematic representation of cultural pressures.
>
> It would seem that your professional training requires no familiarity with the idea that a culture is a cluster of mutually compatible attitudes about authority and social relations, gossip, trust, credibility, and the amounts of food and sleep and exercise a human needs. Still less are the variety of moral and political ideas taken into account. Yet without a systematic approach to culture, how can you hope to interpret the public's reaction to technology?
>
> (1994, p. 17)

Mary Douglas, in her forthright manner, made certain the members of SRA-Europe were aware that, in honoring her, they were not, in her opinion, honoring themselves.[8]

Cosmopolitanism

The story about Mary Douglas and SRA-Europe demonstrates both the seductions and the challenges of culture. In the singular, a culture is seductive because it simplifies our lives and gives them meaning. In the plural, however, cultures are challenging because they appear to each other to be isolated islets of meaning. Even persons of good will and sophistication, such as the members of SRA-Europe, have difficulty in routinely connecting those islets except in the most abstract ways. Are professional anthropologists the only persons among us with the necessary skills to understand culture and to take it seriously? Or is that the problem—we all, aware of it or not, take culture too seriously? A discussion and redescription of the old-fashioned notion of *cosmopolitanism* might help us cope better with the challenges of culture.[9]

The idea of cosmopolitanism was invented in response to the decline of local authority in ancient Greece and the advent of the Hellenistic period. This was a period of great upheavals, conquests, and uncertainty. The limited bonds of trust that had connected clients to patrons were dissolved along with the power of the cities. "The Greek citizen of this time," Pierre Grimal (1962) concludes, "was rather like the adolescent who realizes for the first time that the world is a bigger place than the narrow confines of family life had led him to believe; he was forced to find within himself the support that he no longer found around him and whose presence he deeply missed" (pp. 10, 11).[10] Alexander's conquests had led to the diffusion of Greek culture throughout the known world and to the breakdown of the classical distinction between Greeks and barbarians. Greek culture, always modified by local conditions, became world culture. "Thus a movement began which tended to separate moral and aesthetic values from their national background, to consider them no longer as part of a heritage which was the prerogative of a few privileged men, but to give them a universal significance" (p. 11). A Cypriot of Syrian parentage, Zeno of Citium, the founder of the Stoic school of philosophy, was a member of this movement. And cosmopolitanism—the idea, in brief, that all persons are born equal, owing no allegiance to local authority but only to universal law— was a product of Zeno's school. A version of this original cosmopolitanism is contained in the discourses of the later Stoic, Epictetus who, by turns, was a slave, a freedman and an exile:

> Never in reply to the question, to what country you belong, say that you are an Athenian or a Corinthian, but that you are a citizen of the world. For why do you say that you are an Athenian, and why do you not say that you belong to the small nook only into which your poor body was cast at birth? Is it not plain that you call yourself an Athenian or Corinthian from the place which has a greater authority and comprises not only that small nook itself and all your family, but even the whole country from which the stock of your progenitors is derived down to you? He then who has observed with intelligence the administration of the world, and has learned that the greatest and supreme and the most comprehensive community is that which is composed of men and God . . . Why should not such a man call himself a citizen of the world, why not a son of God . . . To have God for your maker, and father and guardian, shall not this release us from sorrows and fears?
>
> (Discourses 1.9)[11]

In Epictetus's discourse, we can hear the concerns of his listeners, their search for safety in a dangerous world. Their concerns are no different from our own. But whereas the ancients could find unity or the brotherhood of man in God or reason, those transcendent routes to cosmopolitanism are no longer available to us.

As in ancient Greece, cosmopolitanism emerged in modern America in response to turbulent times. For many Americans, the years of the First World War and the great period of European immigration that preceded it were times of rapid, threatening changes. In barest outline, the situation was this. Some people, rooted in notions of a simple, unified American past, were threatened by the changing ethnic mix in America and the resultant pressures toward cultural diversity. Others, young, progressive, optimistic about the future of America and wishing to free themselves from the narrow constraints imposed by the past, welcomed the cultural changes as forces for liberation. For the first group, the war was, in a sense, a godsend—unity based on traditional nationalistic values was imposed by the state; immigration was ended, replaced by deportation. For the second group, the war was more problematical, divisive. Some of them, once "we" were in it, argued that the war was an exciting opportunity, a chance to participate in the remaking of the world. The leading spokesperson for this faction was John Dewey. Others maintained that the war was evil and that nothing good could come of it. Randolph Bourne, a former student and disciple of Dewey, led the much smaller, opposing faction, a lonely, isolated group which shrank to include, in the end, almost only himself as the war deepened.

Like Epictetus, Randolph Bourne was an outsider, eager for change, with no stake in things as they were.[12] Dewey, by origins an outsider, had attained, by the time of the war, his familiar status as a pillar of the establishment's progressive wing.[13] The controversy between Bourne and Dewey centered on the uses of pragmatism in times of turmoil. Bourne presented his arguments against Dewey and his wartime followers in "Twilight of the Idols," a 1917 article in *The Seven Arts*, a short-lived literary magazine, soon snuffed out by the war. Bourne's main point was that technique had come to dominate values in pragmatism. Dewey's followers (and to some extent Dewey himself) had in effect separated means from ends and devoted all of their attention, in the cause of war, to the former. They had become technocrats, mechanics for the war machine. The war and Dewey's pragmatists seemed to have been made for each other. "What is significant," Bourne said, "is that it is the technical side of the war that appeals to them, not the interpretative or political side. The formulation of values and ideals, the production of articulate and suggestive thinking, had not, in their education, kept pace, to any extent whatever, with their technical aptitude" (1964, p. 60). In a time of crisis, pragmatists fell back on technique, scientific method, instrumentalism. The ends, the values, were supplied by the war.

Recalling his days as a pragmatist, Bourne said, "We were instrumental-ists, but we had our private utopias so clearly before our minds that the means fell always into its place as contributory" (p. 60). Bourne acknowledged that Dewey meant his philosophy to start with values. But war allows no room for the creation of values—there is no space for deliberation, discussion, consid-eration. And the pragmatists meekly (or enthusiastically) adjusted to the world as given. All was determined. This is what seems to have saddened Bourne most about the wedding of war and pragmatism—to him, no two ideas could have been more antithetical. Pragmatism needs to be shocked by the new, awakened by the malcontented. "That is why I evoked the spirit of William James, with its gay passion for ideas, and its freedom of speculation," Bourne concluded with stinging irony, "when I felt the slightly pedestrian gait into which the war had brought pragmatism. It is the creative desire more than the creative intelligence that we shall need if we are ever to fly" (p. 64).

At the heart of Bourne's creative, future-focused pragmatism, and what was missing from the pragmatism of the wartime technocrats, was cosmopol-itanism. Bourne's cosmopolitanism, laid out in a 1916 article in the *Atlantic Monthly* titled "Trans-National America," was an argument against a "melting pot" America. For Bourne, war and the melting-pot were, in a sense, func-tional equivalents—both acting to end discussion and inquiry by force rather than persuasion.[14] Force, the melting pot (and the decaying past it represented) had no place in Bourne's transnational, cosmopolitan America. There, advo-cates for competing cultures, including various American nationalisms based on versions of our "tradition," would restrict their efforts to persuasion. In his still-strong, youth-based optimism, and before the war had proved otherwise, Bourne wrote of his American ideal as though it actually existed—"a cosmo-politan federation of national colonies, of foreign cultures, from whom the sting of devastating competition has been removed" (p. 117).

Though he sometimes described his vision as a sort of naïve-seeming league-of-nations America, Bourne had a deep appreciation of culture as a con-tingent, ever-changing product of human activity. His favorite metaphor for cosmopolitan culture was weaving. Immigrants to America should be inter-preted, he said, as "threads of living and potent cultures, blindly striving to weave themselves into a novel international nation, the first the world has seen. . . . Any movement which attempts to thwart this weaving, or to dye the fabric any one color, or disentangle the threads of the strands, is false to this cosmo-politan vision" (pp. 120-121).[15]

Randolph Bourne died young, a victim not of the war but of the great in-fluenza epidemic of 1918. By that time, the war had eliminated any possibility that his cosmopolitan vision of America would be realized. But the idea and practice of cosmopolitanism survived, in small enclaves in America, and most notably among Jewish intellectuals, an affinity that Bourne had noted in one of his essays, "The Jew and Trans-National America." One outsider recognizing other similarly inclined outsiders. As David A. Hollinger (1985) has argued, outsiders such as German-Jewish and other immigrants, together with their American-born children, had several general cultural strategies potentially available to them. The two most popular of these, *assimilation* and *alienation*, were understood to take the existing, dominant American culture as their determinant guide, as though it had the unity, natural status, and function of the North Star. A third, less popular strategy, *cosmopolitanism*, interpreted American culture as being up for grabs, in endless process, being at any time whatever Americans, in all their contemporary and future variety, choose to make of it.

The fourth and final strategy, *cultural pluralism*, a precursor to today's *multiculturalism*, was the only tradition-independent alternative to cosmopolitanism. In a valuable recent article addressing contemporary issues of multiculturalism, Hollinger (1992, pp. 83-84) lays out a set of comparisons between cultural pluralism and cosmopolitanism:

- *Cosmopolitanism* "is willing to put the future of every culture at risk through the critical, sympathetic scrutiny of other cultures, and is willing to contemplate the creation of new affiliations . . ."
- *Pluralism* "is more concerned to protect and perpetuate particular, existing cultures."
- *Cosmopolitanism* "is casual about community-building and community-maintenance, and tends to seek voluntary affiliations of wide compass . . ."
- *Pluralism* "promotes affiliations on the narrower grounds of shared history and is quicker to see reasons for drawing boundaries between communities."
- *Cosmopolitanism* "is more oriented to the individual, whom it is likely to understand as a member of a number of different communities simultaneously."
- *Pluralism* "is more oriented to the group, and is likely to identify each individual with reference to a single, primary community."
- *Cosmopolitanism* "is more suspicious than is pluralism of the potential for conformist pressures within the communities celebrated by pluralists . . ."
- *Pluralism* "is more suspicious than is cosmopolitanism of the variousness and lack of apparent structure in the wider world celebrated by cosmopolitans."
- *Cosmopolitanism* is more open to "arguments offered by universalists that certain interests are shared by many groups. . . ."
- *Pluralism* is "more likely to see in such arguments the covert advancement of the interests of one, particular group."

Following this general outline of cosmopolitanism and pluralism, Hollinger goes on to describe a specific, contemporary form of cosmopolitanism that he calls *postethnicity*. *Post*ethnicity liberates individuals from the claims of their pasts. Hollinger recognizes that group affiliations are central to being human. He simply suggests that these affiliations be interpreted as contingent, contextual, and a matter of individual choice. Thus, postethnicity does for ethnicity what cosmopolitanism does for culture: it gives it life and puts it into play.

In giving us language with which we can separate cosmopolitanism from traditional pluralism, David Hollinger has made an important contribution to our practical handling of culture. *Pluralism* is understood as risk averse, favoring narrow, tight, separate communities, a unitary self, and fixity within traditional cultural limits. *Cosmopolitanism*, in contrast, is risk taking, favoring wide, loose, overlapping communities, multiple selves, and fluidity within universal human limits. These two very different ways of talking about culture are both in prominent use today. Stanley Fish, for example, demonstrates great command of pluralist talk in his recent book, *There's No Such Thing as Free Speech* (Fish, 1994). Although he doesn't use the term, Fish attacks what we call cosmopolitanism by claiming that it requires an "(impossible) act of will," that requires us "to float free of all truths and remain open to innumerable voices" (p. 19). With what does one do this? Fish asks. With "Reason," he replies—if you believe that Reason can be culture-free. But if you believe, as Fish does, that Reason is culture-bound—that is, affected by local concerns— there is no means of escape, no place to go.

What Fish seems to offer as a world-class, slam-dunk argument scores points, on our reading, only within the pluralists' game. According to those rules, the self is unitary and communities are narrow, tight, and separate; one culture to a customer. And that culture is understood to be totalitarian and unchanging. For Fish, the pluralists' is the only game in town; if the rules seem too strict, too bad. But Fish's exclusive franchise is based on a dichotomy between contingency ("historically limited picture") and noncontingency ("a picture that was *not* historically limited") that precludes all competition. Eliminate this dichotomy, admit *multiple* "historically limited pictures," loosen-up the integration within and among these multiple pictures (or selves), and one has a whole new ball game: *cosmopolitanism*.

Our contemporary vocabulary of cosmopolitanism is derived for the most part from the work of Richard Rorty (1991a). Like Stanley Fish, Rorty insists that each of us, in our own ways, is ethnocentric. But Rorty's ethnocentrism is less deadly dogmatic than Fish's. "It amounts," he says, "to little more than the claim that people can rationally change their beliefs and desires only by holding most of those beliefs and desires constant—even though we can never say in advance just which are to be changed and which retained intact" (p. 212).[16] Each of us is constituted or woven (echoing Randolph Bourne) by culture, but we are projects in process, as is culture, not finished products. We are constantly reweaving and being rewoven. To be ethnocentric, "is merely to say that beliefs suggested by another culture must be tested by trying to weave them together with beliefs we already have" (p. 26). Of course, some cultures are more open to change than others. "We can only hope to transcend our acculturation if our culture contains (or, thanks to disruptions from outside or internal revolt, come to contain) splits which supply toeholds for new initiatives. Without such splits—without tensions which make people listen to unfamiliar ideas in the hope of finding means of overcoming those tensions— there is no such hope" (pp. 13-14). Cosmopolitan culture, although "ethnocentric," is loosely woven,[17] with many openings for the emergence of new ways of doing things.[18]

Rorty's description of cosmopolitan culture is based on his interpretation of language. For Rorty, language is not a medium for either expression or description. Language has no purpose; it is simply a contingent product of evolution. "Our language and our culture," Rorty argues, "are as much a contingency, as much a result of thousands of small mutations finding niches (and millions of others finding no niches), as are the orchids and the anthropoids" (1989, p. 16). The history of language is the history of metaphor. "Old metaphors are constantly dying off into literalness, and then serving as a platform and foil for new metaphors" (p. 16). Because they are not members of a normal vocabulary or language game, metaphors have only their literal meanings; they are, therefore, the shockers, the de-centerers, the shakers-up of language, the tools for cultural change. To change the way we talk, Rorty says, is to change "what we want to do and what we think we are. . . . A sense of human history as the history of successive metaphors would let us see the poet, in the generic sense of the maker of new languages, as the vanguard of the species" (p. 20).[19] Cultural change, then, is a matter of metaphorical redescription, not a matter of getting things right. There are no criteria for that. Left to our own devices, Rorty suggests that, "we try to get to the point where we no longer worship *anything*, where we treat *nothing* as a quasi divinity, where we treat *everything*—our language, our conscience, our community—as a product of time and chance. To reach this point would be, in Freud's words, to 'treat chance as worthy of determining our fate'" (p. 22).

One of the great virtues of cosmopolitanism is its murky fluidity, a continuing reminder of change and mix, multiplicity and chance. This, of course, undermines to some extent the complexity-reducing function of cosmopolitanism, making it a more demanding strategy than its purer cultural competitors. Proponents of cosmopolitanism like Rorty can claim only that, as a way of life, demanding as it is, cosmopolitanism is better in vague and uncertain ways than the alternatives. This point is captured in Rorty's phrase, "cosmopolitanism without emancipation."[20] Since there is nothing to emancipate, nothing to be true to, self or order of things, our best strategy is free experimentation—as in science. Emancipators call for revolution with its attendant violence; cosmopolitans use reformist rhetoric to talk about increased tolerance and decreased suffering.

At one point in his discussion of cosmopolitanism Rorty introduces the figure of "linguistic islets." Some people, those we call pluralists, describe these islets as separate, unbridgeable. Others, practitioners of "the sort of cosmopolitan know-how whose acquisition enables [them] to move back and forth between sections of [their] own culture and [their] own history," do what they can to connect the islets. *Contra* Fish, no extraordinary ability to float free from culture is required. "If one sees language-learning as the acquisition of a skill," Rorty points out, "one will not be tempted to ask what metaskill permits such acquisition. One will assume that curiosity, tolerance, patience, luck, and hard work are all that is needed" (1991a, p. 216).

Strong cosmopolitans reject the notion of linguistic or cultural islets, preferring the image of clouds. In a brief, distant view they may seem well defined, separate, and still; experienced more closely and over time, however, their separateness evaporates in the mist, replaced by a single, swirling, boiling mass, constantly changing, appearing, and disappearing toward no end.[21] On this interpretation, our world, our language and our culture, is what we make of it. "There is just as much unity or transparency of language as there is willingness to converse rather than fight. So there is as much of either as we shall make in the course of history" (p. 218).

Cosmopolitans are talkers, not fighters, even though talking as they do will eventually end their way of talking. Whatever the new ways of talking turn out to be, cosmopolitans can only hope that future talkers speak of them in favorable terms. "But they admit," Rorty notes, "that we have no very clear idea what those terms will be. They only insist that, if these new terms have been adopted as a result of persuasion rather than force, they will be better than the ones we are presently using—for that is analytic of their meaning of 'better'" (pp. 219-220). Cosmopolitan cultural change derives from *persuasion*, rhetoric, metaphorical rediscription, and shock. "Rational" cultural reweaving, if one insists on using that term, is nothing more than that which results from persuasion. And, in the spirit of Randolph Bourne, "irrational" is a label one can hang on cultural change imposed by force.[22]

Culture Summary

We have tried to make two main points in our discussion of culture. First, we argued that people's preferences in everyday matters—their judgments of morality and danger for example—are guided by their cultural allegiances. Preferences to a large extent are the products of cultures. A mixture of cultures, as in modern, pluralist societies, produces a mixture of preferences. Disagreement; controversy. This point is important because it explains why there are no universally convincing arguments. Second, we argued that our first point did not imply that communication and persuasion among cultures was impossible. It is simply a matter of "curiosity, tolerance, patience, luck, and hard work." To facilitate this work, a special cultural form, cosmopolitanism, was invented by the ancients and reinterpreted in times of crisis over the years. Cosmopolitanism is a useful strategy for managing cultural conflicts because it takes culture to be an open, future-oriented process: our culture is what we make it. Cosmopolitans are less threatened by cultural change because of this, because they are willing to risk moving away from the past and into the unknown new, and also because, unlike monoculturalists, they speak of themselves in multiple narratives, each narrative connecting them to part of a loosely woven web of cultural communities.[23]

Inevitable cultural conflicts or cosmopolitanism? The main problem with cosmopolitanism, of course, is that it is very demanding. Instead of reducing environmental complexity, cosmopolitanism increases it. As a result, cosmopolitanism may never be practiced by more than a small, intellectual elite.[24] But that possibility is not an argument for restricting the availability of cosmopolitanism. As an ideal and a guide, cosmopolitanism could be liberating to many people, invigorating to many communities.

SOCIAL TRUST: CULTURAL VALUES

Our final functional equivalent to traditional social trust is social trust based on cultural values. We have discussed the traditional interpretation in some detail in earlier chapters. The cultural-values construction of social trust (and its variations) is the primary topic of the remainder of this book. In this chapter, we simply want to make clear the distinction between the traditional and cultural-values interpretations. We do this by placing the two constructions in the same conceptual context—culture. There, the fundamental difference is this:

- *Traditional social trust* is monocultural, adopting rationalism as a universal, transcultural standard incorporating the dual values of competence and responsibility.
- *Social trust based on cultural values* is multicultural, with the values on which it is based varying across cultures as well as across time and social contexts. Within this construction, traditional social trust is a special case.

Social trust based on cultural values thus is a generalized social trust with no predetermined criteria. All that is required is a group of persons with something in common. And having something in common is simply a matter, in the beginning, of living in the world. Beyond that, it is a matter of imagination.

The best plain and clear account of primary level, living-in-the-world social trust has been given to us by Ludwig Wittgenstein. Our interpretation of social trust based on cultural values derives, first of all, from what he had to say. In the main, Wittgenstein's writings on trust—and the related concepts of certainty and doubt—were produced during the last years of his life.[25] The later entries in the second volume of *Remarks on the Philosophy of Psychology*, written in Ireland in 1948 and published in 1980, deal in part with these topics. But it is in *On Certainty*, written in Vienna, Oxford, and Cambridge from 1949 to 1951 and published in 1969, that Wittgenstein concentrates most deeply on issues related to trust.[26] In our discussion of Wittgenstein and trust, we first present and comment on some of his remarks. This will serve to demonstrate his general argument and to provide a context for the contributions of writers who have followed him. We conclude with a discussion of some of these Wittgenstein-inspired treatments of trust and an assessment of Wittgenstein's impact on our language of trust.

Wittgenstein's Remarks on Trust

The focus of Wittgenstein's remarks is the distinction between two types of propositions. One is empirical and descriptive. This type can be recognized by noting if the contrary of a proposition makes sense. If so, then it is a testable statement about things in the world. If not, it is an untestable statement about a conceptual framework, a proposition of the second type. And propositions of this second type cannot be justified or proven correct. Thus, Wittgenstein discusses the relations between evidence and frameworks, between trust and grounds, and between certainty and doubt.[27]

For Wittgenstein, it is basic that evidence is convincing only to persons who share the framework within which the evidence was generated:

> Given the same evidence, one person can be completely convinced and another not be. We don't on account of this exclude either one from society, as being unaccountable and incapable of judgment.
>
> But mightn't a society do precisely this?
>
> For words have meaning only in the stream of life.
>
> (1980, pp. 115-116)

So, we do distinguish among people: those who share our basic worldview and those who don't.

> What is essential for us is, after all, spontaneous agreement, spontaneous sympathy.
>
> (p. 117)

And our agreement and sympathy are groundless:

> I did not get my picture of the world by satisfying myself of its correctness;
> nor do I have it because I am satisfied of its correctness. No: it is the inher-
> ited background against which I distinguish between true and false.
>
> (1969, p. 15)

Because evidence is convincing only within limited frameworks, there can be
no general principle of credibility:

> Perhaps someone says "There must be some basic principle on which we ac-
> cord credence," but what can such a principle accomplish? Is it more than a
> natural law of "taking for true"?
>
> (p. 25)

The worldviews or cultural frameworks that we all live within, that live
within us, provide the basis for trust:

> Do I pay any mind to his inner processes if I *trust* him? If I don't trust him
> I say, "I don't know what's going on inside him." But if I trust him, I don't
> say that I know what's going on inside him.
>
> (1980, p. 104)

Since our worldviews are groundless, our trust is groundless.

> If someone asked us "but is that *true*"? we might say "yes" to him; and if he
> demanded grounds we might say "I can't give you any grounds, but if you
> learn more you too will think the same."
>
> (1969, p. 28)

When a person trusts another person or an institution, grounds are beside the
point:

> . . . If he trusts me he will not only accept my information, he will also draw
> definite conclusions from my conviction, as to how I shall behave.
>
> (p. 88)

Trust is a groundless social bond that nonetheless is necessary to the functioning of society.[28]

Trust doesn't eliminate all doubt. But under normal conditions it restricts
doubt, keeping it away from basic issues:

> That is to say, the *questions* that we raise and our *doubts* depend on the
> fact that some propositions are exempt from doubt, are as it were like hinges
> on which those turn.
>
> (p. 44)

Doubting requires nondoubting. And under extraordinary circumstances it is even possible to doubt oneself, one's worldview:

> I can't be making a mistake,—but some day, rightly or wrongly, I may think
> I realize that I was not competent to judge.
>
> (p. 85)

One's worldview might be "a kind of mythology"—a mythology described by propositions that are learned in action, rules of a game learned in play.

Wittgenstein asks us to imagine some of these propositions as the hardened bed of a river, others as the fluid river itself. Then he asks us to imagine change over time—the hard propositions becoming fluid, the fluid hard.

> I distinguish between the movement of the waters on the river-bed and the shift of the bed itself; though there is not a sharp division of the one from the other.
>
> And the bank of that river consists partly of hard rock, subject to no alteration or only to an imperceptible one, partly of sand, which now in one place now in another gets washed away, or deposited.
>
> (1969, p. 15)

Once again, the shore. And changes in worldview are possible—normally rather slowly, always as a function of social processes.

Wittgenstein's remarks on trust seem at first to be formidably conservative. Social trust is a within-group phenomenon, a guardian of tradition, an inhibitor of growth, a barrier against infiltration and change. The potential of social trust to accompany intergroup conflict seems as great as its likelihood to coincide with intragroup peace. But this would be only a partial reading. In the last set of remarks quoted above, Wittgenstein clearly indicates that it is not necessary to accept one's culture as a unified, static ahistorical whole. Cultures are dynamic and historically contingent; individuals within cultures constantly work to change them. Parts of one's worldview can be used to critique and change other parts. And, most significantly, we can always work within our cultural groups to widen the ways in which we define *we*.

Trust: Following Wittgenstein

The most useful discussion of Wittgensteinian trust is by Lars Hertzberg (1988). Hertzberg bases his analysis on *On Certainty*, but he doesn't confine himself to the content of those remarks. He begins by attacking the "cognitive and intellectual bias" of those philosophers who have confined their comments on trust to matters of believing someone and believing what he says. Trust,

Hertzberg, notes is more basic and general than that. To demonstrate his way of thinking about trust, he defines a distinction between trust and reliance.

Reliance is an exercise of judgment based on evidence: "Relying on someone involves the thought of independent standards by which it is to be judged whether or not my reliance on him was misplaced; reliance is conditional on those standards being met" (p. 312). Trust, in contrast, is an attitude towards a person that is not based on evidence about the person.[29] As a consequence, "Nothing can force a person to give up his trust in another; in order to do so he must *change*" (p. 314). We take this to mean that trust is based on a bond of *similarity* between persons; the bond is broken when similarity changes to dissimilarity: "When I trust someone, it is *him* I trust; I do not trust certain things *about* him. When I trust someone, he as it were *embodies* goodness, or reason, for me" (p. 315). That is, their bond is based on shared cultural values.[30]

Hertzberg uses his distinction between reliance and trust to discuss why the latter is often interpreted as a weakness. It turns on a failure to consider the place of responsibility in the two cases. An error in reliance is an error in judgment for which the person making the judgment is responsible. An error in trust, in contrast, is failure on the part of the person trusted: "The reason for this is that, unlike reliance, the grammar of trust involves a perspective of justice: trust can only concern that which one person can rightfully demand of another" (p. 319). And, of course, justice, like trust, is a matter of shared cultural values.

Norman Malcolm, a close friend of Wittgenstein's, has also commented on the remarks on trust contained in *On Certainty* (1988). Malcolm's argument, summarized in three points, is that there is a form of skepticism in Wittgenstein's certainty: "When truly we cannot be making a *mistake*, when we regard it as *nonsensical* to suppose our assertion might be false, when we do not even understand *how* it could be false—then there is an overwhelming temptation to believe that reality *must* agree with our certainty. Wittgenstein is telling us that this is not so" (p. 286). Malcolm's second point is that "Most of what we know, or think we know, about science and history, rests on *belief* in various authorities, on our *trusting* what we read and are told, and not on anyone's personal verification" (p. 286). The final point is that "There can be no *guarantee* that one will not be 'contradicted on all sides' by the testimony of others; or that 'unheard-of' events will not disrupt the regularities of nature" (p. 286). Wittgenstein, Malcom reminds us, is cautioning us (at the same time he is insisting on the necessity of certainty) about the contingency of all we know.[31]

The Impact of Wittgenstein on Trust

Thinking about the impact of Wittgenstein on trust, on how we think and talk about trust, we are tempted toward the extremes. Either Wittgenstein has had no impact whatsoever, or Wittgenstein's impact is so pervasive that we don't notice it. In many respects, the latter is true. Much of what Wittgenstein says seems common sense to us now. After all, his ideas and those of others affected by him have been circulating through our culture for decades. For many of us, he is in our bones. He is one of us. But if someone asks for evidence, then we are in trouble. We have none. We search psychology. Nothing. Sociology. The same. And even in philosophy, if we are looking for Wittgensteinian trust rather than Wittgenstein, we will not find him.

We know Wittgensteinian trust is here, but there is no evidence. This is no mystery. We know trust is here because Wittgenstein was talking about what is in us and in our social world. If we examine ourselves and our society, we find it. But psychology and sociology are somewhere else, playing different games—theoretical games that Wittgenstein deplored. Much of the discourse of social science is simply separated from the everyday facts of life.[32] Thus, theories of trust fly off here and there, guided (if by anything at all) by the ritualistic logic of normal science, completely out of touch with the world.

The separation of social science from social life is not the only reason for Wittgenstein's lack of impact on the way we talk about trust. There is also our deep ambivalence toward trust. In contrasting reliance and trust, Lars Hertzberg says, "In relying on someone I as it were look down at him from above. I exercise my command of the world. I remain the judge of his actions. In trusting someone I look up from below. I learn from the other what the world is about. I let him be the judge of my actions" (1988, p. 315). We are ambivalent toward trust, when we think about it, because it is risky. When we trust we are giving something up in order to gain something else in return. We give up a bit of control over ourselves: We become less monadic and more social. We risk losing our individuality, and nothing is more important than that.

So social science comes to the rescue and domesticates trust, tames it, sanitizes it, and makes it safe for Americans, safe for democracy. Trust no longer is risky. Trust no longer threatens your self-control. Trust no longer robs you of your individuality. Trust no longer is Wittgensteinian. Trust *is* no longer—it has been rationalized out of our lives. Distrust, afterall, is a better bet.

Social trust based on cultural values is an attempt, first, to make trust Wittgensteinian again and, second, to make it risky.

SUMMARY: CULTURE, SOCIAL TRUST/PLURALISTIC, COSMOPOLITAN

In this chapter, we have discussed two community-focus, low-resource-demand strategies: culture and social trust based on cultural values. These are the strategies, among all those that we have considered, that should be most effective in uniting individuals in support of social goals. Available evidence supports this conjecture, particularly in the case of culture: the judgments of individuals are strongly guided by the cultural worldviews that they have learned and to which they contribute. Thus, on many social issues that we may consider significant, many people act similarly to one another without thinking or doing too much about it. Social trust based on cultural values should also operate in a similarly effective and efficient manner. Both culture and social trust can be powerful tools in the management of public problems.

But to what end? One way of talking about the ends of culture is to argue as we have that cultural diversity can be interpreted in two general ways, *pluralistic* and *cosmopolitan*:

- *Pluralistic* cultural diversity is risk averse, favoring narrow, tight, separate communities, a unitary self, and fixity within traditional cultural limits.
- *Cosmopolitan* cultural diversity, in contrast, is risk taking, favoring wide, loose, overlapping communities, multiple selves, and fluidity within universal human limits.

Pluralism and cosmopolitanism are, of course, end points on a continuum—provisional simplifications for conversational convenience. They help us understand, in the plainest way, that culture can be used to either move groups of people apart or to move them together.

Following from our understanding of culture, social trust based on cultural values can take two general forms—pluralistic and cosmopolitan. Pluralistic social trust is the social trust of the present—the normal, common form based on *existing* group values.[33] Cosmopolitan social trust, in contrast, is based on *emergent* group values. Understanding this is the beginning, the first step toward a better future. To contribute usefully to the solution of social problems, however, we have to learn how to move from pluralistic social trust, with its rigid, defensive solitudes, toward cosmopolitan social trust, with its fluid, inclusive interweavings. We have to learn how to move into futures that we can't describe because we have liberated them from their ties to our pasts. We have to learn, in sum, how to *create* social trust. This future social trust is the subject of Part III.

Part III

SOCIAL TRUST: FUTURE

In "Part III, Social Trust: Future," we attempt to describe a way social trust can help us move toward a cosmopolitan society. There are three chapters. In Chapter 8, we describe and provide empirical support for our concept of social trust based on cultural values. We identify two types of social trust—pluralistic (within group) and cosmopolitan (across group). Only the latter is useful to the solution of social problems. Chapter 9 is devoted to the general topic of narrative thinking. We discuss the general importance, functions, and uses of narrative in human life, in psychology and science, and in social trust. We describe science as a model cosmopolitan community, a community based on the narrative of cosmopolitan social trust. In Chapter 10, our last chapter, we attempt to outline the development of social trust from the present to the future, from a pluralist society to a cosmopolitan society. We contrast two forms of public participation—pluralist and cosmopolitan. Four elements contribute to the working of cosmopolitan public participation—cosmopolitan leadership, a model cosmopolitan community, use of narrative, and imagination. We conclude with a brief reconsideration of the distinction between pluralist and cosmopolitan societies and the difficulties of moving from the one to the other.

8

Social Trust Based on Cultural Values

In this chapter, we describe our concept of social trust based on cultural values. Our interpretation differs from the traditional construction of social trust in two significant ways. First, we understand social trust to be a *risk judgment*. That is, we take social trust to entail a movement from a limited, relatively controlled condition to one that is broader and less controlled. Social trust, on our account, entails risk. This is opposed to the traditional formulation, which limits social trust to moves the safety of which can be guaranteed by the standard rules of rationality.[1] To be properly justified, that is, social trust must be based on the fundamental values of competence and responsibility. This is our second significant departure from tradition. Our construction removes the constraints of standard rationality. Social trust, in our interpretation, can be based on *any* values—whatever happens to be salient to a person at a certain time, in a given context. This formulation is saved from chaos by noting that removal of standard rationality constraints does not deprive us of guidance. Each of us is constituted by cultures that are shared by groups of similar others. Our cultures identify the values we use to make judgments, with the values varying across cultures. Thus, competence and responsibility are not excluded from our interpretation; they are included—as are all other sets of values—as a particular case with no special privilege. In addition to describing social trust based on cultural values, we also briefly outline some of the empirical support this new formulation has thus far received. We conclude the chapter with a discussion of the two general types of social trust—pluralistic and cosmopolitan.

SOCIAL TRUST IS A RISK JUDGMENT

The notion that social trust is a risk judgment is based on a wedding between our work on risk judgment (e.g., Earle, Cvetkovich, and Slovic, 1990) and Niklas Luhmann's (1979) work on trust. In his discussion of trust as a complexity-reducing strategy, Luhmann insists that trust requires risk:

> We . . . formulate the problem of trust as a gamble, a risky investment. The world is being dissipated into an uncontrollable complexity; so much so that at any given time people are able to choose freely between very different actions. Nevertheless, I have to act here and now. There is only a brief moment of time in which it is possible for me to see what others do, and consciously adapt myself to it. In just that moment only a little complexity can be envisaged and processed, thus only a little gain in rationality is possible. Additional chances of a more complex rationality would arise if I were to place my trust in a given future course of action of others . . . If I can trust in sharing the proceeds, I can allow myself forms of co-operation which do not pay off immediately and which are not directly visible as beneficial.
>
> (p. 24)

In our interpretation, following Luhmann, social trust is a risk judgment that assigns to other persons (agencies, organizations, institutions, etc.) the responsibility for working on some necessary task. In making a judgment of social trust, an individual accepts the risk that the entity being trusted will act as expected. Our account of social trust as a risk judgment means that trust is a conscious act and that trust is transitory, limited in time to the period required to make the judgment.[2]

In making a social trust judgment, an individual in effect moves from State A (in which the person is faced with an environment that threatens to overwhelm him with complexity) to State B (in which the cognitive demands of the individual's environment are reduced to manageable size). For the individual who makes the social trust judgment, trust acts as a *bridge* from State A to State B, from disequilibrium (an unbalanced, "nonnormal" state) to equilibrium (a balanced, "normal" state). Trust, therefore, offers the individual two general types of benefits: it reduces cognitive complexity while at the same time enabling a person to move from an old normal state that has become disturbed by some problem to a new, steady normal state that provides increased behavioral alternatives as a result of the complexity incorporated in it by social trust. Internal (cognitive) complexity is reduced while external (environmental) complexity is increased. The risk in trust is that the new normal state may not develop as expected. Also, the trust judgment may simply be wrong. But trust has done its job: Cognitive complexity has been reduced. As Luhmann describes it in his systems terminology, "The system substitutes inner certainty for external certainty" (p. 27). It is the reduction of complexity and the risks associated with it that are central to trust, not the specific values on which it is based: "Trust is not concerned with knowing the essential truth about a matter but with the success of the reduction of complexity" (p. 69).[3]

Our interpretation of social trust as a risk judgment is directly opposed to the traditional account of social trust as a continuous, ongoing basis for social relations. In the traditional formulation, risk is minimized or eliminated entirely, ruled out by rationality. But social trust without risk, we argue, is no trust at all. It is risk that makes trust work; in economic terms, it is reducing costs while increasing benefits. With regard to the role of risk, our understanding of social trust is similar to Aaron Wildavsky's account of safety: "Conceiving of safety without risk is like seeking love without courting the danger of rejection" (1988, p. 228). Social trust, in Wildavsky's vocabulary, is a *resilient* strategy: it seeks the reduction of cognitive complexity, and the attendant enlargement of social benefits, by taking risks. To trust is to risk.

The Classical Origins of Trust as Risk

Social trust is associated primarily with modernity, and during the modern period every attempt was made, following enlightenment orthodoxy, to set it on a universal and unassailable rational base. This involved, among other cleansing initiatives, the separation of trust from risk. The result was traditional social trust, a concept divorced from all but the highest of human interests, competence, and responsibility. But trust was not always so pure.

In ancient Greece, when trust was limited to interpersonal relations, risk and trust were claimed by some writers to be intimately intertwined. A number of classicists such as Arlene Saxonhouse (1988) and Darrell Dobbs (1987) have discussed the relations between trust and risk in ancient times. But it is Martha Nussbaum who has most thoroughly and usefully interpreted the ancient texts on these topics, freely moving between the poets and the philosophers. In her 1986 book *The Fragility of Goodness*, Nussbaum begins her analysis of "luck and ethics" by posing three fundamental questions on life's contingencies. First, to what extent is it rational to open one's life to vulnerability and chance in the form of personal and political relations? Second, to what extent are these vulnerabilities compatible—or can there be conflicts among them? In her third question, Nussbaum confronts us with the great ignored problem of risk and trust, "the ethical value of the so-called 'irrational parts of the soul' . . . appetites, feelings, emotions" (p. 7)—those parts which, untamed and troubling within us, link us to the untamed and troubling without. Should they, in the name of self-sufficiency, be brought under rational control? Reading Nussbaum, we are shocked into a realization of the hollow, useless abstractness of so much of our talk about trust and risk. Where are our bodies, where are our emotions when we talk? They are split apart from us for simplicity's sake, for some dream of rationality—and for safety. If we are seriously interested in affecting our lives in good ways, Nussbaum warns us, we need to consider all of what we human beings are.

By basing her account on both poetry and philosophy—literature and science—Nussbaum, more than any modern social scientist, is able to address problems of risk and trust in the rich complexity of lives as they are lived. As she unfolds her argument, drawing on her understanding of Aristotle and the tragic poets, she makes these startlingly contemporary, useful points:

- Human cognitive capacities are limited.
- Self-sufficiency is impossible.
- Luck plays an irreducible role in the shaping of human life and values.
- Humans tend to have multiple, incommensurable values, creating a complexity that we want to reduce.
- Within the realm of human problems, scientific, technical reasoning cannot be substituted for practical reason.[4]
- The vulnerable life is the best life.

In sum, a good life, according to Nussbaum, is, in part, one that includes vulnerability to other people—one that includes, in other words, a form of trust that entails risk. Enmeshed as most of us are in modern forms of life devoted to the rational elimination of risk, Nussbaum, in her interpretation of the ancient Greeks, reminds us of what we are missing, of what risk and trust can add to our lives.

SOCIAL TRUST IS BASED ON CULTURAL VALUES

To say that social trust is a risk judgment does not imply, of course, that it is a judgment made blindly or arbitrarily. On the other hand, judgments of social trust needn't be based on large amounts of certain kinds of information, as was the case in the traditional construction. As we noted earlier, Ludwig Wittgenstein claimed that trust was *groundless*. By that he meant that trust was a matter of culture, not of evidence, of shared worlds rather than argument. We trust persons whom we take to be similar to us in salient ways, persons who share our cultural values. Social trust based on cultural values is multicultural in the sense that it can be based on any values: in contrast to traditional social trust, there are no predetermined criteria. Cultural values, the bases for social trust, vary across groups of persons and within groups across time and social contexts. As a final complication, the arguments of Martha Nussbaum and the notion of multiple selves remind us that cultural values also vary, and at times conflict, within individuals.

Table 8.1
General Questionnaire Contents

Page	Contents	Forms
1	Title	One
2	Instructions	One
3	Story #1	Three
4, 5	Questions Regarding Story #1	One
6	Social Trust Items for Story #1	One
7	Story #2	Three
8, 9	Questions Regarding Story #2	One
10	Social Trust Items for Story #2	One
11	Culture Items	One
12	Background Items	One

Half of the subjects receive a questionnaire with Story #1 first; for the other subjects, Story #2 is in first place. With the three different forms for each story, there are therefore 3 (form of Story #1) x 3 (form of Story #2) x 2 (order of stories) = 18 different forms of the questionnaire.

Supporting Evidence: Empirical Studies

One of the cultural groups we belong to is the world community of social scientists. Prominent among the values of this group is the exposure of one's hypotheses to empirical test. In support of this, we have conducted several studies of social trust judgments over the past three years with the primary purpose of examining in various ways the general hypothesis that social trust is based on cultural values. Instead of reciting the technical details of these studies, we will informally outline a typical research procedure and describe some central results.[5]

Most of our studies have a simple, basic form that we call a "survey experiment." That is, we use surveylike methods and materials, but we manipulate the contents of the materials (questionnaires) so that they create the structure of an experiment. A typical study, for example, may include 300 to 400 subjects (primarily college students but with a good percentage of older nonstudents as well). Each subject completes one questionnaire. Systematic variations among the questionnaires, however, result in the subjects being randomly assigned to experimental groups. A page-by-page description of a typical questionnaire may be helpful. The questionnaire centers on two short, simulated newspaper stories. Each of the stories is followed by sets of questionnaire items designed to measure various theoretical constructs.[6] In Table 8.1, we give the page number, the general contents of the page, and the number of forms those contents take.

Our simulated newspaper stories are based on current risk-management issues; the "news" in each story is a description of a proposed risk-management strategy. In our example, Story #1 concerns AIDS, and Story #2 deals with nuclear waste management. For both stories, the three forms, the three risk-management strategies, are each designed to express a different cultural orientation. These three worldviews—Hierarchical, Individualist, and Egalitarian— are drawn from the work of Mary Douglas and Aaron Wildavsky (1982) and Karl Dake (1992). In the AIDS story, for example, the Individualist strategy calls for:

1. A program encouraging voluntary testing for the AIDS virus (HIV) among high-risk groups;
2. More open access for infected persons to experimental drugs for the treatment of AIDS;
3. Prosecution of infected persons who knowingly place others at risk; and
4. Increased efforts to educate the public, particularly high-risk groups, in safe-sex practices.

In contrast, the Hierarchical strategy was more top-down, controlling and punitive, while the Egalitarian plan was more accepting and communitarian.

The "Culture Items" on page 11 of the questionnaire are designed to measure the cultural-value orientations of the subjects. Karl Dake (1992) has very thoughtfully and methodically worked to transfer the ideas of culture theory into questionnaire items (as well as other methods of measurement). In our work, we have adapted and amended Dake's items, the result being the following simplified set (responses to all items are given on seven-point, agree/disagree scales):

Hierarchical
    a. I'm for my country, right or wrong.
    b. The police should have the right to listen in on private telephone conversations when investigating a crime.
    c. Centralization is one of the things that makes a country great.

Individualist
    a. Environmental and other problems would be more readily solved if there were less government intervention.
    b. Most of what I value in life is achieved through my own efforts; my community and the place I live in contribute little.

Egalitarian
a. Much of the conflict in this world could be eliminated if we had more equal distribution of resources among nations.
b. I support a tax shift so that the burden falls more heavily on corporations and persons with large incomes.

Based on their responses to these items, each subject is given a score on the three cultural orientation scales (i.e., the average score per item). Each subject is then given a (provisional) cultural identity based on her highest score. She is identified as an Egalitarian, for example, if her score on that scale is greater than her scores on the other two scales.[7]

As outlined thus far, our procedure presents us with: two sets of risk management strategies that are classified according to cultural orientation; and a set of subjects that is classified according to cultural orientation.

Since the subjects are randomly assigned to the strategies, we produce an experimentlike design: we can assess the effects of the "interaction" between the cultural orientation of the strategies and the cultural orientation of the subjects. That is, we can determine whether the evaluation of a story with a given cultural orientation is affected by the cultural orientation of the evaluator. Evaluations for Story #1 are given by subjects in response to the questions on pages 4 and 5; an identical set of questions for Story #2 is on pages 8 and 9. These story evaluation items produce data for our model of risk communication. Since these data do not directly address questions of social trust, we will not describe them here except to note that the two sets of cultural orientations (story and subject) do interact on some measures—indicating that subjects with a given cultural orientation give their highest evaluations to stories that express that culture.

For our present purposes, the questions on pages 6 and 10, the social trust items, are most important. These items, divided into two sets for each story, are very simple. For the nuclear-waste-management story, the first set of items begins with this question:

The proposed new federal organization described in the story is the Nuclear Waste Management Agency (NWMA). Based on what you have read here, how do you feel about the NWMA?

An appropriately modified question is used with the AIDS story. In both cases, the question is followed by the same six-item trust-values scale. Each of the six items consists of a seven-point response scale anchored by bipolar descriptors of the relations between the story and the subject.

For example:

Shares my values	_|_|_|_|_|_|_	Different values
In line with me	_|_|_|_|_|_|_	Wrong direction
Same goals as me	_|_|_|_|_|_|_	Different goals
Supports my views	_|_|_|_|_|_|_	Opposes my views
Acts as I would	_|_|_|_|_|_|_	Acts against me
Thinks like me	_|_|_|_|_|_|_	Thinks unlike me

By simply summing the responses (ranging from 7 to 1, left to right) on these six items, we have a measure of subjects' judged value similarity between themselves and the story. The second set of social trust items consists of a single question and its accompanying response scale. For the nuclear waste story, the set was this:

Based on what you have read here, would you say you would trust the NWMA?

Would not trust the NWMA at all	_|_|_|_|_|_|_	Would trust the NWMA completely

This single item gives us a general, first-approach indicator of subjects' trust judgments.

With these sets of social trust items embedded in our survey questionnaires, we are in a position to explore the cultural-values social trust hypothesis from two directions. First, we can examine both the trust values and trust judgment data for an interaction between the cultural orientations of the stories and the cultural orientations of the subjects. (For simplicity, we confine our description of results to the nuclear waste story; the results for the AIDS story are similar.) For both measures, trust values and trust judgments, the results are the same—a very strong interaction between story and subject cultural orientations.[8] All three groups of subjects give their highest marks to the story that matched their cultural orientation. The effects of story cultural orientation varied across subject groups, however. Egalitarian subjects, for example, were affected most by story variations: they gave very high marks on both scales (an average item score approaching 5) to the Egalitarian story and very low marks to the Hierarchical story (the average dipping to close to 3); the Individualistic story was given marks midway between the others.[9] The Hierarchical subjects were similar to the Egalitarians, but they distinguished less between the stories expressing orientations they opposed. In contrast to those two groups, the Individualist subjects put the least distance between their favored Individualist story and the other two, which they lumped together. In other words, the Individualists had the least variation in their responses, neither trusting a great deal within their culture nor resolutely withholding it across cultures.

Another way we can use results from this study to explore the cultural-values social trust hypothesis is to examine a model for the prediction of trust judgments. The procedure is very simple. According to the cultural values hypothesis, trust judgments are best predicted by judged similarity of values between the subject and the object, the "truster" and the "trustee." Using the data generated by the AIDS story, we can construct the following model:

We have already discussed three of the elements in this model: story culture (or cultural orientation), trust values, and social trust.[10] Story credibility is derived from a subset of the story evaluation questions contained on pages 4 and 5 and 8 and 9 of the questionnaire.[11] This new element is included in the model as an alternative to cultural values. Credibility, as in the case of competence and responsibility (which, unfortunately, we have no measures of), is often informally equated with social trust or suggested as a predictor of it.

As it is shown in the figure above, the model contains all of the theoretically justified paths to the prediction of social trust. In this condition, the model does its job very well.[12] Statistical tests of the model indicate, however, that the trust values element has five times the impact on social trust that the credibility element does. In addition, the effect of trust values on credibility is more than three times greater than the effect of credibility on social trust. Another way to examine the importance of the relationship between trust values and social trust is to eliminate the path between these two elements and observe the effects on the performance of the model. With no direct path between trust values and social trust, the model fails miserably.[13] Even in this condition, with trust values having to travel through credibility, the latter has only about double the effect of the former on social trust. The impact of trust values on credibility is roughly the same as the impact of credibility on social trust. Taken together, the two sets of results we have described provide strong, if preliminary, support for the cultural values notion that individuals use values similarity as the basis for their judgments of trust.[14]

In addition to the relatively controlled, micro-level evidence that we have outlined in support of the cultural values hypothesis, we have been continuously engaged for the past several years in the application of this interpretation of social trust in various community contexts. Although they are perhaps more engaging than the experimental studies, they are less well defined and require more space to describe. Here, we simply identify and very briefly describe these ongoing efforts:

Lynden Community Forums

Lynden is a small community in northwestern Washington. Like all communities, large and small, in the state, Lynden is required to develop a growth management plan. Our involvement in the development process has centered on the use of narrative-generation techniques for the identification of community values. For example, three community forums were held in which several visions for Lynden's future were presented. Questionnaires were used to assess audience members' acceptance of the individual presentations and also their judgments of value similarity between themselves and each of the presenters. Results on these measures showed that acceptance was highly related to judged value similarity.

Whatcom County Critical Areas

Whatcom County is located in northwestern Washington, on the Canadian border. Like every county in the state, Whatcom County is required to develop a "critical areas ordinance" for the protection of environmentally sensitive areas such as wetlands. Public hearings were held in which individuals expressed their opinions about a draft ordinance prepared by the County Council. Much of this testimony was negative, centering on the "rights of property owners." Nonetheless, the council approved the ordinance unchanged. In response, property rights groups drafted their own, less restrictive version of the ordinance and had it placed on the ballot for the upcoming election. Voters approved that version of the ordinance. The question of which of the two ordinances has force is now being decided in court. Our work in this matter has involved the identification of the values expressed in the public testimony and in the two ordinances. We concluded that a lack of shared values between the first version of the ordinance and the public testimony indicated an absence of trust between significant segments of the public and the Council on this issue. The second version of the ordinance, expressing a different set of values, resulted. The lesson for the Council and others is that care and effort must be taken to assure that sets of broadly shared values are expressed in potentially controversial legislation. This does not suggest a mechanical identification of existing commonalties. It points instead to the need for civic leadership in the imaginative creation of emergent commonalties designed to cope with the specific problem at hand.

The Northwest Timber Summit

This is another case involving public hearings, the issue here being the rate of logging in federally owned forests in the northwestern states. The testimony included statements from the standard set of competing groups: loggers, environmentalists, federal agencies, logging-dependent business and towns, etc. Following the "summit" (so-called because President Clinton and several of his cabinet members had participated), an interagency task force was formed to draft a logging plan designed to address the concerns that had been expressed. The completed plan was given good marks by commentators not directly involved in the dispute. Many of the original stakeholders denounced the plan, however, claiming that it did not express their values. That is, the groups of stakeholders based their trust judgments, their acceptance of the plan, on their traditional, within-group values, and the plan, of course, was based on an amalgam of cross-group values. As in the Whatcom County critical areas case, our analyses indicated that little had been done by the leaders of the process to encourage the creation of emergent sets of values that would move stakeholders beyond their traditional, entrenched positions.

The empirical work and the application efforts that we have outlined here all contribute to our confidence that social trust is based on cultural values. We are reminded, however, that confidence based on the familiar should be kept open to revision.

SOCIAL TRUST: PLURALISTIC AND COSMOPOLITAN

Our distinction between pluralistic and cosmopolitan social trust turns, in a sense, on the notions of familiarity and suspicion. Within pluralistic social trust, individuals rely on the familiar and suspect what is different; within cosmopolitan social trust, individuals attempt to reverse these relations—to suspect the familiar and to rely on what is different. We say *attempt* here because movement away from the familiar toward what is different is, for most persons, movement against the established flow of their lives. It is (or appears to be, is interpreted as) a movement away from simplicity toward complexity. As such, it is resisted.

Both pluralistic and cosmopolitan social trust are compatible with our cultural values construction. Both forms of social trust are based on cultural values. The difference between the two is the difference between pluralistic values and cosmopolitan values. Pluralistic values are associated with *existing* groups; there is a satisfied acceptance of (or insistence on) things as they are (or as people believe they once were), the fundamental rightness of one's group. Cosmopolitan values, in contrast, are associated with *emerging* groups; there is an insistence on reflexivity, mixture, and reformulation in response to useful new ways of being in the world, in response to the wrongness of any single way. Understanding these differences between pluralistic and cosmopolitan values is central to making social trust a useful tool for the management of social problems. Toward that end, we explore, for the remainder of this chapter, several different ways of talking about the pluralistic/cosmopolitan distinction.

Pluralistic Social Trust

One way to talk about pluralistic social trust is as *group cooperation*. According to Robin Dawes and his colleagues, group cooperation is the product of group identity and group discussion: "Why? Because people make promises to each other which they feel obligated to keep. . . . It is the ethical feeling of obligation that drives the behavioral effects observed" (Tyler and Dawes, 1991; p. 11). But where does group identity come from? Is it based on individual benefits? No. "Our experiments have led us to conclude that cooperation rates can be radically affected by one factor in particular, which is independent of the consequences for the choosing individual. That factor is group identity: Such identity—or solidarity—can be established and consequently enhance cooperative responding in the absence of any expectation of future reciprocity, current rewards or punishments, or even reputational consequences among other group members" (Dawes, van de Kragt, and Orbell, 1990, p. 99).

Dawes argues that groups provide people with self-identities. Group identity is the complement of self-identity: individuals create the group, and the group creates the individuals. "Having taken on a self-identity linked to the group, people voluntarily behave in ways that benefit the group. . . . In situations without strong social bonds, people are egotistical. Once a group identity is created, however, people are increasingly responsive to group-centered motives" (Tyler and Dawes, 1991, p. 21). In a manner similar to cultures and cultural values, then, groups and group values function to reduce the cognitive complexity of their members.

In sum, group cooperation appears to work in this way: group identity plus group discussion produces an ethical feeling of obligation and this results in cooperation. This scenario is an echo from David Hume:

> When each individual perceives the same sense of interest in all his fellows, he immediately performs his part of any contract, as being assured that they will not be wanting in theirs. All of them, by concert enter into a scheme of actions, calculated for common benefit, and agree to be true to their words; nor is there anything requisite to form this concert or connection, but that every one have a sense of interest in the faithful fulfilling of engagements, and express that sense to other members of the society. This immediately causes that interest to operate upon them and interest is the first obligation to the performance of promises.

> Afterwards a sentiment of morals concurs with interest, and becomes a new obligation upon mankind.
>
>   (Hume, [1740] 1969, p. 574)

This Dawes-Hume "ethical feeling of cooperation," obviously beneficial (for a time) within groups, can lead to difficulties among groups. Evidence for this is everywhere in our daily lives. In the San Francisco Bay Area, for example, an official for the regional government claimed recently that "we are one of the most aggressive debating societies in the world. . . . We're operating on an idealized version of democracy in which everyone gets what they want. Each individual views himself as part of some minority, fostering fractionalization of the community. The result is political gridlock" (San Francisco Chronicle, May 18, 1992, p. A6). Such comments are typical expressions of a growing concern about and disenchantment with interest-group politics, politics based on the too-limited constructions of group cooperation and pluralistic social trust.[15]

Another way to talk about pluralistic social trust is in terms of values, conflicts among values, and pluralism.[16] Although we have chosen not to give it any specific, technical meaning, the term *values* has played a prominent role thus far in our discussion as part of the term *cultural values*. In contemporary social science, *values* is hard to escape. Charles Lindblom (1990) managed that feat in a limited sense, by creating his own value-like concept of "volitions" to play an important role in his theory of inquiry. And researchers who do use *values* seldom agree on its meaning. Some, such as Ronald Inglehart (1990), interpret values as durable, cross-situational dispositions. Others, like Jon Hurwitz and Mark Peffley (1987), use values in more context-specific ways: "We find core values like ethnocentrism and the morality of war to structure foreign-policy postures like militarism, anticommunism, and isolationism; which in turn are important determinants of individuals' preferences across a wide range of specific policies, such as defense spending, Soviet relations, involvement of U.S. troops overseas, international trade, and nuclear arms" (pp. 1113-1114). Our work is more in line with this latter understanding, an important implication of which is an emphasis on the heuristic use of values as aids to judgment and decision making. That is, the use of values as judgment aids reduces the need for "expensive" information gathering and processing. It does, that is, if there are no conflicts among values.

We claimed earlier, however, that intrapersonal value conflicts are inherent to any well-lived life, the life of a person who accepts the necessity of risk and trust. Similarly, interpersonal and intergroup value conflicts are unavoidable in any society. "These collisions of values," as Isaiah Berlin puts it, "are the essence of . . . what we are" (1991, p. 13). The question, of course, is how one interprets them and what one does about them. In a classic pluralist statement, Berlin says of those who would do away with value conflicts that theirs "is a world altogether beyond our ken . . . principles which are harmonized in this other world are not the principles with which, in our daily lives, we are acquainted; if they are transformed, it is into conceptions not known to us on earth. But it is on earth that we live, and it is here that we must believe and act" (p. 13).

Because Berlin is most concerned about the imposition of one group's "correct" solution on members of other groups—a concern we, of course, share—he tends, we think, to be overly accepting of existing conditions and conflicts, pessimistic about the possibilities of change: "Our values are ours, and theirs are theirs," he insists (p. 11). At times, Richard Rorty talks this way as well, as when he says, referring to his *Contingency, Irony and Solidarity*, "The fundamental premise of the book is that a belief can still regulate action, can still be thought worth dying for, among people who are quite aware that this belief is caused by nothing deeper than contingent historical circumstance" (1989, p. 189). Both Berlin and Rorty base their liberal positions on group solidarity. But Rorty more often talks about enlarging the group, widening the span of "we," than he does of dying for contingent beliefs.[17]

We will not attempt to argue the grand issues of liberalism and pluralism here. We want only to make a very simple point about the form of pluralism that we associate with pluralistic social trust. It is this: the premise that neither individuals nor society must conform to predetermined designs does not necessarily lead to the conclusion that each of us, as individuals and groups, should accept what is as what should be and fight for its continued existence if not for its dominance over other ways of life. For us, this type of pluralistic conclusion is too simple, too stupid, too *monopolistic*. This form of pluralism is plural only in the most naïve sense—that there are several groups or ways of life or cultures in the world. But that set of groups is settled in, they hope, for the long run, joined together in a conspiracy against change, against the new. In turn, they encourage each other to defend their "rights," then they scream and threaten each other. But it's just a game. Beginning, middle, end. Nothing's happened. Let's play two![18]

The primary problem with pluralism is lack of imagination: it mistakes, or thoughtlessly accepts, what is for what should be. Pluralism is necessary, of course, but nothing else is. As Amélie Oksenberg Rorty (1990) has brilliantly demonstrated, pluralism can be interpreted in many different ways—cultural, racial, demographic, class and power, political, psychological, intellectual, moral, etc. Rorty describes these varieties of pluralism as fluctuating, superimposed fields within a society. Under the best conditions, conditions fostering life and growth, these fields float freely among one another, continually generating new, unpredictable, useful combinations in individuals and groups. Under the worst conditions, the conditions leading to decline and death, the fields become aligned in polarized ways that permit them to collapse into a unity that appears universal and eternal. The task, then, is to identify and encourage conditions that are closer to the first set than the second.

Amélie Rorty describes four ways of going about this. Arranged in order of inclusiveness on the pluralism-to-cosmopolitanism continuum, they are: communitarianism; liberalism; a system of checks and balances, and the polyphonic or dialogic mode. It is this last, most inclusive way, Rorty argues, that offers us the best chance of usefully harmonizing our polyphonic pluralisms—if, that is, we can make practical, applied sense of the metaphors. They were created by Mikhail Bakhtin, for whom dialogue is neither a static, within-group validation nor a chaotic, between-group flip-flop in which one trades one's original culture for a new one. Dialogue is about change, of course, but it is an ordered, reasonable change based on persuasive conversation between persons who differ. Change based on understanding. Thus, in order to change, Bakhtin says (along with Wittgenstein, Richard Rorty, and others) you must remain the same: "*Creative understanding* does not renounce itself, its own place in time, its own culture" (Bakhtin, 1986, p. 7). But you must talk with someone who is different: "We raise new questions for a foreign culture, ones that it did not raise itself; we seek answers to our own questions in it; and the foreign culture responds to us by revealing to us its new aspects and new semantic depths" (p. 7). Mutually enriched; mutually changed. After the dialogue, neither participant is the same as before. Bakhtin moves us toward cosmopolitan social trust by describing dialogue as a generative process, a process through which new bases for connections between people can be created.[19]

Cosmopolitan Social Trust

Pluralistic social trust, its embracing label aside, is based on the singular; its users must therefore be committed to fight for survival. Cosmopolitan social trust emerges from the multiple; its users have no need to fight—they can go on with life. Speaking of Rome, speaking of us, Michel Serres says, "It is necessary to leave in order to found somewhere else, not to keep aside—on the side of one's brother, one's city, or one's enemies; on the side of discipline or of familiar or habitual thought." In this way, Serres moves beyond Bakhtin toward cosmopolitan social trust, toward the multiple, toward maximal freedom to change. To stay at home is to be captured by the singleton. "The only real trap," Serres says, "is war, hatred, the polemic" (1991, pp. 261-262). To be singular is to invite war: "The reign of *sameness* must be suspended; either the others, together, form an orchestral mixture, or else the single other takes over, which is the beginning of exclusion or war, where vengeance will never end" (1993, p. 271). Cosmopolitan social trust is the *orchestral mixture*; pluralistic social trust is the *single other*. [20] How does one move from the latter to the former? The first step, as with Serres's Anaximander, is to abdicate, to leave one's fortified enclosure. Then, we suggest, one should do what one can to communicate with the multiple.

Cosmopolitan social trust depends on communication. More specifically, in risk management, our primary context of application, cosmopolitan social trust depends on risk communication. This relationship can be demonstrated in a simple social dilemma situation:

- Two persons may both be inclined to cooperate.
- But, owing to lack of communication, they are unaware of their matching values (i.e., at minimum, to cooperate).
- Fearing defection based on value differences, they therefore fail to trust.
- With communication, however, they can create values to share.
- Without communication and the resultant trust, defection, and mutual loss are inevitable.

Communication does not, of course, always lead to cosmopolitan social trust, but without communication there is no possibility of it.

Communication depends on social trust. If the communication occurs within an established group, it depends on pluralistic social trust; if it is between groups, it depends on cosmopolitan social trust. The dependence of communication on social trust can be demonstrated in several ways. Social trust, we have argued, is based on cultural values. That is, a necessary condition for social trust is a match between the currently salient values of the person making the trust judgment and those of the entity being trusted. A parallel condition holds for communication: a necessary condition for communication is a relation of *relevance* between the participants. [21] Relevance, like social trust, is based on shared cultural values; the former is a special case of the latter. In this sense, then, communication is dependent on social trust.

In the case of risk communication—a form of risk management—both social trust and communication are concerned with risk. Risk is inescapable. People engage in risk communication in order to develop common strategies for managing their uncertain environments. Judgments of social trust are made for the same reason: to manage uncertain environments by enlisting the help of others. Social trust can be achieved only if environmental risks are managed through the acceptance of social uncertainty; environmental uncertainty can be managed if people are willing to risk social trust. Risk management—safety—requires risk taking.

Social trust is a medium of communication. This can be taken in a literal, McLuhan sense. Social trust is an extension of man, and social trust is the message. What is the content of social trust? Community. When a person trusts socially, he communicates community. And the meaning of community is value equivalence, sharing. Similarly, in risk communication one is communicating not only about environmental uncertainties but also about community: we are in this together, and we will cope together. But we come to an apparent paradox. Social trust, based on shared cultural values, is necessary for community, which is also based on shared cultural values. Community is necessary for the communication of community. How does one get from here to there? With leadership and, for a creative community, imagination. And, through them, with the gradual establishment of a social norm for cosmopolitan social trust.

Leadership is necessary for the growth of creative communities because people need help in becoming aware of *possible* communities, *possible* sets of values they could share. Leadership, on this interpretation, is a general form of communication. The central responsibility of leaders, according to Robert Reich, is "to provide the public with alternative visions of what is desirable and possible, to stimulate deliberation about them, provoke a reexamination of premises and values, and thus to broaden the range of potential responses and deepen society's understanding of itself" (1988, p. 4). This is what makes leadership creative and creative communities possible. Contrary to prevalent populist rhetoric, the form of leadership advocated by Reich is not a matter of determining existing public values and designing actions based on them. It entails instead "the creation of contexts in which people can critically evaluate and revise what they believe" (p. 6). Leadership is about the future and it is about change—the creation of new futures.

This type of leadership is based on cosmopolitan social trust. It is a *resilient* process in Aaron Wildavsky's (1988) terms, designed not to provide precooked answers to supposedly well-understood problems but to articulate possibilities and facilitate their discussion. As Ronald Heifetz and Riley Sinder (1988) put it, "Leadership mobilizes groups to do work. Often this demands innovation in defining problems, generating solutions, and perhaps foremost, locating responsibility for defining and solving problems" (p. 193). In contrast, leadership based on pluralistic trust is *anticipatory* (Wildavsky, 1988), based on power and authority rather than creative process. This is the central problem of leadership—moving from pluralism to cosmopolitanism—refusing to reproduce the past, insisting instead on the creation of a new future. This requires that people work, change. As a consequence, this type of leadership is often rejected. Heifetz and Sinder are correct in emphasizing the centrality of public work in cosmopolitan leadership. But they neglect one critical point. The successful cosmopolitan leader is the person who can, through whatever creative means, make the necessary public work somehow *easier*.

When is change easier? We can only say what is perhaps obvious. Change is easier when what is past is considered contingent and what is new is judged to be useful. Consider two schematic examples, one in rather ordinary circumstances, the other in extreme conditions. The first is the case of immigrants to America. The arriving generation may not consider their cultures of birth to be contingent. To a great extent, they are what they are, only in new places. And many of the immigrants may expect to return, periodically or permanently, to their countries of birth. As a result, some immigrants preserve their native cultures in static and dead ways, as museum pieces, in contrast to the usually more dynamic cultures of their relatives who stayed at home. For the second generation, however, the contingency of culture becomes evident. Most of them learn that in order to flourish in their new homes they will have to adopt ways of being that differ in certain aspects from their parents' ways. And many eagerly do so. This need not be assimilation; it often is a cosmopolitan mixture of the old and the new. One's evaluations of these changes aside, the lesson is plain.

The same lesson can be drawn from our second example, the case of the Western hostages in Lebanon. Survival strategies varied among the hostages, even among those who were confined to the same cramped space. Some, such as Terry Anderson, clung to their pasts. "Seeking shelter from the terrors around him," Michael Massing writes, "Anderson took refuge in his Catholicism; rather than serving as a bridge to others, however, it became another source of division" (Massing, 1993, p. 126).[22] Others, such as Brian Keenan, let go of their pasts in order to create, with others, something more useful for their futures. Massing describes how Keenan, the Irishman, dealt with his forced attachment to McCarthy, the Englishman:

> Despite his keenly felt Irishness, he refused to be confined by it. In the end, it was his ability to transcend nationality, as well as class and all the other particularistic allegiances of the modern era, that enabled him to make his empathetic leap toward McCarthy and his imaginative leap from their cell. "In the circumstances in which we found ourselves physically chained together," Keenan writes, "we both realized an extraordinary capacity to unchain ourselves from what we had known and been." In a world swept by ever-narrowing categories of self-identification, Keenan's unchaining stands as a powerful example of how, in even the most adverse circumstances, a sense of universality can prevail. But the memoirs of his fellow-prisoners show just how difficult those chains can be to sunder.
>
> (p. 126)

Changing: unchaining. These brief examples of the conditions of change, one in ordinary circumstances and one in extreme, suggest a role for the cosmopolitan leader. To do the work that needs to be done, people need to be encouraged to interpret their pasts as contingent and to make their futures from the best materials available where they are. The cosmopolitan leader encourages unchaining, encourages future-focused cosmopolitan cultures of change.

More specifically, the cosmopolitan leader encourages:

An acknowledgment of one's personal limitations. Belief in self-sufficiency is harmful to oneself and a barrier to social trust. We are all wrong in our own ways.

An acknowledgment of the contributions of one's community(ies) to one's life. Every person is a product of the communities to which he belongs. Without communities, human life and accomplishments are impossible.

A social-process understanding of knowledge. Knowledge is a product of social interaction. The purpose of knowledge is coping with reality, not representing it.

A willingness to take risks. Social trust is a risk judgment. Environmental risks cannot be managed without necessarily taking social risks.

These four points—that individuals and what they know are limited products of communities and that management of community problems depends on social trust—are common to both forms of social trust. Individuals are encouraged to think of themselves as irredeemably social. But two points remain:

An acknowledgment of the limitations of one's community or culture. Belief in community-or culture-sufficiency is harmful to one's community or culture and a barrier to cosmopolitan social trust. Our communities and cultures are all wrong in their own ways.[23]

A willingness to create commonalties with persons from other communities and cultures. Cosmopolitan social trust is based on shared cultural values. Without commonalties, there can be no social trust. With sufficient tolerance, hard work, and imagination, however, commonalties can always be created.

These final points take us from pluralistic to cosmopolitan social trust: communities and cultures are limited and the management of societal problems depends on cosmopolitan social trust. Individuals living in communities and cultures are encouraged to think of them as contingent, always open to useful changes.

There is nothing new in any of these aspects of cosmopolitan leadership. They are in sympathy, most deliberately, with the general thrust of the American pragmatism of John Dewey and William James. The influence of this native American way of thinking on a broad range of academic and applied disciplines has increased dramatically recently. Pragmatism's emphasis on individual fallibilism, contextualism, and the close social examination of ideas has been particularly important. Hilary Putnam (1990), for example, notes that pragmatists promote a fallibilistic attitude toward "visions" and ideals. "But, more importantly," Putnam continues, "pragmatists insist on the idea of taking ideals seriously. That's what pragmatism is about. One of William James's most telling observations is that academics and intellectuals tend to give themselves a great deal of credit because they have such wonderful ideals, but the trouble is they do nothing about them" (pp. 1915-1916). Similarly, Margaret Radin (1990) points out that "pragmatism recommends that we take our present descriptions with humility and openness, and accept their institutional embodiments as provisional and incompletely entrenched. Pragmatism recommends this openness in the only way pragmatism can—because it seems to work best for human beings" (pp. 1725-1726). Further useful interpretations of American pragmatism can be found in the work of Richard Bernstein (1992), Martha Minow and Elizabeth Spelman (1990), Richard Rorty (1982, 1989, 1991a), John Stick (1986), and Cornel West (1989).

As we have noted, cosmopolitan social trust can be very demanding—much more so than pluralistic social trust. The former requires self-reflexivity and a willingness to change, neither of which is demanded by the latter. Still, cosmopolitan social trust is less demanding than the strategy of compassion recommended by Martha Nussbaum (1992). Here is a comparison between the two:

Cosmopolitan Social Trust	Compassion
Complexity-increasing	Complexity-increasing (temporarily)
Transfers burden to self	Transfers burden to self (temporarily)
Based on shared cultural values	Based on shared human values essence
Contextual and contingent	Universal and uncontingent

The key differences are these. As indicated by the parenthetical modifier on the first two descriptors, cosmopolitan social trust is dynamic, a bridge between two successive states. The increases in complexity and self-burden are *temporary*. In the case of compassion, however, these increases are apparently unending. On this interpretation, cosmopolitan social trust is much less demanding than compassion. Another important difference concerns the last two descriptors. Cosmopolitan social trust results from specific work—it emerges from particular circumstances evoking specific cultural values—it is constructed by the persons who use it. Compassion, in contrast, is an abstract ideal—based on "a belief in a common humanity" and "respect for the dignity of humanity"—that must somehow be found in specific circumstances. Cosmopolitan social trust is made and compassion is found. And finding is singular, limiting, past-bound; making is multiple, improvisitory, future-shaping.

SUMMARY

Our aim in this chapter was to begin talking about social trust in new ways. We borrowed concepts from a variety of sources for our vocabulary—risk, vulnerability, change. We claimed that social trust is based on contingent sets of values, varying across contexts, cultures, and time. And we offered some preliminary evidence supporting this claim.

We identified two types of social trust: pluralistic and cosmopolitan. Pluralistic social trust is singular, rooted in the pasts of existing groups. Since it is a within-group phenomenon, pluralistic social trust is not useful in the management of complex societal problems. Cosmopolitan social trust is multiple, created in the emergence of new combinations of persons and groups. These new combinations are based on new sets of values that are constructed for the solution of specific societal problems.

Cosmopolitan social trust is a demanding process; it requires that people unchain themselves from their pasts and move into uncertain futures. It demands change. To make change easier, cosmopolitan social trust relies on leadership. The role of the cosmopolitan leader is to encourage people to think about their pasts as contingent and to consider beneficial uses of the new. The cosmopolitan leader encourages the creation and discussion of possible futures. How can this be done? Robert Reich (1988) offers a hint in his description of the art of policy making. The art, Reich says, is "in giving voice to . . . half-articulated fears and hopes, and embodying them in convincing stories about their sources and the choices they represent" (p. 5). This is the central point. The art of leadership is in *story telling*. And the basic tool of the cosmopolitan leader, the means by which she encourages cosmopolitan social trust, is *narrative*. Narrative—its general characteristics and how it is used in human life—is the subject of the next chapter.

9

Narrative, Human Life, and Social Trust

We ended the previous chapter with the claim that cosmopolitan leadership depends on the use of narrative. Accept for the moment that a narrative is simply a story, an account of events occurring over time, with a beginning, a middle, and an end. Why is narrative so important? Our answer, in brief, is this. The lives of people are constituted by narrative. Most people, most of the time, think in narrative form. And communication, to be maximally effective, should also be structured on the narrative form. This is a significant conclusion because an important type of communication—scientific—is often structured to avoid narrative form. We address this issue and others in our longer answer, which constitutes the remainder of this chapter. We begin with a discussion of the general significance of narrative in human life. Then we describe some of the specific functions that narrative serves. During the past decade, narrative has played an increasingly important role in a growing number of academic disciplines. We briefly outline some of the uses of narrative in some of these disciplines. And we conclude with comments on the uses of narrative in psychology and in science.

THE IMPORTANCE OF NARRATIVE

Consider two contexts of human life, one small in scale and one rather large. The small scale context was created by A. Michotte (1963) as the first experiment in his long series of studies of the perception of motion:

> The observer sits at a distance of 1.50 metres from a screen, in which is cut a slit 150 mm. long and 5 mm. high. Immediately behind this screen is a uniform white background, on which stand out two squares of side 5 mm. One, a red square, is in the centre of the slit; the other, a black square, is 40

mm. to the left of the first. We shall call the black square 'object A,' and
the red square 'object B'. The subject fixates object B. At a given moment
object A sets off and moves towards B at a speed of about 30 cm. per sec. It
stops at the moment when it comes into contact with B, while the latter then
starts and moves away from A, either at the same speed or, preferably, at an
appreciably lower one, e.g. 6 or 10 cm. per sec. Then it stops, after covering
a distance of 2 cm. or more, according to the speed adopted.

(pp. 19-20)

The question in this experiment is, What do the subjects say they see? Michotte
reports that, "observers see object A bump into object B, and *send it off* (or
"*launch*" it), *shove it forward, set in motion, give it a push.* The impression is
clear; it is the blow given by A which *makes* B go, which *produces* B's movement" (p. 20). The words in italics (Michotte's own) are key here. They
indicate that subjects interpreted what they saw, two simple objects in motion,
as a whole, as a unitary phenomenon. And they talked about that phenomenon
in narrative form. People need to simplify even the simplest situations, it
seems, to unify them and give them meaning.

Narrative also operates in more familiar, larger-scale human contexts. A
football game, for example. Albert Hastorf and Hadley Cantril (1954) showed
the film of a game to supporters of the two opposing teams and then asked them
to describe the action. Narrative structure is built into a football game, of
course, so it is not surprising that the two sets of supporters constructed sto-
rylike descriptions of the game. What is interesting about the results of this
study are the *differences* between the stories produced by the supporters of one
team compared to the stories produced by the supporters of the opposing team.
Each group of supporters constructed stories in which their team represented
"good" and the other team represented "evil." The events in the two sets of
stories differed systematically to produce different narrative unities and meanings, and to support the opposing conclusions. Thus, people don't use narrative
to structure their experience in some standard way, to give it some standard
meaning. Hastorf and Cantril demonstrated that people use narrative to express their values and emotions, those of the groups to which they belong.[1]

We all know this, but we also want to deny it. We know that life is "a tale
told by an idiot," but we want it to have some transcendent sense. If life is a
story, we want it told, not by an idiot or by ourselves, but by god. Or by science. Some guarantor of meaning—*the* meaning. So we make up some more
inclusive story, a transcendental narrative, to underwrite our local versions.
That's how important narrative is: the harder we work to escape it, the more
tightly we wrap it around us.

In human life, narrative is inescapable, indispensable. "Narrative is present in every age," Roland Barthes says, "in every place, in every society; it
begins with the very history of mankind and there nowhere is nor has been a

people without narrative. All classes, all human groups, have their narratives
. . . Narrative is international, transhistorical, transcultural: it is simply
there, like life itself " (1982, pp. 251-252). All human groups use narrative.[2]
Narrative form is woven so deeply into human life that for a person to be unable (or to refuse) to use it is to be in danger of (or to risk) exclusion from
human groups.[3] Oliver Sacks (1993) describes the case of an autistic person,
Temple Grandin, who is unable to use narrative, unable to understand stories.

> What is it, then, I pressed her further, that goes on between normal people,
> from which she feels herself excluded? It has to do, she inferred, with an
> implicit knowledge of social conventions and codes, of cultural presupposi-
> tions of every sort. This implicit knowledge, which every normal person
> accumulates and generates throughout life on the basis of experience and
> encounters with others, Temple seems to be largely devoid of.
>
> (p. 116)

Sacks does not make plain what he means by "accumulates and generates"
here. In context, however, he contrasts this form of knowing with the inferen-
tial processes used by Grandin. We take him to mean narrative.

> Lacking it, she has instead to "compute" others' feelings and intentions and
> states of mind, to try to make algorithmic, explicit, what for the rest of us is
> second nature. She herself, she infers, may never have had the normal so-
> cial experience from which a normal social knowledge is constructed.
>
> (p. 116)

Grandin cannot understand social discourse. Allusions, presuppositions, irony,
metaphors, jokes—the vocabulary of life passes her by. Because she cannot use
narrative, Grandin "feels excluded, an alien." It is the ability to use narrative
that enables us to feel human. "My mind is like a CD-Rom in a computer," she
says. Without narrative, Granden experiences little in the way of emotions—in
response to people, music, visual scenes. "In autism," Sacks says, "it is not
affect in general that is faulty but affect in relation to complex human experiences, social ones predominantly, but perhaps allied ones—aesthetic, poetic,
symbolic, etc." (p. 123).

An autistic person like Temple Grandin tends to have a "wholly causal or
scientific view of the universe" and a "'scientific' notion of God . . . as something like order out of disorder." But even she, almost totally deprived of
narrative support, not knowing what it feels like—even she longs for it, knows
somehow, deeply, that it is what she needs. "I've read that libraries are where
immortality lies," she says toward the end of her time with Sacks. "I don't
want my thoughts to die with me. . . . I want to have done something. . . . I'm
not interested in power, or piles of money. I want to make a positive contribution—know that my life has meaning. Right now, I'm talking about things at

the very core of my existence" (p. 125). Temple Grandin is a master of one way of thinking, one way of life—call it "scientific" or "paradigmatic." But the construction of a meaningful life, she knows, requires narrative.

THE FUNCTIONS OF NARRATIVE

Much of what we consider "human" about ours lives depends on the functions of narrative. We are narrative animals. As such, being constructed from narrative, we tend not to notice it or talk reflectively about it. And when we do discuss it, on those rare occasions when we examine the stories we use every day, we tend to speak pejoratively, not about the content of the stories but of our need to use stories at all. We try to escape to what we hope will be less arbitrary forms. But if we want to remain fully human, we can't. As a reminder of our dependence on narrative, we briefly outline some of its crucial, human functions.

Narrative Structures Time

In one of the classic discussions of narrative, Paul Ricoeur (1984) identifies the central function of narrative as the structuring of time. "Time becomes human," Ricoeur says, to the extent that it is articulated through a narrative mode, and narrative attains its full meaning when it becomes a condition of temporal existence" (p. 52). For us, time requires narrative, and narrative requires time. Narrative is the tool we use to cope with time, to control it, to escape from it.[4]

Narrative Simplifies Complexity and Generates Meaning

Narrative structures time by simplifying it and giving it meaning. As in the writing of history. Hayden White (1987) contrasts two ways of writing history, as annals and as narrative. In the annals, years are listed consecutively and events considered important during each year (if any) are identified. There is some structure here, and, certainly, much simplification. But there is little meaning because the events are simply taken as real. The entries in the annals are tokens of reality, but they do not constitute a historical account. Only a narrative account, one among several possible stories about a given set of events, generates meaning by claiming to be the true account. By reducing complexity, by selecting and rejecting.[5] By saying—this is the meaning, this is the moral. And that is what we need to know. "The value attached to narrativity in the representation of real events arises out of a desire to have real events display the coherence, integrity, fullness, and closure of an image of life that is and only can be imaginary" (p. 24). Because we are constituted by narrative, we want life to be like a story.

We want life to be meaningful, and that is what stories are all about. Stories, as Thomas Leitch (1986) has argued, "are not primarily a means of communicating information but a transaction designed to arouse and satisfy the audience's narrativity, a sense of themselves as existing in a world of contingent meanings which encourages guesses about its order with intimations whose authority is never final" (p. 199). This domination of meaning over information (or the serving of the former by the latter) in narrative is well demonstrated in the form known as "urban legends." Jan Harold Brunvand (1981) describes urban legends as believable stories set in contemporary times and involving ordinary human beings. Many of the legends that Brunvand relates achieved, in certain times and places, great popularity. Brunvand attributes this to the "true, worthwhile and relevant information" they seem to contain. Contrary to Brunvand, we maintain that what is believable and popular about the stories he describes is not the information they contain but the meanings they express. They are believable and popular primarily because they express populist values and moral judgments such as distrust of what is foreign, fear and envy of elites. Urban legends, of course, express the values of their users.

Narrative Constitutes Ourselves and Our Communities

Without narrative our lives have no meaning. Through the use of narrative, we can create meaning. As we noted in our discussion of self-knowledge, many contemporary philosophers and psychologists agree that self-representations take the form of narratives. Our lives are constructed, given meaning, through story-telling processes. Narratives are used, first, by communities to construct community members, persons who will, in their turn, re-create their communities.[6] And narratives are used by individuals to construct themselves, to re-invent, re-create, re-interpret, to re-narrate themselves in ways that differ from those offered by the narratives used in their home communities. Finally, narratives are used by individuals to create commonalties that can serve as the bases for the construction of new communities.[7] In contemporary societies, an individual can belong to a dynamic mix of communities, each expressing its own set of narratives. These narratives may differ in significant ways. An individual, therefore, may maintain and recite multiple, inconsistent narratives about himself. This multiplicity suggests contingency. Interpreted in this way, as multiple self-narratives, an individual can become dynamic and creative—making communities as well as being formed by them.[8]

Narrative Guides Action

If an individual (or community) understands her life as a story, then she has a pretty good idea of what comes next. In the event, her life may not turn out as she expected, but that's not important. What matters is simply being able to think about the future, to penetrate the unknown, to structure the chaos. Just as narrative structures our pasts, it structures our futures. Each of us is *in* our story—living it out or making it up—revising it, as we go along. The guiding function of narrative has traditionally been discussed in social science through the use of the *drama* metaphor.[9] Individuals are said to have *roles* and to follow *scripts* in public *performances*, etc. The social drama is a particular type of narrative, but its power and ubiquity can easily be experienced by deliberately violating a script's directions.[10] What happens, of course, is an awakening: the show is over, and we have to return to a somewhat less structured life. The simple, routine order of the original script is gone, and the players must cast about for an alternate script—or improvise on the spot.[11]

The guidance function of narrative isn't limited to the mundane world of the social drama, of course. Narrative guides us everywhere, at times in subtle ways. How does an artist decide what to do, for example. Or a scientist. Some artists and scientists simply form themselves on the shapes of other artists and scientists and continue doing what these models seem always to have done. Others construct (or borrow) a narrative of their art or science, place themselves in it, and move off in the direction indicated. As Ian Hodder (1993) demonstrates in his studies of Sitagroi (northeastern Greece) artifacts dating from 5500 to 2200 B.C., the practice of narrative guidance has a long history in the production of material culture.

Narrative Comprises Values

The term *values* has played a central role in our story. We have described our interpretation of social trust as being based on "cultural values." But we haven't had much to say about what we meant by cultural values. Our reluctance until now to be more explicit about values derives from our skepticism about the usefulness of the term. Traditionally, *values* has been taken to refer to the most basic level of preference in a person or institution, etc. In the process of making decisions, a person was informally said to "have" values and to be able to "refer to" or "get in touch with" them. Mixing tactile and visual metaphors, a person having difficulty getting in touch with his values could have them "clarified." These and many other familiar ways of talking were based on the mother metaphor of a card catalogue or listlike memory. It was simple. Each of us had our master list of values. When a problem popped up, all we had to do was flip through the cards or scan the list to find the correct answer, the basic value that would determine our response.

Recent psychological research, however, has demonstrated that values are not so simple.[12] The card catalogue has been replaced by a modern, multi-process production line. As John Payne and his colleagues (1992) conclude in an authoritative review, values are not referred to; they are constructed. And although individuals may have a variety of preference-generation methods available, it is likely that all these methods have one attribute in common—that they demand less from the user than the "card catalogue" method.[13] But in Jerome Bruner's (1990) memorable phrase, "We don't shoot our values from the hip, nor are they the product of isolated individuals." "Rather," Bruner continues, "they are communal and consequential in terms of our relations to a cultural community. They fulfill functions for us in that community" (p. 29). We demand less of a user and his values if we describe both as *socially* constructed: individuals and communities are constituted by narratives—and values are embedded in narratives.

Our claim, in brief, is this. Values are abstractions that are inferred from narratives for the purpose of justification. Behavior is guided primarily by narratives (as well as by habits, imitation, etc.), not by values. Values, of course, can be reified for use as behavior-guiding principles. As such, they are attractive in their seamless purity, but they often prove to be blunt, unwieldy tools in use. In our account of values, people tend to use them, to invoke them, for rhetorical purposes—to make themselves and their opinions appear to be simple, well organized, and rational.[14] To speak of values is to appeal to fundamental, universal principles cleansed of any taint of parochial culture.[15] The flight from culture is the flight from narrative. Values are abstracted from narrative and interpreted as though they have some intrinsic meaning. But meaning is produced by, within, narrative. Separate the value from the narrative, and the meaning is lost. Life is lived in context.

Values are rhetorical devices. Our simple point is that they are ineffective. Values are ineffective rhetorical devices because they constrict conversations to narrow ranges of possibilities. Narrative, in contrast, is open to all constructions of our pasts and our futures, including those that express new visions, and new values—ways of moving beyond our devisive pasts into more inclusive futures.

Narrative Expresses Emotions

The story of philosophy could be told as an account of successive attempts to separate people from emotions. People experience and are troubled by emotions. Gods do not experience emotions. People should strive to be godlike, to transcend the limitations of humanity. Martha Nussbaum (1990) outlines such a story, according to which, "We should allow the call of theoretical reasoning about universals to draw us upwards, away from the cognitive and emotional responses typical of the merely human being, and seek pure intellectual deductions such as a god might perform. Above all, we should avoid appeals to emotion, and we should eschew storytelling" (pp. 388-389). We should avoid narrative because it is there that we learn to be vulnerable, emotional human beings. Contrary to the philosophers who advise us to escape from emotions, Nussbaum commends us to embrace them, to live with them in an active process of inquiry and criticism—criticism based not on logical argument and evidence; criticism based on narrative. "Stories first construct and then evoke (and strengthen) the experience of feeling," Nussbaum tells us. "So a criticism of emotion must be, prominently, an unwriting of stories" (pp. 293-294). We are our stories, emotions and all. But neither our stories nor our emotions are privileged; they must be open to rewriting. New, imaginatively useful stories can create places unknown to us, unknown to logic—emotion-rich, human futures.

Narrative Is Persuasive

Martha Nussbaum identifies two types of critical activity: the scientific and the narrative. Stanley Fish (1980) does the same, and he calls them *demonstration* and *persuasion*. In the demonstration model, interpretations are supported or not by independent sets of facts. In the persuasion model, interpretations and facts are linked. Richard Rorty (1991a) calls his forms of inquiry *objectivity* and *solidarity*. Objectivity is practiced by people who describe themselves in direct relation to nonhuman reality. Solidarity is practiced by people who describe themselves in relation to a human community. Both Fish and Rorty argue that the dualisms they have described are not useful and that all critical activity should be described, in Fish's case, as persuasion or, in Rorty's case, as solidarity. In other words, our knowledge is inescapably social, the product of contingent, narratively-constituted communities. Our knowledge is inescapably narrative.[16]

Stanley Fish puts it this way: "No one can claim privilege for the point of view he holds and therefore everyone is obliged to practice the art of persuasion" (1980, p. 368).[17] The art of narrative. Richard Rorty echos for a moment the sociological abstractions of Niklas Luhmann when he says, "We view all inquiry as a matter of responding to the incoherence among beliefs produced by novel stimuli" (1991a, p. 109). All inquiry is complexity reduction. All inquiry is recontextualization. All inquiry is narrative. We can stop arguing about method and start talking about values. Start recontextualizing—start rewriting our stories. What is characteristic of us, as literate democrats, Rorty says, "is the desire to dream up as many new contexts as possible. This is the desire to be as polymorphous in our adjustments as possible, to recontextualize for the hell of it. . . . All I can do is recontextualize various developments in philosophy and elsewhere so as to make them look like stages in a story of poeticizing and progress" (p. 110). And that's all any of us can do. Recontextualize. Rewrite. Move away from theory, the singular, and move toward narrative, the multiple. That is the way of change, and that is the way of leadership. "The novel, the movie, and the TV program," Rorty points out, "have, gradually but steadily, replaced the sermon and the treatise as the principal vehicles of moral change and progress" (1989, p. xvi).

The basis for persuasive leadership now is imagination, not argumentation, the creation of the new, not the emancipation of the old. And Rorty makes himself the model of what he advocates, recontextualizing for the hell of it—but also because it's the best thing he can do, the best anyone can do. "What political utopians since the French Revolution have sensed is not that an enduring, substratal human nature has been suppressed or repressed by 'unnatural' or 'irrational' social institutions but rather that changing languages and other social practices may produce human beings of a sort that had never before existed" (1989, p. 7). Narrative is persuasive because it can change one's life, one's world.[18]

THE USES OF NARRATIVE

During the last fifteen years, there has been a dramatic shift within a number of academic disciplines away from reliance on models based on what Jerome Bruner (1986, 1990, 1991) calls "paradigmatic" knowing and toward models based on narrative. Our aim in this section is simply to indicate the scope and multifariousness of this movement by very briefly identifying some of the contributors to it in several disciplines and topics of study. This short survey is followed by separate outlines of the uses of narrative in psychology and in science generally.

In the Social Sciences

Donald Polkinghorne (1988) has produced a comprehensive general introduction to narrative and its uses in history, literature, and psychology. Also included in Polkinghorne's book is a useful guide to the practice of narrative analysis. *The Rhetoric of the Human Sciences* (Nelson, Megill and McCloskey, (Eds.), 1987) contains several provocative essays on narrative, including "Science as Solidarity" by Richard Rorty.

History

The works of Hayden White (1973, 1978, 1987) are the most prominent on the narrative side of the debate against those historians who aspire to "scientific" status. Also at issue is the question of whether events have some intrinsic narrative structure—as opposed to that imposed by historians.

Literary Criticism

Stanley Fish (1980), mentioned in earlier sections of this book, is a leading antitheorist (pronarrativist) in this field, but the number of contributors is vast on all sides.

Communication

Walter Fisher (1987) has had a strong influence on the establishment of a narrative model of human communication. Among the good advice that Fisher offers is that which he directs to technical experts who would enter public policy debates: "Once this invasion is made, the public, which then includes the expert, has its own criteria for determining whose story is most coherent and reliable as a guide to belief and action. The expert, in other words, then becomes subject to the demands of narrative rationality" (p. 73). And this is so, the experts' claim to a separate rationality—paradignamic or scientific—not withstanding.

Values Analysis

Since values are embedded in narratives, any valid analysis of values would seem to have to involve narrative analysis somewhere along the line. A number of studies have demonstrated the usefulness of this connection. Marsha Vanderford and her colleagues (1992), for example, analyzed the values embedded in the narrative discourses of HIV patients and their doctors before and after an ethics education project. Results showed that the project was successful in encouraging more positive evaluations in both directions between the two groups.

Moral Development

This is one of the most active areas of research in narrative studies as well as being an area with close ties to practical application. All this indicates a broad consensus on the significance of stories in the development of moral sensibility. Among the prominent contributors are Carol Witherell and Nel Noddings (1991) and Mark Tappan and his colleagues (Tappan and Brown, 1989; Tappan and Packer, 1991).

Jury Deliberations

Studies of narrative structure in jury deliberations date back at least to W. L. Bennett (1978) and constitute, methodologically, one the strongest sets of narrative studies. The very careful and thorough work of Nancy Pennington and Reid Hastie (1986, 1988, 1990, 1992) is exemplary. Other interesting studies in this area include those of Karin Aronsson and Claes Nilholm (1990)—examining the deliberations of lay judges—and of A. Cheree Carlson (1991)—a case study of the Henry Ward Beecher scandal in post-Civil War New York. These three sets of narrative studies use distinct methodological approaches, but all three produce interesting and useful results.

Social Movements

Several researchers have recently applied narrative analysis to the study of political leadership in social movements. Richard Couto (1993), in his examination of the use of narratives by American civil rights leaders, stresses the need for "free spaces," places apart from the mainstream to which activists can temporarily retreat in order to create useful new ways of talking, new narratives to guide their movements.[19] William Kirkwood (1992) discusses the development of a "rhetoric of possibilities" through which leaders of social movements might be able to encourage people to change, to become what they are not—to recontextualized themselves.

Environmental Management

After years of domination by the paradignamic model, workers in environmental management are rapidly becoming aware of the importance of narrative. Timothy O'Riordan (1991), for example, has provocatively proposed a new "vernacular science of environmental change" that would unite two ways of interpreting the natural world, "environment" (i.e., objective, scientific) and "nature" (i.e., the world as sacred): "Vernacular science is not just participatory science: it is a science that transcends national boundaries and generations" (p. 151). As an emergent practice, vernacular science would require the development of a new vocabulary. O'Riordan urges caution here—the translation of existing vocabularies, the slow, experimental development of a new, common discourse. And he recommends the use of "the common languages of the creative arts"—narrative. In a less ambitious mode, Dominic Golding and his colleagues (1992) also recommend—and test (not entirely successfully)—the use of narrative in environmental management, specifically in risk communication. Among other environmental studies involving narrative are Sheldon Ungar's (1992) useful analysis of the social construction of "global warming" as a social problem and the investigations of land-use decisions by David Maines (1993) and by Maines with Jeffrey Bridger (1992).

NARRATIVE IN PSYCHOLOGY

A broad history of the use of narrative in psychology is given by Donald Polkinghorne (1988) in his general introduction to narrative in the human sciences. And a brief rundown of some recent developments is provided by Susan Fiske (1993) as part of her Annual Review article on social cognition.[20] Narrative has been a part of psychology for a long time, with widely varying levels of effect. As indicated simply by its inclusion in Fiske's review, narrative is now entering a period of high-level influence. The resurgence of narrative is due to the work of many people, but the contributions of four psychologists—Theodore Sarbin, Kenneth Gergen, Mary Gergen, and Jerome Bruner—stand out.

Theodore Sarbin's association with narrative stretches from his early work in role theory (Sarbin, 1943) to his recent advocacy of narrative as a "root metaphor" for psychology (Sarbin, 1986). In the latter, he proposes what he calls "the narratory principle: that human beings think, perceive, imagine, and make moral choices according to narrative structures" (p. 8). Psychology, according to Sarbin, *is* narrative. As an example of psychology as narrative, Sarbin discusses self-deception (p. 17). A narrative account of self-deception, he notes, has no use for the traditional mechanistic metaphors of "repression" and "dissociation." Instead, understanding self-deception requires that one enter the person's self-narrative. And helping a person to cope with self-deception entails encouragement in the process of narrative reconstruction.

Kenneth Gergen and Mary Gergen have been prolific contributors to the use of narrative in psychology over the past decade. Among their very influential work, some is devoted to general critiques of past practice in psychology and to suggestions on how matters could be improved through the use of narrative (e.g., Gergen and Gergen, 1986; K. Gergen, 1989). Their writings also include narrative analyses of specific topics such as the self (Gergen and Gergen, 1988) and relationships (Gergen and Gergen, 1987). Throughout, the Gergens have managed to mix their very wide-ranging interests with sharp, useful interpretations of the specific. Kenneth Gergen says of self-knowledge, for example, that "It is not, as is commonly assumed, the product of in-depth probing of the inner recesses of the psyche. . . . Rather, it is a mastery of discourse—a 'knowing how' rather than a 'knowing that' (Gergen, 1989, pp. 75, 76). By interpreting the self as narrative, Gergen provides us with tools and methods for self- and community-reconstruction.

Jerome Bruner is the author of several of the most influential books and articles in twentieth-century psychology. Two of Bruner's recent books, *Actual Minds, Possible Worlds* (1986) and *Acts of Meaning* (1990), are devoted to his account of narrative in psychology. In the first of these, Bruner describes two modes of thought: paradignamic and narrative. The paradignamic mode "deals in general causes, and in their establishment, and makes use of procedures to assure verifiable reference and to test for empirical truth. Its language is regulated by requirements of consistency and noncontradiction. . . . It is driven by principled hypotheses" (1986, pp. 12-13). The narrative mode, in contrast, deals in "good stories, gripping drama, believable (though not necessarily 'true') historical accounts. It deals in human or human-like intention and action and the vicissitudes and consequences that mark their course. It strives to put its timeless miracles into the particulars of experience, and to locate the experience in time and place" (p. 13). In short, Bruner's two modes of thought are the traditional rationalism of science (paradignamic) and what the rest of us do (narrative). Bruner embeds the latter in what he calls "folk psychology" in his book *Acts of Meaning.* In that book, Bruner recalls the history of modern psychology as a movement away from the rationalist and toward the folk, a movement away from a psychology of science and toward a psychology of people (including scientists).[21]

NARRATIVE IN SCIENCE

When Jerome Bruner talks about scientific, or paradigmatic, thinking, he tends to separate it sharply from narrative. We can speculate that he does this because he is reacting against the established "psychology of science" and wants to replace it with a "psychology of people"—he wants to point up the differences, the improvements of the new over the old, the narrative over the paradignamic. Thus, the dualism. Another, antidualist, way to demonstrate the priority of narrative over paradignamic is simply to absorb the latter into the former. That is what Paul Feyerabend (1992) does, for example, when he claims that, *"nature as described by our scientists is a work of art that is constantly being enlarged and rebuilt by them"* (p. 3).

This is the point. Since meaning is the product of narrative, paradignamic thinking on its own—if it could be on its own—is meaningless. And narrative, as we have discussed it here, is not just a mode of thinking; it is the way we live, it is the way scientists live. It is only within narrative—broadly conceived—that science makes sense to scientists or to anyone else. And attempts to denarrativize science, to purify and devalue it, to remove it from life, are, of course, futile. Scientists live *in* narrative; it is narrative that makes science—scientific activity—possible.

Science is narrative through and through, in the large and in the small. Science is narrative in the large in that there is a shared understanding among most scientists (and many nonscientists) about "science-as-narrative"—a generalized sequence of events that leads to the continuing, unforced reconstruction of local scientific narratives. Science-as-narrative is the science that Richard Rorty (1991a) describes, the community and its institutions: "Reference to such institutions fleshes out the idea of 'a free and open encounter'—the sort of encounter in which truth cannot fail to win. On this view, to say that truth will win in such an encounter is not to make a metaphysical claim about the connection between human reason and the nature of things. It is merely to say that the best way to find out what to believe is to listen to as many suggestions and arguments as you can" (p. 39). Science-as-narrative, in brief, is the story of people working together in peace to achieve shared, emergent goals—the story of people freed from the past, moving into a future constructed from their own imaginations. It is the story of a form of social trust.

Science is narrative in the small in that the activities of scientists within fields of study are guided by locally constructed narratives. "The intelligibility, significance, and justification of scientific knowledge," as Joseph Rouse (1990) has noted, "stem from their already belonging to continually reconstructed narrative contexts supplied by the ongoing social practices of scientific research" (p. 181).[22] Scientists' activities are intelligible to themselves and others because they are interpreted within local narrative structures. And narrative serves all the functions for scientists in science as it does for anyone else in any other field of activity. Thus, science advances through processes of narrative reconstruction, recontextualization. As Rouse points out, this "explains the rapid obsolescence of the scientific literature, and the fact that even graduate students learn all but the most recent science from updated textbooks rather than journals" (p. 191).[23] Paradigmatic thinking is embedded in narrative, and critical inquiry in science, as in other fields, is a matter of persuasion, not demonstration.[24]

As part of the persuasion process, the paradigmatic mode used by scientists in their formal communications comprises a set of narrative conventions that serve as signs of community membership. As such, these signs provide a basis for judgments of social trust, a basis for community solidarity. This argument, offered by Rom Harré (1990) among others, identifies another way in which science is like all communities—a model community. The behavior of scientists, of course, is very different from their written descriptions of their activities (Latour and Woolgar, 1979). Should the reader base his trust on the written description or on the actual behavior? The written description is designed to eliminate the personal (but in most cases much that is personal remains). The behavior is the personal (but may be unknown to the reader).

Harré (1990) concludes from several sociological studies that the knowledge value of results is based on the moral status of the scientists who generate them. Because it is more variable, trust dominates truth. "Trust in someone's results depends very much on our faith in that person, whereas truth, so it seems to me, ought to be tied to trust in a methodology, regardless of who uses it, provided they use it competently" (p. 91). By "faith," Harré means something close to competence and responsibility, the bases for traditional, or rationalist, trust. And Harré's notion of truth is, of course, also rationalist. But this seems too narrow and neat. Too consistent. One's judgment of moral status, even in science, can be based on any set of values. And those values derive, of course, from the historically contingent local narrative of scientific activities in which one happens to live—and which one may be struggling, in heated competition with others, to reconstruct toward certain ends.

Narrative, we have claimed, is in science in the large and in the small, in grand and local forms. And both forms provide the bases for the social trust on which science depends, the social trust which constitutes scientific communities and which encourages their continuing reconstruction. Social trust is the fundamental narrative of science.

SUMMARY

In this chapter, we discussed the importance, functions, and uses of narrative in a wide range of human activities. We argued that narrative is inescapable and indispensable. The penalty for the inability or refusal to use narrative is exclusion from human communities. The rewards for the effective use of narrative can include the reconstruction of oneself and one's community. These rewards are nowhere more evident than in scientific communities, models of continuing narrative reconstruction—freedom from the past and openness to the new—models of cosmopolitan social trust. And that is why cosmopolitan leadership, the goal of which is community reconstruction, must depend on narrative. As in science, cosmopolitan leadership must construct a narrative of social trust and use it, in the large and in the small, to constitute new, cosmopolitan communities. In our final chapter, we explore some ways in which this might be done.

Social Trust: Moving from a Pluralistic to a Cosmopolitan Society

In Chapter 1, as part of our introduction to social trust, we described and evaluated parts of the U.S. Department of Energy's (1993) plan to "earn public trust and confidence" for its management of radioactive wastes. Our discussions of social trust in the intervening chapters have elaborated on the brief points of criticism we made in our opening chapter. We can now say that the DOE plan will likely fail because it relies on flawed interpretations of social trust:

- The DOE plan relies on *traditional social trust*. We have argued that the traditional, rationalist construction of social trust is invalid and that it results in the generation of social distrust.
- The DOE plan relies on *pluralistic* (within-group) social trust rather than *cosmopolitan* (across-group) social trust. We have argued that pluralistic social trust generates across-group social distrust and that cosmopolitan social trust is necessary for the solution of social problems.

The DOE plan seems—on these points at least—more suited to the generation of social distrust than social trust.[1] But this contrary tendency is not limited to details of interpretation—it characterizes the general approach to social trust in the DOE plan, an approach we call *strategic*.

Throughout most of this book, we have used the term *strategy* to tie social trust together with a number of functionally equivalent procedures such as social distrust, confidence and hope etc. What these activities—described in Part II—have in common, we said, is that they are all strategies for the reduction of cognitive complexity, strategies for simplicity. But strategy, we now note, implies a level of forethought and care and a distancing—a calculatedness—that seems, for the most part, to be missing from social trust and its rivals. Strategy, in brief, is too rational. We suggested a more appropriate term in Chapter 9 when we described social trust as a *narrative*. The distinction between *strategy* and *narrative* is this: A strategy is an isolated technique that is imported into a problem context for a specific purpose. By itself, a strategy has no meaning; its meaning is derived from the contexts in which it is used. A narrative, in contrast, generates meaning and defines contexts. A strategy is a part; a narrative is a whole. Thus, attempts to use social trust strategically are likely to fail because the meaning of social trust is undetermined, up for grabs. Social trust can only succeed as a narrative—that is, as a generator, not a recipient, of meaning.

In this final chapter we outline the movement of social trust from a pluralistic toward a cosmopolitan society, from the present to the future. First, we use the distinction between strategy and narrative to further explicate difficulties in the pluralistic DOE social trust plan. Of course, a narrative approach to social trust would not, in itself, guarantee success. Some narratives lead to what you call success, some to what you call failure. We illustrate the latter, in the second part of this chapter, by discussing the traditional narrative of *public participation* in planning and decision processes—as, for example, in environmental risk management. We conclude by describing a prospectively successful narrative—the narrative of public participation based on cosmopolitan social trust, the narrative of a cosmopolitan society.

A STRATEGIC APPROACH TO SOCIAL TRUST

One way to show that the U.S. Department of Energy's approach to social trust is strategic rather than narrative consists simply of pointing out that DOE wants to solve its social trust problems without changing in any basic ways. A strategic approach is a partial approach, a fiddling around with whatever moves most easily without disturbing the existing whole. A narrative approach disturbs the existing whole, creates a new one. The DOE's reluctance to change is not hidden. It is stated straightforwardly in the findings of the DOE Task Force on social trust.

The first of the task force's eight general findings is that DOE has a social trust problem:

> There is widespread lack of public trust and confidence in the Department of Energy's radioactive waste management activities.
>   (U.S. Department of Energy, 1993, p. 34)

The next finding states that there have been some recent improvements—that is, under the management of Secretary Watkins, the convener of the task force, and his successor. Findings 3 through 7 claim in various ways that the social trust problem is the result of bad experiences the public has had with DOE and that only trustworthy behavior by DOE can remedy the situation. These findings demonstrate, in other words, that the task force has adopted the traditional interpretation of social trust.

Finally, in Finding 8, the social trust accorded any unit within DOE is said to be linked in certain ways to that accorded other units:

> Actions taken by any one unit within DOE influence the level of public trust and confidence in other units. That coupling is strong when the effect of the action is to reduce trustworthiness; the coupling is quite weak when the effect of the action is to strengthen trustworthiness.

> (p. 38)

This conclusion is a restatement of a notorious social trust myth—the myth of asymmetrical trust exchange: trust is easy to lose but hard to gain. What does this mean? It could mean that evidence counts in the loss of trust but not in the gain of trust. This would be a combination of social trust interpretations— traditional (on the loss) and cultural values (on the gain). Or it could mean that, in the case of social trust, people are conservative hypothesis testers—that is (interpreting only the gain—not the loss—of trust as a risk), they require overwhelming evidence to counter their aversion to the risk of trust, to eliminate the risk. This would be the standard, traditional interpretation of social trust. Finally, unlikely, it could mean that evidence counts in neither the gain nor the loss of social trust—the talk of evidence on the loss of trust (and the lack of such talk on the gain) being simply a matter of *post facto* justification. This would be a thoroughgoing cultural values interpretation of social trust. Regardless of interpretation, asymmetrical trust exchange remains a myth— yes, a narrative—believed by many, supported with evidence by no one.[2]

The eight general findings in the DOE social trust plan are followed by three findings with respect to organization. Only the first of these is significant to our purposes:

> The behavior of organizations responsible for managing radioactive waste and the results they produce will be far more important in creating or inhibiting public trust and confidence than will be their organizational forms and structures.

> (p. 38)

This is something of a summary statement. It expresses a strategic approach to traditional social trust: *traditional* because social trust is said to be based on (competent and responsible) behavior; *strategic* because social trust is said not to be based on organizational forms. This latter means that the DOE plan rejects change. The task force opts for stasis, for known problems rather than unknown solutions: "It believes that the more extensive any reorganization is, the more uncertain will be its effects" (1993, p. 39). Who could write a clearer, more concise statement of tradition and strategy in social trust? And who, writing about social trust, could—by denouncing risk and change—conjure subtler support for social distrust?

PUBLIC PARTICIPATION: THE TRADITIONAL NARRATIVE

Public participation in the United States, as it is generally understood and practiced now—and as it is described in the dominant narrative—derives from traditional American culture, particularly from that ideal American narrative, "participatory democracy" (see, for example, Mansbridge, 1980). In this narrative, participation can take many forms. The simplest of these is voting; voting behavior can therefore be used as an easy, if coarse, indicator of the contemporary power of the general participatory narrative. Robert Jackman (1987) claims, for example, that, "Where institutions provide citizens with incentives to vote, more people actually participate; where institutions generate disincentives to vote, turnout suffers. Thus, the meaning of national differences in voter turnout is rather clear: turnout figures offer one gauge of participatory political democracy" (p. 419). By this measure, participatory democracy in the United States, relative to other industrial democracies, is rather weak. Other indicators such as membership in voluntary associations, however, have traditionally been used to demonstrate strong participatory democracy in the United States (Gittell, 1980). In addition, public participation in the United States (and in other industrial democracies; see Nelkin, 1977) was given a boost in the 1970s by environmental and other legislation that mandated various forms of citizen involvement in policy making and implementation (Langton, 1978). In brief, the strength of the participatory democracy narrative is contextual; strong for some groups in some areas of interest and weak elsewhere.

In any case, quantitative indicators of public participation are not what we need. We need to get at what, according to the narrative, it means to participate—what the specific behaviors are and what values they are meant to instantiate. In his discussion of U.S. citizen participation in the management of environmental risks, Daniel Fiorino (1990) adopts such a qualitative approach. He assesses a variety of participatory mechanisms (public hearings, initiatives, public surveys, negotiated rule making and citizen review panels) against a set of "democratic process criteria." According to Fiorino's criteria, a participatory mechanism should:

- Allow for the direct participation of amateurs in decisions.
- Enable citizens to share in collective decision making.
- Provide a structure for face-to-face discussion over some period of time. Discussion, deliberation, the search for shared values, the opportunity to transform conflict into more constructive directions through

mutual talk and persuasion—all are important attributes of a participatory process.

- Offer citizens the opportunity to participate on some basis of equality with administrative officials and technical experts.

(Fiorino, 1990, pp. 229-230)

Fiorino's criteria seem to do a good job of outlining the main points of the American public participation narrative. "The case for participation should begin with a normative argument," Fiorino concludes "that a purely technocratic orientation is incompatible with democratic ideals. If administrative institutions and processes do not reflect the ideals of a democratic society, then we may want to rethink their acceptability on analytical or efficiency grounds alone" (pp. 239, 240). We take Fiorino to mean that if an institution does not reflect the ideals of a democratic society, then it should not be used—regardless of the technological benefits claimed for it. This seems fair enough—so long as the ideals are in order—since, in the absence of any external criteria, democratic processes, free and open encounters, are our best way of finding out what to do. But this is where Fiorino's analysis falls down—at its start—in its identification of democratic ideals.

Fiorino's ideals derive from the work of various "participation theorists," including Benjamin Barber (1984). Barber has developed a strong and useful understanding of traditional American culture, which he calls "thin democracy." In addition, Barber's interpretation of politics, while narrow and perhaps misleading in some settings, is solid and pragmatic, useful in the contentious and potentially dangerous context of risk management: "What shall we do," he asks, "when something has to be done that affects us all, we wish to be reasonable, yet we disagree on means and ends and are without independent grounds for making the choice?" (pp. 120-121). Barber's response is *strong democracy*—conflict resolution "through a participatory process of ongoing, proximate self-legislation and the creation of a political community capable of transforming dependent, private individuals into free citizens and partial and private interests into public goods" (p. 132).

The second half of Barber's book is devoted to spelling out the implications and implementation of his interpretation of our democratic tradition. A central problem with Barber's account is his rejection of representation—and therefore of social trust—because, he claims, it is incompatible with freedom, equality, and justice.[3] Our claim, of course, is the opposite—that representation, in the form of social trust, cannot only be compatible with, but in many cases may be necessary for, freedom, equality, and justice. The traditional public participation narrative, on Barber's account and as expressed in Fiorino's criteria, is thoroughly, romantically individualist. And there is little evidence that it works.[4] The traditional narrative's lack of efficacy can be attributed in large part, we believe, to the demands of individualism—no division of labor and no accommodation to human limitations.

No Division of Labor

The traditional public participation narrative excludes provisions for division of labor and leadership.   Aaron Wildavsky (1979) at one point, for example, describes a vision of citizens acting as policy analysts.   But Lyn Kathlene and John Martin (1991) stress the central importance of leadership to the success of public participation.   And, as John Dunn (1988) points out, any expectation for equal participation from everyone is based on a never-instantiated ideal and is more likely, particularly in modern, stratified societies, to produce negative than positive effects (pp. 88-89).   Thus, it would seem a reasonable, minimal obligation of any institutional narrative that it accommodate such inescapable social conditions as division of labor.   It is evident that the traditional public participation narrative does not.

The task, then, is to develop a narrative that can work, a new narrative that can constitute a form of public participation that is compatible with existing conditions.   Referring to the reconstruction of political parties, John Dunn argues that it "would have fully to acknowledge the reality of the distinction between leaders and led; and it would have to give a much clearer account of the attributes that leaders need to display if trust in them is to stand any chance of proving well founded.   It would need to construe the party as agency of representation more as a medium of social identification and less as a structure for the manipulative pursuit of interests" (p. 89).   The point is very simple—but difficult.   The traditional public participation narrative is filled with characters who are indistinguishable from one another—all are simply unconnected, self-expressive individuals.   Work, however, like any good story, requires diversity and connection.   The central meaning of the traditional narrative is individuality.   Work—the solution of social problems—requires community.

No Accommodation to Human Limitations

Also absent from the traditional public participation narrative are any provisions to accommodate the limits of human capacities.   The reality of human life is that we are faced with competing demands on limited resources. These demands range from those associated with the physical survival of our persons to the maintenance of the communities we live in, and beyond.   Most of us tend to deal with matters of personal survival first, then family, and so on. Any narrative, such as traditional public participation, that makes clearly unrealistic demands on people is a narrative designed for failure.

The negative implications that limited human capacities have for traditional public participation are described in a number of studies. Marilyn Gittell (1980), for example, thoroughly documents the negative effects of limited personal resources such as money and time. The relations between cognitive limitations and participation are Shawn Rosenberg's (1988) concern. Whereas, in the traditional narrative, equal cognitive performance is expected from all participants, Rosenberg, in her structural theory, argues that people vary in the ways they think about politics, and that this has strong implications for participation. Another way in which the traditional theory ignores cognitive limitations is in its advocacy of relativism, "The view," as Richard Rorty (1982) describes it, "that every belief on a certain topic, or perhaps about any topic, is as good as every other. No one holds this view. Except for the occasional cooperative freshman, one cannot find anybody who says that two incompatible opinions on an important topic are equally good" (p. 166). This relativism is a consequence of the individualism in the traditional narrative. One's knowledge is one's own, and we all are equal. In practice, contrary to the traditional narrative, we are not all equal, and we do not treat the opinions of all persons equally; if we did, we would not survive.

A striking example of the distance between the traditional public participation narrative and practice is the case of a person speaking for himself. According to the narrative, a person's testimony is taken at face value. Richard Rorty, however, makes the obvious—if unpopular—point that it is "a mistake to think of somebody's own account of his behavior or culture as epistemically privileged. He might have a good account of what he's doing or he might not" (p. 202). Here Rorty makes clear that the usefulness of knowledge is social, judged by participants in conversation. Individuals are not excluded from participation on these grounds, however. "It is not a mistake," Rorty continues, "to think of [personal testimony] as morally privileged. We have a duty to listen to his account, not because he has privileged access to his own motives but because he is a human being like ourselves. . . . We do so because he is, after all, one of us" (p. 202). Rorty's narrative is antitraditional—socializing the individual, embracing diversity and community.

Another version of this argument against personal epistimic privilege is given by Scott Brewer (1990) with regard to "oppressed" persons. "To indulge in the fiction of a superior oppressed perspective or vantage point or situated embodiment," Brewer claims, "is to deny victims of oppression their right to be wrong as well as to be right. . . . One should not argue for the inclusion of the perspectives of oppressed group members on the assumption that they have some special insight; rather, the proper argument for inclusion is that every person deserves to have the opportunity for his or her perspective to enter the fray of debate" (pp. 1761-1762). The key point here is that the traditional public participation narrative is contentless, an atavistic ritual.[5] By treating all participants equally, the traditional narrative is in effect saying that no one has anything of value to contribute and that public debate serves no useful function. At the end of the traditional narrative is another story—a coda following a standard plot, one ending in cynicism, distrust and withdrawal.[6]

The notion of human limitations, and especially of variations in cognitive capacity and performance, is of course anathema to the traditional public participation narrative. We deliberately raise these matters because we believe that the traditional narrative, unrealistic in both demands and incentives, positively discourages public participation. It seems almost to be a story written to encourage distrust. Societies that want to discourage distrust construct narratives that conform to human limitations. It is a sad irony for us that ancient Greece, the source to which many advocates mistakenly trace the ideal of public participation, was instead a society that deeply understood the need for living within human limits. "It is their instinct," Martha Nussbaum (1986) points out, "that some projects for self-sufficient living are questionable because they ask us to go beyond the cognitive limits of the human being; and, on the other hand, that many attempts to venture, in metaphysical or scientific reasoning, beyond our human limits are inspired by questionable ethical motives, motives having to do with closeness, safety, and power" (p. 8).

The traditional public participation narrative fails because its public is not fully social and its participants are not fully human. Society is complex and requires division of labor; the traditional narrative denies division. People must live within human limits; the traditional narrative ignores limits. Public participation can work only if the narrative that guides it is fully social and fully human.[7]

PUBLIC PARTICIPATION: THE COSMOPOLITAN NARRATIVE

This is our problem. The traditional public participation narrative can be replaced only by a better narrative, one that is more persuasive. But the persuasive power of the traditional narrative is devoted to the service of individualism, not public participation; the traditional narrative, we maintain, discourages public participation. And this may be what the majority of American people want at this time—a form of public participation that is neither too public nor too participatory.

The social analog of the individualism on which the traditional narrative is based is pluralism—diversely separated individuals—risk averse, favoring narrow, tight, separate communities, a unitary self and fixity within traditional cultural limits. All of these characteristics—descriptive of the American mainstream narrative—are antithetical to what we would call effective public participation. The construction and communication of a public participation narrative that is both effective and more persuasive than the traditional narrative will therefore be a very difficult task.

On our account, effective public participation—public participation that acknowledges both human limitations and the need for leadership—requires a guiding narrative based on cosmopolitanism—diversely related individuals—risk taking, favoring wide, loose, overlapping communities, multiple selves, and fluidity within universal human limits. Cosmopolitan social trust is such a narrative, comprising the values of the cosmopolitan leader—acknowledgment of personal and community limits, the social self, and a willingness to create commonalties.

Our problem, then, is this. We must persuade a society that is dominated by pluralistic cultural narratives to consider adopting—in small ways at first—the cosmopolitan public participation narrative. We must persuade people—perhaps many people—to move away from pluralism and toward cosmopolitanism. How can this be done? By using the tools at hand: cosmopolitan leadership, a model cosmopolitan community, narrative, and imagination.

Cosmopolitan Leadership

The cosmopolitan narrative of public participation explicitly recognizes the need for leadership—leadership based on cosmopolitan social trust. The cosmopolitan leader tries to live and exemplify the life, the narrative, of cosmopolitan social trust—the life of the *emergent multiple*—a life based on these values:

- An acknowledgment of one's personal limitations
- An acknowledgment of the contributions of one's community(ies) to one's life
- A social-process understanding of knowledge
- A willingness to take risks
- An acknowledgment of the limitations of one's community or culture
- A willingness to create commonalties with persons from other communities and cultures

The cosmopolitan leader is distinguished by a refusal to reproduce the past and an insistence on the creation of useful new futures. The job of the cosmopolitan leader is to encourage useful change in others and to help people cope with human limitations. To make change easier, the cosmopolitan leader encourages people to interpret their pasts as contingent and to construct their futures from the best materials available where they are. The cosmopolitan leader encourages future-focused cosmopolitan cultures of change—cosmopolitan communities.

A Model Cosmopolitan Community

Our model cosmopolitan community is science, a community constituted by the narrative of cosmopolitan social trust.[8] Although they share values, cosmopolitan leaders need not be "scientists," of course—nor can all scientists be cosmopolitan leaders. As a cosmopolitan community, science is guided, in the large, by the summary values of the cosmopolitan social trust narrative—*freedom from the past* and *openness to the new*. According to this narrative, movement into the future, into the unknown, is guided by free and open encounters among persons from diverse communities. Science itself is composed of diverse communities, each of which is guided, in the small, by its own locally constructed narrative. These local narratives are saved from becoming pluralistic—singular and rooted in the past—by their being embedded within *science* and its narrative of *cosmopolitan social trust*. To be viable, according to this encompassing narrative, all local narratives must be open to continuing reconstruction based on unconstrained persuasion. And the only way to reconstruct a narrative, to persuade, is to replace the existing narrative with (what is agreed to be) a new and better one. Persuasion, in science as elsewhere, is narrative.

Cosmopolitan Narrative

The foremost advocate of cosmopolitan narrative—the use of literature to move toward a cosmopolitan society—is Martha Nussbaum.[9] For the past ten years Nussbaum has written prolifically and brilliantly on the relations between philosophy and literature and on the application of an Aristotelian ethical procedure to contemporary social problems. The focal question for Nussbaum, as for Aristotle (and the starting point of their procedure) is "How should a good person live?" A basic concern for Nussbaum is the type of information or knowledge that should be used in addressing that question: philosophic and/or poetic; scientific and/or literary; social and/or individual? How can we know what is good and how to live?

In her 1986 book *The Fragility of Goodness*, Nussbaum begins her account of the moral dilemma inherent in human life with a description of Pindar's vine tree image of a good person needing support from other persons. Opposing this appreciation of contingency in Greek poetry is the Greek philosophical tradition in which reason was to be used to control the course of life. Nussbaum provides this useful summary of these two ways of thinking about human life in the world (p. 20; the headings are ours):

Self-Sufficiency	Risk/Trust
Agent as hunter, trapper, male	Agent as plant, child, female (or with elements of both male and female)
Agent as purely active	Agent as both active and passive/receptive
Aim: uninterrupted activity, control; elimination of the external	Aim: activity and receptivity; limited risk; living well within a world in which the external has power
Soul as hard; impenetrable	Soul as soft, porous, though with a definite structure
Trust reposed in the mutable and unstable	Trust reposed in the mutable and unstable
Intellect as pure sunlight	Intellect as flowing water, given and received
Solitary good life	Good life along with friends, loved ones, and community

In this account, Nussbaum associates Plato primarily with Self-Sufficiency, Aristotle with Risk/Trust, and the Greek tragic poets with both (but arguing for the human values in the latter). Nussbaum identifies herself as an Aristotelian, a practical thinker interested in encouraging Risk/Trust as a social norm. But she insists that Aristotelian dialogue be informed by tragic drama. These plays deal with particular human lives in all their complexity and contingency—vital details that we tend to exclude from our more analytical approaches to problems, when we tend to be pushed toward the self-sufficiency norm. We need the encouragement of full, complex human dramas to support a consideration of the Risk/Trust way of life. We need narrative guidance: "A tragedy does not display the dilemmas of its characters as pre-articulated; it shows them searching for the morally salient; and it forces us, as interpreters, to be similarly active" (p. 14).

The idea of inserting drama (or other forms of literature or art) into the public participation process must seem to some people, if only because of its contrast with current practice, to be odd and somehow unserious. But for Nussbaum, and for us, the use of art for public purposes is a serious proposal for coping with serious problems—problems made serious in part by our past neglect of knowledge that could be generated by public discussion of art.[10] Nussbaum shows us how public art, literature, can work in the resolution of conflicts. "A tragic poem," for example, "will be sufficiently distant from each reader's experience not to bring to the fore bias and divisive self-interest; and yet . . . it can count as a shared extension of all readers' experience. It can, then, promote self-inquiry while also facilitating cooperative discussion" (pp. 14-15). Public discussion of art in America can be about more than Jesse Helms and Robert Mapplethorpe—a classic pluralist tug-of-war; it can be about the creation of a cosmopolitan community.

In the Aristotelian ethical procedure advocated by Nussbaum, there is always a tension between rule-based decisions and improvisation.[11] Unfortunately, in our desire to reduce complexity, we are too often drawn to the former. "For there is a tendency, both in philosophy and in life," Nussbaum explains in *Love's Knowledge* (1990), "to seek out theories that fix things in advance. It seems both shameful and dangerous to have accomplished so little and to have left so much to the occasions of life" (p. 97). But middle paths of coping have evolved to guide us as we improvise: these are our emotion and value-bearing stories of practical wisdom. Nussbaum has in mind the complex narratives of writers such as Henry James. Of course, few of us will ever learn as much from—or want to read as much of—Henry James as Nussbaum has. Still, her general point is clear: communication about human concerns should include emotional information, and emotional information is best conveyed in narrative form. That is how we all learn about emotions, of course—not necessarily from Henry James, but certainly not through logical argument. It is not Nussbaum's point, we must emphasize, that narrative knowledge is privileged. It can and should be criticized, just as logical arguments are. But it takes a new, better story to replace an old one, not a set of facts or a chain of logic.

The cosmopolitan character of Nussbaum's work derives from her general notion of the human being and the human way of life. It is a cosmopolitan way of life. "Narratives, especially novels," Nussbaum says, "speak to the reader as a human being, not simply as a member of some local culture; and works of literature frequently cross cultural boundaries far more easily than works of religion and philosophy" (1990, p. 391). Narrative literature itself, for Nussbaum—she refers to a certain "good" kind of literature (all her examples are generally recognized serious works) without clearly distinguishing it from the "bad"—is cosmopolitan. Good narrative literature is cosmopolitan, a mixture of the particular and the general—a weaving together of what is human.[12]

Imagination

In the cosmopolitan narrative of public participation, participants are encouraged, first, to free themselves from the past. We call this process *de-individualization* or *de-centering*, meaning a freeing from, a letting go of a particular, dominant self-narrative, a self-narrative rooted in the past. This is not a loss of individuality. It is simply a reinterpretation of one's self as a contingent rather than a necessary product of past events. Things in the past could have been otherwise. Things in the future can be different. For the most part, the future can be what one makes it. To be viable, however, the future cannot be the past.[13]

How can an individual or a group of individuals—public participants—engage the process of de-individualization? Michel Foucault (1983, pp. ix-xiv) has provided a set of principles:

- Free political action from all unitary and totalizing paranoia.
- Develop action, thought, and desires by proliferation, juxtaposition, and disjunction, and not by subdivision and pyramidal hierarchization.
- Withdraw allegiance from the old categories of the Negative (law limit, castration, lack, lacuna), which Western thought has so long held sacred as a form of power and an access to reality. Prefer what is positive and multiple: difference over uniformity, flows over unities, mobile arrangements over systems. Believe that what is productive is not sedentary but nomadic.
- Do not think that one has to be sad in order to be militant, even though the thing one is fighting is abominable. It is the connection of desire to reality (and not its retreat into the forms of representation) that possesses revolutionary force.
- Do not use thought to ground a political practice in Truth; or political action to discredit, as mere speculation, a line of thought. Use political practice as an intensifier of thought, and analysis as a multiplier of the forms and domains for the intervention of political action.
- Do not demand of politics that it restore the "rights" of the individual, as philosophy has defined them. The individual is the product of power. What is needed is to "de-individualize" by means of multiplication and displacement, diverse combinations. The group must not be the organic bond uniting hierarchized individuals, but a constant generator of de-individualization.
- Do not become enamoured of power.

Foucault: a cosmopolitan leader. His principles are the values expressed in his cosmopolitan narrative, his cosmopolitan life.[14]

As they free themselves from the past, participants following the cosmopolitan narrative are encouraged to open themselves to the new. The gap between the no longer useful past and the unknown future is bridged by cosmopolitan social trust. And cosmopolitan social trust depends on *imagination*. To solve their problems, participants must change. In changing, they must create something new—they must make their own futures. Unchained from the past, imagination—rewriting, recontextualizing, creating—is all they have. Imagination is everything. Perhaps we overstate the case—imagination isn't everything. It's just the most important—and neglected—thing. "In every area," Michel Serres (1989a) says, speaking generally, "imagination strikes the first blow; reason—method and rigor—is always second. Invention takes place everywhere, especially where one does not expect it" (p.7).

Without invention, life is death. But only Michel Serres can avoid—through continuous, endless, brilliant invention—the experience, in life, of numerous periods of lifelessness.

> Invention is the only true intellectual act, the only intelligent action. The rest is copying, cheating, disloyalty, laziness, conventionality. Invention is the only proof that one truly thinks the thing one thinks, no matter what that is. I think, therefore I invent. I invent, therefore I think. The only proof that a scientist is exercising his science is that he invents. Lack of invention proves, by counterproof, the absence of works and of thought. He who does not invent is working elsewhere than in the realm of intelligence.
>
> (p. 17)

Tough words—true words. Our problems are the product of our lack of imagination. We can't imagine a past different from the one we made, so we cling to that past, and we die there. We can't imagine a future different from our past—so we cling to what was and we die there. Our best hope for life, in Serres's sense, is in a new future, free from the past—if we can imagine it—a cosmopolitan society, a free, flourishing multiple, embracing the new, continually changing into the unknown.

SUMMARY AND CONCLUSION

Summary

In this final chapter we tried to outline the development of social trust from the present to the future, from a pluralistic to a cosmopolitan society. We used the U.S. Department of Energy's plan for "earning public trust" to represent an approach to social trust in a pluralistic society. This plan, we concluded, was an attempt to use social trust *strategically*—an attempt to solve problems requiring change by refusing to change. The Department of Energy is wed to stasis, we claimed, and its plan is bound to fail. We also discussed the traditional American form of public participation, a narrative of participatory democracy in a pluralistic society. This form of public participation cannot succeed, we argued, because it provides neither for division of labor—no leaders, everybody equal—nor for human limitations. Finally, we discussed the cosmopolitan public participation narrative, a story of change—from past to future, from pluralism to cosmopolitanism. And we briefly described four elements that help make the cosmopolitan narrative work—cosmopolitan leadership, a model cosmopolitan community, the use of narrative and imagination. Throughout this discussion, we relied heavily on three cosmopolitan leaders—Martha Nussbaum, Michel Foucault, and Michel Serres—guides to a cosmopolitan society.

Conclusion

Even with the help of social trust and cosmopolitan leaders, the path from a pluralistic society to a cosmopolitan society is long and difficult. And we have just begun. How do you end a beginning? We cannot provide any grand summing-up. We don't know enough; we have only started learning. Perhaps we had best end simply by hoping that we got off on the right foot. We have tried to free ourselves from the past and open ourselves to the future. We have tried to be good cosmopolitans. And we have tried to make this book a sustained argument for change. We suspect, however, that our criticisms of the past have been more imaginative—and persuasive—than our prospectus for a cosmopolitan future. Research presently underway, including our own on the functions of narrative in social trust processes, should certainly help. Benefiting from that research, future discussions of social trust will provide more useful direction than we have been able to here. If we have generated some interest in social trust and in a cosmopolitan society, if we have stimulated some research on these topics, we have succeeded.

This has been a book about change, about movement from a pluralistic past to a cosmopolitan future. One way to talk about this sort of change is to say that it is the privilege of "those who are lucky enough to live in the wealthy West." That is what Michael Ignatieff (1993, p. 13) says.[15] Ignatieff claims that it is the power of Western nation states that makes cosmopolitanism possible in such cities as Paris, London, New York, and Los Angeles. Take away the power of the state, and ethnic, racial, national violence will result. "The people of Sarajevo were true cosmopolitans" Ignatieff claims (p. 13). They took to killing each other only because they lacked support—imposed restraint—from the big powers in Europe and America. Cosmopolitanism is dependent on the power of the state and always will be.

Ignatieff, of course, is not talking about cosmopolitanism at all, as we use the term. And he's not talking about movement or change either; he's simply describing pluralism controlled and pluralism uncontrolled. None of the cities he nominates—Paris, London, New York, Los Angeles, Sarajevo—is remotely cosmopolitan. Some—many—cosmopolitan individuals live in each of them, no doubt. Certainly, however, most of the people in each of those cities identify with narrow cultural groups to the exclusion of others. So long as that is true, they are living in the past, and they have a ways to go to become cosmopolitan. Ignatieff acknowledges the importance to individuals of belonging to communities, but the only options he recognizes are the traditional—ethnic, racial, national. This is an error due to lack of imagination, an error mired in the past.[16]   Cosmopolitanism is not a tamed pluralism.   It is a *rejection* of the old, static categories; it is the *creation* of new, fluid multiplicities—not categories at all—flowing into one another, mingling, changing.

Notes

CHAPTER 1

    1.   In *Searching for Safety* (1988), Wildavsky argues convincingly that the complexity of modern social systems makes the identification of "safe" conditions all but impossible.

    2.   Our emphasis on the problem of complexity, and in particular on the problem of complexity as it relates to social trust, derives from the work of Niklas Luhmann and, through him (with a phenomenological spin), from Talcott Parsons. Luhmann says, for example: "The only problem that does arise is the relation of the world as a whole to individual identities within it, and this problem expresses itself as that of the increase in complexity in space and time, manifested as the unimaginable superabundance of its realities and its possibilities. This inhibits successful adaptation to the world by the individual, for, viewed from within, the world presents itself as unmanageable complexity, and it is this which constitutes the problem for systems which seek to maintain themselves in the world" (1979, p. 5).

    3.   Much of the confusion concerning the relations between social trust and social distrust can be attributed to two points of interpretation. First, social trust and social distrust can be described at the level of either the individual or of some social aggregate. At the individual level, a person, on our interpretation, cannot both trust and distrust the same object at the same time. In this narrow sense, trust and distrust are linked. At the social level, the number of individuals who trust a given object at a certain time would be linked to the number who simultaneously distrust that object only if trust and distrust were the only options available to individuals. And this is the second point. Social trust and social distrust can be described as two mutually exclusive and exhaustive states into one of which each of us must fall. Or they can be described, more modestly, as only two of many available options. In our attempt to open up the discussion of social trust, we talk about social trust at *both* individual and social levels—the individual in social context; neither makes sense without the other. Similarly, we discuss social trust within its context of strategies available to individuals to help them cope with social complexity. Within that context, social trust and social distrust are interpreted as independent competitors (along with the other strategies) for attention, approval, and adoption by individuals and groups.

4.   Note that McGarity made these comments in the mid-1982, in the heart of the Reagan administration.

5.   Our disagreement here is based on McGarity's framing of the problem. For McGarity, social trust seems to be some vague general bond between "the public" and "regulatory agencies." Given this understanding (which we do not accept), he argues that interest group representation will "increase" social trust. It is this with which we disagree. Clearly, other formulations of social trust may change its relations with interest group representation.

6.   Robert Reich, Secretary of Labor in the Clinton administration, has edited a very useful book, *The Power of Public Ideas* (1988), which recognizes and endorses the positive role ideas (such as social trust) could play in public policy and government: "In our revised philosophy of policy making, ideas about what is good for society occupy a more prominent position. The core responsibility of those who deal in public policy— elected officials, administrators, policy analysts—is not simply to discover as objectively as possible what people want for themselves and then to determine and implement the best means of satisfying these wants. It is also to provide the public with alternative visions of what is desirable and possible, to stimulate deliberation about them, provoke a reexamination of premises and values, and thus to broaden the range of potential responses and deepen society's understanding of itself" (pp. 3-4).

7.   The general plan for this program is described in *Earning Public Trust and Confidence: Requisites for Managing Radioactive Waste* (U.S. Department of Energy, 1993). This document is the final report of the Secretary of Energy Advisory Board Task Force on Radioactive Waste Management, a distinguished group of academics and representatives of stakeholder groups convened by former Secretary James D. Watkins in 1991.

8.   The restriction of trust to "those with whom one interacts" would seem to limit the DOE program to *interpersonal* as opposed to *social* trust. But the program is specifically to "earn" the trust of the "public," many of whom will interact very little if at all with the DOE. We interpret this contradiction as an indicator of a general tendency in discussions of trust, particularly in America, to back away from the social and slide into the interpersonal.

9.   The processes by which benefits and compensation are distributed to affected parties also, of course, encourage the maintenance of traditional positions.

10.   The requirement for changes in interests can be finessed by making a distinction between interests and positions, with change being absorbed in the latter—thus permitting interests to remain static. We prefer the exposure of interests, however—a direct, unbuffered, mutual consideration of change by all parties. This insistence on reflexivity and talk about change seem more likely to us to lead to positive states than to approaches committed to preserving the past.

11.   This description of societal systems is taken from Niklas Luhmann. Accounts of the differentiation of social systems can be found in many of Luhmann's works; for example, Luhmann 1990 (p. 177).

12.   Although the availability of opportunities for learning does distinguish interpersonal from social trust, the learning on which trust is based can, in both cases, be of a very simple sort. Thus, for example, one person may trust another not on the basis of evidence accumulated over time but on a "groundless" judgment of similarity between

them. Such a judgment of similarity can result simply from knowing the two share the same culture.

13. Giddens (1990) draws on the work of Irving Goffman in his discussion of the facework commitments involved in interpersonal trust working in conjunction with and supporting the faceless commitments of social trust (p. 80).

14. Of course, it is not simply a matter of social trust adapting to changing social conditions. The differentiation of social relations can be interpreted as being a consequence of the development of social trust. That is, the increasing availability of the language of social trust supported the growing complexity of society.

15. We say "unflinching" because of the all but universal presumption (Eisenstadt and a few others exempted) that social trust and elites, at least in modern democracies, are antagonistic forces. For good or ill, we, along with Eisenstadt, describe social trust as being to a great extent dependent on the activities of elites.

16. Fortunately, there are a few subarguments and extensions that we can attend to. But the striking fact remains that Eisenstadt's highly useful description of social trust has been all but ignored by contemporary writers on the subject.

17. Eisenstadt doesn't explicitly talk about distrust, but the social situation he describes, one dominated by lack of solidarity and lack of shared cultural values, is one in which distrust might flourish (1984, p. 300).

18. Gallant notes that discussion of forms of trust "are not prominent in the sources" (1991, p. 146).

19. Gallant (1990) stresses the discontinuity between the Hellenistic period and that preceding it. Paul Veyne, in contrast, in his vast, detailed description of client-patrol relations in the Greek and Roman worlds, emphasizes continuity in the role of the local elites: "The role of the sovereign city was over. But as an autarchic entity the city triumphed in the Hellenistic period, and even more under the empire, when the Mediterranean world, henceforth urbanized, lived under a regime of local autonomy (p. 41).

20. Our outline of trust in feudal society is based on Canfield's (1989) intriguing analysis of English literature from the Middle Ages to the Restoration.

21. John Dunn (1988) provides another useful interpretation of the transitions in understanding of trust in the seventeenth and eighteenth centuries, with emphasis on the contributions of John Locke to a rationalist, individualist conception: "In legitimate political socieites, accordingly, governmental power is in fact conceived both by rulers and ruled as a trust and (with whatever modifications are due for the moral and cognitive limitations of both rulers and subjects) the psychic relations between rulers and ruled can also consequently aspire to be one of trust: confidence, the giving and receiving of clear, veridical, and carefully observed mutual understandings, a relation of trust deservedly received and trust rationally and freely accorded" (p. 83).

22. Harold Laski (1962) sums up the transition from feudalism to capitalism as "movement from a world in which individual well-being is regarded as the outcome of action socially controlled to one in which social well-being is regarded as the outcome of action individually controlled" (pp. 21-22).

23. For both research programs, trust was just one of many topics of interest. As a result, trust, although very significant, dominates neither book.

24. The "learning theory" followed by the Yale group was the then prominent and now all-but-forgotten theory of Clark Hull (1943). The influence of Freudian theory in

academic psychology has also greatly diminished.   Only social psychology, though greatly changed, has grown and prospered.

25. The Yale program lives on in modified form in the work of leading contemporary researchers such as Richard Petty and John Cacioppo (1986).

26. The significant but normally ignored problems of the external validity of experimental models are most deeply addressed in the work of Kenneth Hammond; for example, Hammond (1986) and Hammond, Hamm, and Grassia (1986). Hammond's work builds on the psychology of Egon Brunswik.

27. The interpretation of responses as constructions is part of the general "social construction" approach to social psychology and related disciplines. The work of John Zaller (1992) is an excellent application of this approach to the study of public opinion in politics.

28. The classic statements of this position are by Solomon Asch (1940, 1952). Although Hovland and his colleagues did briefly discuss Asch's position, they remained loyal to their learning theory interpretation as opposed to Asch's Gestalt interpretation.

29. Although long resisted by the psychological mainstream, the effect of culture on judgment in all areas of life, as ably demonstrated by Alan Fiske (1991a, 1992), is rapidly becoming a basic tenet of social psychology.

30. Of course all researchers have to make compromises between complexity and simplicity. The trick is to avoid erasing the phenomena in which one is interested. In tackling persuasion, Hovland and his colleagues were confronting vast social complexity. To make it manageable, i.e., to domesticate it for the psychological laboratory, they had to simplify it; but in doing so, they eliminating most of what made it difficult and interesting in its natural settings.

31. Even the best contemporary work on persuasion retains limiting aspects of the Yale program. See, for example, Zaller's (1992, pp. 46-47) comments on Petty and Cacioppo.

32. Noting this impact with due ambivalence, Deutsch says "It take no credit (or blame) for spawning the enormous research literature that has utilized this game since these intitial studies" (1973, p. 179). Descriptions of the game and its use in research are given in Deutsch's book.

CHAPTER 2

1. We have in mind here what Joel Wolfe calls Individualistic Democracy: "Designates individuals acting to maximize their self-interests (utility) through decision-rules that aggregate preferences on issues. Participation is inclusive and agents are independent, rational individuals; the decision-rules yield the collective preference that constitutes policy" (p. 9). The strong relations of this interpretation of democracy to American social science theory and practice are most evident in studies influenced by "self-interest" economics. The contributors to Beyond Self-Interest, edited by Jane Mansbridge (1990), offer criticisms and alternatives to this approach.

2. One of the conditions identified by Parsons (1970) is shared values.

3. Also among the pioneer investigators of social trust within risk management are Paul Slovic (1993) and his colleague James Flynn (Flynn, Burns, Mertz and Slovic, 1992).

4. Of course, not all studies of trust share this tradition. An interesting example is Russell Hardin's Bayesian, "rational theory" approach: "You trust someone if you have adequate reason to believe it will be in that person's interest to be trustworthy in the relevant way at the relevant time. One's trust turns not on one's own interests but on the interests of the trusted. It is encapsulated in one's judgment of those interests." And "I trust you because it is in your interest to do what I trust you to do" (1992, pp. 505, 506). Since Hardin's analysis is totally abstract and psychologically uninformed, all this turns out to be vacuous and uninformative. The title of Hardin's article, "The Street-Level Epistemology of Trust," would seem to be appropriate only on those thoroughfares closed to all persons save economists.

5. One research program with a useful approach to this task is that of Robert Bellah and his colleagues. See, for example, Habits of the Heart, 1985.

6. The term unitary democracy is used by Jane Mansbridge in her extensive critique of adversary democracy (1980).

7. These developments in America recapitulate, of course, the general history of social trust as societies became more complexly differentiated.

8. This point is made by Richard Merelman in his book on culture and politics in America (1984).

9. An admiring account of this movement, applauding the role of social distrust in American democracy, is provided by Virginia Hart (1978).

10. This argument is made by another admirer of social distrust, Bernard Barber (1983).

11. In his very important book, *Structures of Social Life* (1991a), Alan Page Fiske describes in brilliant detail the function of tradition in a wide variety of cultures. Commenting on the Moose, whom he has studied, Fiske notes that: "The culture *is* tradition, the distinctive implementation rules of the community. Like many other peoples, Moose assert that their paramount goal in social relations is to maintain and reinforce their corporate solidarity, sharing communally among the living and with their dead progenitors, thereby perpetuating the immutable, immanent community of tradition. We ought to take their word for it" (p. 380). Of course, in modern societies, tradition tends to be mutable, a necessary but changeable guide. And at the opposite end of the continuum from the Moose is the postmodern liberal described by Richard Rorty: "To see one's language, one's conscience, one's morality, and one's highest hopes as contingent products, as literalizations of what once were accidentally produced metaphors, is to adopt a self-identity which suits one for citizenship in such an ideally liberal state" (1989, p. 61). In their attitudes toward and reliance on tradition, we believe most Americans fall somewhere in between the Moose and Rorty.

12. Charles Lindblom exemplifies this spirit of inquiry as he questions American attitudes toward their Constitution: "Since in decades thereafter elites thought it advisable to present their designed constitutional order as a great accomplishment of democracy rather than as a superbly designed halfway house to democracy, American thought has ever since been unable to think clearly about the constitutional order" (1990, p. 286). Writing about the general relations between tradition and rationality,

Robert Nozick expresses similar ideas: "Even when there is a known reason for something's survival, and even when some of the functions it performs are worthwhile, that does not settle the question of whether its continuance is desirable. That will depend upon whether we can devise and institute an alternative that it is rational to believe will be better and be worth its attendant risks" (1993, p. 130).

13. Thus, in his discussion of future directions, Freudenberg says, "there is a need for more systematic thought about the kinds of institutional arrangements that are most and least likely to foster recreant behavior, and about the factors that can foster or frustrate the efforts of recreant officials and organizations to evade the responsibility for their failings" (1993, p. 927). *Recreancy* is Freudenberg's neologism for "the failure of institutional actors to carry out their responsibilities with the degree of vigor necessary to merit the societal trust they enjoy." Freudenberg's is a populist realism.

14. The domination of theory by method in Flynn's study is indicated by his conflation of trust and distrust: "The issue of trust implies its opposite, distrust. On the continuum from absolute trust to absolute distrust, what degree of trust is required for an agency or organization to overcome public concerns about potential hazards? In cases of sites that are perceived as dread and potentially catastrophic, such as nuclear facilities, how much distrust will the public tolerate?" (Flynn, Burns, Mertz, and Slovic, 1992). Along with the odd locutions, we note that trust and concern, shown by their data to be strongly related, are apparently treated here as though they were independent.

15. In their article, Parker and Parker quote from a source which we hadn't been aware of, *Home Style: Representatives in Their Districts* (1978), a book by Richard Fenno: "When a constituent trusts a House member, the constituent is saying something like this: 'I am willing to put myself in your hands temporarily; I know you will have opportunities to hurt me, although I may not know when these opportunities occur; I assume—and I will continue to assume until it is proven otherwise—that you will not hurt me; for the time being, then I'm not going to worry about your behavior'" (p. 56). Fenno's account of trust is closer to ours than is the Parkers'.

16. Herbert Simon's pioneering ideas on human cognitive limitations can be found in Models of Man (1957) and in many of his other works.

17. This pervasive psychological principle is fundamental, for example, in the theories of persuasion developed by Richard Petty and John Cacioppo (1986) and by Shelly Chaiken (Chaiken, Liberman, and Eagly, 1989).

18. As psychologists, we certainly do not believe that psychology is the queen of the social sciences. Psychology is no more basic than the others; it's simply another (internally very diverse) way of talking. And as with every discipline, most of that talk is not of much use to anyone.

19. Cultural chauvinism in mainstream American psychology, both historical and contemporary, is under increasing attack. A promising alternative is the *cultural psychology* being developed by, among others, Richard Shweder and his colleagues (see, for example, Shweder and LeVine, 1984; Shweder, 1991; Shweder and Sullivan, 1993; and Stigler, Shweder, and Herdt, 1990).

20. An useful interpretation of the relations between American social science and American individualism is provided by Barry Schwartz in *The Battle for Human Nature: Science, Morality and Modern Life* (1986).

21. *Habits of the Heart* (1985), by Robert Bellah and his colleagues, is an important recent discussion of American values. Following some law of irony, the book was criticized for not using methods (quantitative surveys, etc.) based on values the authors were intent on criticizing.

22. What we want to emphasize here is the general *distancing of social science from life* that is manifested in the traditional construction of social trust. In this distancing process, social science, ironically, becomes separated from itself. As Paul Feyerabend noted with respect to physics: "Some of the older historians (Goethe, Burtt, Koyré) already suspected that scientists may do one thing and act as if they were doing another. The resulting conflict between scientific reports and the actual procedures used became obvious in the twentieth century when interviews, computer printouts, records of telephone calls were added to letters and notebooks. Scientists themselves now emphasized the unsystematic and opportunistic nature of scientific discovery (Einstein), the role of paradox and the need for "crazy" ideas (Bohr), and the fraudulence of research papers (Medawar). Most important, however, was the discovery to what extent familiar features of scientific practice depend on cultural factors" (1993, p. 28). The studies of Bruno Latour are instructive on the (ironic) relations between science and scientists. See, for example, *Laboratory Life* (Latour and Woolgar, 1986).

23. Robert Hughes, born in Australia, has said of Americans, for example, that we "have a real problem in imagining the rest of the world. [Americans] are not the only ones—most things are foreign to most people—but considering the variety of national origins represented in their vast society, its incuriosity and proneness to stereotype can still surprise the foreigner, even (in my case) after twenty years' residence in the U.S." (1993, pp. 96, 97).

24. Or, as Richard Rorty calls it, anti-anti-ethnocentrism: " It urges that ideals may be local and culture-bound, and nevertheless be the best hope of the species" (1991a, p. 208).

25. Mary Ann Glendon has demonstrated that our American unwillingness to look abroad for useful ideas extends even to our most prestigious institutions, the Supreme Court and the law: "Ironically, what we have missed through our insularity is the opportunity for rediscovery of our own tradition, with its tremendous potential for self-renewal and for creative adaptation to new and challenging circumstances" (1991, p. 170).

26. Of course, American culture can also be described as diverse, composed of many different subcultures, etc. Triandis's simplification is "temporary and convenient, what works in particular circumstances" (Feyerabend, 1993, p. 29). It is not asserted to be real.

27. A number of American social scientists are engaged in the interesting task of demonstrating that people in general, and Americans in particular, are not motivated by self-interest. That they claim success in this is due largely to the fact that they strip individuals of all social relations—they are treated as isolated monads—and of anything of interest to think about. David Sears and Carolyn Funk, for example, admit in their remarkable argument that "self-interest may well operate more strongly on local 'doorstep' issues, such as the 'NIMBY' (not in my back yard) resistance to threatening local projects . . . Unfortunately, exploration of such issues is not as glamorous as matters of war and peace, presidential elections, or the control of Congress, and so research

on them, to the extent that it is done at all, tends to be relegated to the less prestigeful academic venues and outlets" (1991, pp. 78-79). Thus speaks the American academic tradition. For a more useful, culturally informed discussion of this issue, see Fiske 1991b.

CHAPTER 3

1. And Veyne, of course, believes that we share this basic human problem and response with the Greeks: "We can get a glimpse of it in the work of Freud. It is amazing that the strangeness of his work startles us so little: these tracts, unfurling the map of the depths of the psyche, without a shred of proof or argument; without examples, even for purposes of clarification; without the slightest clinical illustration; without any means of seeing where Freud found all that or how he knows it. From observing his patients? Or, more likely, from observing himself?" (1988, p. 30).

2. Note that "complexity" in this context indicates a *simplification*, a structuring, of unordered "chaos."

3. In his many volumes of work, Luhmann has analyzed an enormous variety of social issues, from love to law, from religion to environmental communication, from art to social trust. Luhmann's theory of social systems is a unique amalgam of Parsonian systems theory, cybernetics, phenomenology, and biology. We make use of parts of Luhmann's theory here, but we make no attempt to explicate it. Useful guides into Luhmann are provided in the translator's introductions to several of his books; for example, *Religious Dogmatics and the Evolution of Societies* (1984, translated with introduction by Peter Beyer) and *Ecological Communication* (1989, translated with introduction by John Bednarz, Jr.).

4. Victor Ottati and Robert Wyer (1990) describe the general model of social cognition in useful detail in their recent account of the relations between social cognition and political choice.

5. As individuals search for simplicity, traditional, rationalist assumptions about human judgment tend to fail. James Kuklinski and his colleagues, for example, give us this description of how individuals may cope with a question: "They may ask themselves: 'How should I know whether this particular action is good or bad? I don't really know all that much about politics. Well, anyway . . . how do I feel about this?' Consulting their feelings, they find a negative (or positive) reaction, based on the affect the group elicits. They read this gut reaction as a response to the full sentence (group plus action), the result being a snap judgment that reflects group affect without any of the considerations of the 'I dislike X' type" (Kuklinski, Riggle, Ottati, Schwarz and Wyer, 1991, p. 5). Thus, individuals may base judgments, even presumably important political judgments, on simple affect. But this may not be as dismal an account as it first appears to be: "The results we reported suggest that reason need not always yield a more tolerant, just, or fair society. To the contrary, the people in our experiments asked explicitly to consider consequences actually expressed less tolerance, on the whole, than did those who reacted from the gut" (pp. 22-23). On the other hand, traditional, participatory democracy may suffer: "If emotions and passions indeed are a—perhaps the—critical and inevitable link between elected representatives and citizens, can they, like

considered thought, lay claim as a legitimate component of U.S. politics? In short, given the inevitability, is there a case for desirability? We hope other empirical researchers will find this question as enticing and challenging as do we" (p. 24). We certainly do. Our concept of social trust deals with exactly these problems: the link between representatives and citizens, what it is based on and its social desirability.

6. This is an important example of what we mean by "psychological realism."

7. A basic point from Luhmann: "Statements concerned with complexity become productive only when they are turned from unity to difference. The distinction of system and environment can be used to do this. It enables one to make the statement . . . that for any system the environment is always more complex than the system itself" (1989, 11).

8. Steven Neuberg and Jason Newsom (1993) suggest that people achieve cognitive simplicity in two fundamental ways, avoidance strategies and structural strategies. There are two kinds of structural strategies, behavioral and cognitive. According to this scheme, social trust is a strategy based on cognitive structuring. Its functional equivalents would fall into that or other of Neuberg and Newsom's categories. In their empirical studies, these researchers demonstrate that individuals differ in their desire for simple structure, and they suggest that these differences may have important social implications.

9. Of course, increased social benefits are normally bought at the cost of increased social risks.

10. Traditional—or rationalized—interpretations of social trust seem to be in the ironic, self-defeating position of both risking stasis through oversimplification (interest-group politics, for example) *and* demanding increased information processing effort. The U.S. Department of Energy social trust program, outlined in Chapter 1, is an example of this.

CHAPTER 4

1. We use the terms *social distrust* and *distrust* interchangeably here. Regardless of the term used, the social focus of this strategy is *individual*—that is the concern of the distrusting person is focused on himself as a separate individual.

2. Aaron Wildavsky's most sustained discussion of anticipatory and resilient risk management strategies can be found in *Searching for Safety* (1988).

3. Rajiva Verma (1986) suggests reading the Shakespearean tragedies *Macbeth* and *Antony and Cleopatra* as accounts of inner certainty—its lack coupled with distrust in the first play, its presence coupled with trust in the second.

4. The relationship of the Furies to Athenian justice, as described by Aeschylus in *The Eumenides*, is a rough metaphor for our contrast between social distrust and social trust.

5. Carol Ember and Melvin Ember, for example, present cross-cultural evidence from 186 societies demonstrating a positive relationship between socialization for distrust and war (Ember and Ember, 1992).

6. Inglehart's studies of political culture attempt to associate changes in cultural values with shifts toward advanced industrialization within various societies (1988,

1990). Distrust is associated with relative lack of progress toward advanced industriali-zation. Diego Gambetta has produced an extensive account of the contemporary workings of the Mafia in Southern Italy in *The Sicilian Mafia: The Business of Private Protection* (1993).

7. William Pfaff, for example, claimed in an editorial column that "the specific character of Reaganism was to hold government responsible for society's ills and to refuse to fund it or respect it" (1992, p. A28).

8. We want to stress here that we are interpreting *culture* as a dynamic, changing set of skills that are learned, used, and in some cases discarded in favor of more useful replacements. We share Diego Gambetta's (1993, pp. 10-11) concern that *culture* not be used in any static, deterministic way.

9. We us the term *American romantic distrust* because of the sentimental nos-talgia with which Barber, along with Vivien Hart, Richard Merelman, and others, discusses the role of distrust in American Populism, a movement whose resurrection (under the more modern rubric "participatory democracy") these authors advocate. Barber, commenting approvingly on Hart's (1978) analysis, concludes that, "political distrust is the product of the public's realistic and accurate perception of deficiencies among their leaders with respect to competence, fiduciary responsibility, or both (Barber, 1983, p. 72). In this brief statement, Barber manages both to capture the tra-ditional American spirit of social distrust and to describe that spirit's congenial companion, the traditional American account of social trust.

10. The prime mover among the cultural theorists is Mary Douglas, who based her theoretical position on the work of Emile Durkheim. See, for example, *Implicit Mean-ings: Essays in Anthropology* (1975) and *Risk and Culture: An Essay on the Selection of Technical and Environmental Dangers* (Douglas and Wildavsky, 1982).

11. This culture-theoretic account, or the worldview that it expresses, can *itself* be interpreted as a source of social distrust. Jeffrey Goldfarb (1991, p. 137), for example, claims that what he calls "ideological critique" produces "cynicism." In defense of culture theory, we need only point out that distrust or cynicism are not associated with *all* forms of social relations: it is possible to live in a society that both accepts culture-theoretic ideas and is not dominated by social distrust. How to get from here to there is the problem.

12. Note what happens when art and politics are conflated in this way: The artist's self becomes a static entity with certain concrete attributes—sex, race, etc.—that de-mand expression. All attention is turned reverently inward. But then the irony: The more narrowly focused the artist is on herself, the more convinced she becomes that she is gazing deeply into the heart of society. The more self-absorbed she is, the more con-vinced she is of the universal truth in her vision. And these are darkly conservative consequences.

13. Friedman's excellent *Crime and Punishment in American History* ranges from the colonial period to the present. His chapter on the twentieth century is titled "Crimes of the Self" (1993, pp. 435-448).

14. On the relations among individualism, self-expression, and crime, see Jack Katz's book, *Seductions of Crime: Moral and Sensual Attractions in Doing Evil* (1988). Katz helps us understand crime in America by inviting us to consider the obvious at-tractions in it. In order to maintain barriers between us and bad people, we tend not to

want to think about these matters. On the other hand, we devour enormous quantities of these forbidden pleasures vicariously. On this matter, Lawrence Friedman points to television and the culture it teaches: "The culture certainly stresses the self, the individual; it does not invite people to submerge themselves in some higher cause or entity. It invites them, on the contrary, to be *themselves;* it is individualistic with a vengeance. We have referred to the result as 'crimes of the self'" (1993, pp. 455-456).

15. We are using *culture* in a loose and general way here. Under most circumstances, it is more useful to refer to specific subcultures or cultural groupings in America. In this context, however, we want to make some general points about the dominant culture shared in varying degrees by most Americans.

16. The critical importance of political discourse is not uncontroversial even among critics of American culture. Both Robert Hughes and Mary Ann Glendon, for example, cite Václav Havel to bolster their nonparallel arguments. Hughes asks, "Did Václav Havel and his fellow playwrights, intellectuals and poets free Czechoslovakia by quoting Derrida or Lyotard on the inscrutability of texts? Assuredly not: they did it by placing their faith in the transforming power of thought—by putting their shoulders to the immense wheel of the word" (1993, p. 72). Glendon, in contrast, reports that, "When Václav Havel in 1989 gained a platform from which to address the world, he chose to deliver one of his first major speeches on 'the mysterious power of words in human history.' The Czech president's message was a somber one, for his purpose was to remind us that while exhilarating words like 'human rights' recently have electrified society 'with their freedom and truthfulness,' one need not look far back into the past to find words and phrases whose effects were as deadly as they were hypnotic. Most sobering of all, said Havel, the very same words that can at some times be 'rays of light,' may turn under other circumstances into 'lethal arrows'" (1991, p. 11). Why the difference? Is it due simply to the fact that Hughes is referring to Havel before and Glendon to Havel after the fact of liberation?

17. Sampson is inconsistent on the crucial point of whether, as dialogic partners, the dominators and the oppressed should speak in their own voices. The oppressed, of course, should always speak in their own voices, whatever they are. As for the dominators, in the passage just quoted Sampson seems to suggest that they in some way adopt the language of the oppressed. Earlier, however, appealing to Mikhail Bakhtin, Sampson maintains that "experts can neither abandon their perspective nor presume it has primacy" (1993, p. 1227).

18. The demands of "identity politics" have much in common with American rights talk as described by Mary Ann Glendon: "its penchant for absolute, extravagant formulations, its near-aphasia concerning responsibility, its excessive homage to individual independence and self-sufficiency, its habitual concentration on the individual and the state at the expense of the intermediate groups of civil society, and its unapologetic insularity" (1991, p. 14). The strongest case for control over one's self-description is given by Richard Rorty: "To be a pragmatist rather than a realist in one's description of the acquisition of full personhood requires thinking of its acquisition by blacks, gays and women in the same terms as we think of its acquisition by Galilean scientists and Romantic poets. We say that the latter groups invented new moral identities for themselves by getting semantic authority over themselves. As time went by, they succeeded in having the language they had developed become part of the language everybody

spoke. Similarly, we have to think of gays, blacks and women inventing themselves rather than discovering themselves, and thus of the larger society as coming to terms with something new" (1991b, p. 249).

19. Niklas Luhmann has developed a useful account of the power of communications media and the revolutionary effects of changes in those media. For Luhmann, society consists of nothing but communications, and society evolves through communications, through self-reference. Since nobody is outside society to plan and direct it, changes in society are uncontrollable and unpredictable. Though he can't resist a few stabs at prognostication ("science fiction"), Luhmann prefers describing emerging problems such as "an increasing gap between control capacities and goal attainment which leads, among other things, to increasing disappointments and negative feelings toward society" (1990, pp. 105-106).

20. The power of print to divide is powerfully demonstrated in Benedict Anderson's *Imagined Communities*, an account of the contributions of printed vernacular languages to the formation of nations (Anderson, 1991).

21. Alan Fiske has identified (and thoroughly documented with data from cultures throughout the world) what he calls the four elementary forms of human relations. In its entirety, Fiske's scheme is extensive and elaborate, addressing all facets of human life. As a brief example, we note the type of social identity that Fiske has associated each of the four models: communal sharing—self defined in terms of ancestry, race, ethnicity, common origins, and common fate; authority ranking—self as revered leader or loyal follower; equality matching—self as a separate but co-equal peer, on a par with fellows; market pricing—self defined in terms of occupation or economic role (1991a, pp. 44-45).

22. We are not referring here to class identity in the classic sense, which obviously isn't strong in America. Instead, we want simply to point to the remarkable class selfishness that dominates America and that we share with our neighbor, Haiti (see Geertz, 1993, p. 64).

23. The failure of established authority in eastern Europe, for example, was—for most of us—a cause for celebration. What has replaced it—thus far—is not.

24. Significant, perhaps increasingly important, supporting roles are played by "talk radio" and segments of the Internet.

25. Niklas Luhmann argues that the selection principles used by television editors to determine what is news, for example "new" and "conflict," have significant distrust-building effects: "It must be assumed that such principles, which constantly stress discontinuity as opposed to continuity, tend to undermine confidence. It is quite conceivable that they stimulate simultaneous demands for protection against and participation in change, thus generating both fears and claims" (1990, p. 96).

26. Sheila Jasanoff provides us with a crisp contrast between a risk-management process based on "a system of trust" (in Great Britain) and a system based on distrust (in America). She concludes, however, that "the British methods of dealing with technical uncertainty, despite their many attractions, cannot readily be assimilated into the U.S. policy process. The tensions and paradoxes that mark the analysis of risk in America are to a large extent unavoidable by-products of a legal and political environment that prizes openness and diversity along with scientific rationality. In this pluralistic society, political arguments, including esoteric arguments about scientific

evidence, must necessarily be resolved through negotiation and debate among many competing interests" (1991, p. 45). What Jasanoff fails to note, however, and what we have tried to stress here, in agreement with Lindblom and others, is the extent to which what may appear to be "pluralistic" debate consists very simply of multiple manifestations of the American individualistic cultural norm.

27. In a pioneering study of "racial mistrust and deviant behaviors among ethnically diverse black adolescent boys," Frank Biafora and his colleagues present evidence in support of their hypothesis that "Mistrust may be maladaptive for [some black adolescent boys] in that it may motivate them to withdraw from activities that are essential if they are to access the opportunity and reward structures of the dominant society—for example, school completion and/or seeking employment" (Biafora, et al., 1993, p. 894).

28. Martha Nussbaum provides a brilliant analysis of the relations between control and risk in *The Fragility of Goodness* (1986).

CHAPTER 5

1. The best exemplar of this irony is *The Confidence Gap: Business, Labor, and Government in the Public Mind*, an extensive study of social trust and related concepts written by Seymour Martin Lipset and William Schneider (1983). No social science book could be more empirically based than Lipset and Schneider's: thousands of results from hundreds of public opinion polls covering a period of many years are analyzed and discussed in exhausting detail. What we won't find in any of Lipset and Schneider's dozen chapters, however, is any serious discussion of the concepts that were more or less blindly used by the polling organizations. For these arch-empiricists, data, evidently, are data. But it's not just a matter of the lack of critical curiosity about the concepts they are discussing. In addition, Lipset and Schneider use interchangeably such presumably distinctive concepts as social trust and confidence. It is in ways such as these that social science contributes to the perpetuation of the past.

2. This is the term used by Owen Flanagan in his critique of ethical theories (1991).

3. As F. G. Bailey points out in his valuable book on truth and lying, *The Prevalence of Deceit*, Bok claims to be writing practical, usable ethics while she describes situations few humans encounter, those involving "clear-cut lies."

4. In this quotation Richard Rorty (1991a) is referring to "knowledge" and "truth." With regard to the latter, Rorty restates the words of William James: "The pragmatist says that there is nothing to be said about truth save that each of us will commend as true those beliefs which he or she finds good to believe" (p. 24).

5. At its base, "truth," of course, is simply another complexity-reduction strategy. But "simply" is the wrong adverb since truth is at *the heart* of all of the other strategies, their driving force. F. G. Bailey (1991) has neatly connected politics, truth, and simplicity: "Contest is the central feature of politics, but there would not be such a contest if we did not have so strong a need to wrap ourselves around with a *habitus*, to find "the truth," to find a place on which to stand, to settle comfortably with one answer and relieve ourselves of the anxiety aroused by questioning, doubt, and uncertainty" (p. 128).

6.   Held (1984) further restricts her definition of trust (correctly we believe) by insisting that it be both voluntary and risky: "The trust I am talking about is voluntary trust, the trust that is possible between conscious, autonomous persons who are able to trust or not trust and able to betray or not betray. To trust is not merely to rely on and to predict accurately the behavior of another. Trust arises in situations of uncertainty more clearly than in situations of certainty. We trust another person who *could* betray us not to do so" (p. 66).

7.   Seymour Martin Lipset and William Schneider (1983) provide an empirical account of this point, for what it's worth. In *The Confidence Gap,* Lipset and Schneider argue that at the same time Americans became increasingly dissatisfied with the performance of their institutions, they maintained an overall confidence in the system: "[There is no] evidence to suggest that Americans feel there are fundamental defects in their systems of democratic government or free enterprise" (p. 384).

8.   In her discussion of trust, Virginia Held helps us to understand how *all* traditional accounts of social trust are expressions of moral philosophy rather than social science, normative rather than descriptive, even when their authors claim or assume otherwise.

9.   Lars Hertzberg (1988) has given us a particularly interesting interpretation of trust in children, but this is different from Baier's infant trust. With Hertzberg, we have a human mind at work: "The child's readiness to go along with what is intimated to him cannot be thought to derive from any more basic consideration: what others suggest will matter to the child simply *because* they suggest it, or because it is *they* who suggest it. It seems, then, that the idea of something speaking in favour of an action can only acquire meaning for a child through *someone's* speaking in its favour. In this way, coming to have an understanding of good and bad, of things mattering, presupposes a fundamental dependence on other people" (p. 311). But the child's dependence on others, and his trust, are basically no different from our own.

10.   A common example of this situation is choosing to vote for a candidate, as Jeffrey Smith has demonstrated in his *American Presidential Elections: Trust and the Rational Voter* (1980).

11.   But competence and responsibility are hard to escape. At the end of her essay, Baier (1986) sums up her position: "Trust, I have claimed, is reliance on others' competence and willingness to look after, rather than harm, things one cares about which are entrusted to their care. The moral test of such trust relationships which I have proposed is that they be able to survive awareness by each party to the relationship of *what* the other relies on in the first to ensure their continued trustworthiness or trustingness" (p. 259). But by saying "competence and willingness" in this context, Baier seems to be making a general gesture toward unspecified values. We would contend, though Baier obviously does not, that, in general, a person's reasons for trusting are unknown to him. *Post facto* justifications, of course, are always available.

12.   We should note also that we use *confidence* only in reference to a strategy for the reduction of cognitive complexity. We never use it here, as others might elsewhere, to refer to a personality trait.

13.   Our discussion of confidence as well as of trust derives from the various writings of Niklas Luhmann. It is important to note, however, that our interpretation of these matters, in most instances, is not identical with Luhmann's. Aside from being

very highly developed theoretically and thoroughly integrated across contexts, Luhmann's writings, in general, are much more nuanced and attuned to contextual specifics than we can attempt here. In his essay *Familiarity, Confidence, Trust* (1988), for example, Luhmann makes a distinction between familiarity and confidence that draws too fine a line to be useful to us in this project.

14. When we refer to management in both situations, confidence and trust, we include both individual (by the person) and social (by other members of her community).

15. The difficulties inherent in confidence and overconfidence have recently been usefully described by Lee Ross and Richard Nisbett in terms of construal processes (1991, p. 87).

16. A convenient review of these techniques is provided by the National Academy of Sciences in *Risk Assessment in the Federal Government: Managing the Process* (1983).

17. A number of dramatic and costly failures in large-scale technological systems over the past two decades have encouraged several attempts by researchers to understand risk assessment errors. Paul Slovic, Baruch Fischhoff, Sarah Lichtenstein, and colleagues, for example, have used insights derived from cognitive psychology and decision analysis to account for such errors; see, for example, *Acceptable Risk* (Fischhoff, Lichtenstein, Slovic, Derby, and Keeney, 1981). A pioneering sociological account of risk assessment errors is given in *Normal Accidents: Living with High-Risk Technologies* by Charles Perrow (1984). A good general source on the study of human error is the book by that title by James Reason (1990).

18. Our account here, to emphasize what we think is an important a point, is one-sided. Anticipatory risk assessment obviously has its place, particularly used in conjunction with policies based on resilience. As Aaron Wildavsky points our, "Anticipatory strategies, justified by fear of regret, have an outstanding rhetorical advantage: their proponents can claim that they are aiming directly at safety by seeking to prevent expected harm from taking place. Adherents of resilience face a corresponding rhetorical disadvantage: by encouraging risk taking they are apparently opposed to safety, offering mainly indirect capacities to cope with the unexpected" (1988, p. 226). Think, for example, about the contemporary American debate about the management of crime.

19. As George Priest has demonstrated, treating safety as a condition, as though you knew how to produce it, inevitably results in unforeseen (and in some cases regrettable) consequences. "The vast expansion of the liability of manufacturers, professionals, and municipalities," Priest points out, "has derived from the belief that these defendants were almost always in the relatively better position *both* to prevent injuries and to insure for them. The widespread withdrawals of products and services consequent to the expansion of liability shows this presumption to be wrong" (1990, 226).

20. "From Resilience to Anticipation: Why the Tort Law is Unsafe," the chapter on tort law in Aaron Wildavsky's *Searching for Safety* (1988), was co-written by Daniel Polisar.

21. One of these problems is the proliferation of results-oriented (i.e., anticipatory) legislation. In the German context, Niklas Luhmann has concluded that, "Results-

oriented practice is the most important single source of complexity within the system. . . . Result orientation will, to a large extent, not achieve its ends and will produce unintended side effects" (1990, p. 240). But note, also in Germany, what the Federal Constitutional Court had to say about the Atomic Energy Law in a 1978 decision: "Firm legal determination of a specific safety standard by means of formulation of rigid rules would . . . were it possible to provide, inhibit rather than promote technical development and the proper securing of constitutional rights. It would mean a step back at the expense of safety" (Kuhlman, 1986, p. 396).

CHAPTER 6

1. All quotations from Voltaire's *Candide* are taken from the translation by Robert Adams (Voltaire, 1966).

2. The few sentences that we can devote to Ernst Bloch obviously can only hint at what he produced. Ronald Aronson has written an excellent brief review of *The Principle of Hope* (1991). Bloch's son, Jan Robert Bloch, has written on Bloch and his relations with the German Democratic Republic and the Soviet Union (Bloch, 1988). Wayne Hudson's book *The Marxist Philosophy of Ernst Bloch* is an orthodox but detailed account of Bloch's philosophy (Hudson, 1982).

3. Ronald Aronson contends that Bloch deliberately avoided rational argument: " In the end we do not have hope communicated to us: we are pummeled by hope" (Aronson, 1991, p. 224). But "rational argument," preferred by many philosophers and others, is not the only, nor in all cases the best, form of persuasive communication. Aronson recognizes this. After attacking Bloch for alleged irrationality, he notes that, "Bloch's thought is ultimately an all-inclusive faith in the dawning of a better world, one neither demonstrated nor demonstrable, drawing much of its sustenance from religion. It expresses this faith by taking totally seriously—indeed, more than many religious thinkers—the hope bubbling up in the Jewish and Christian Bibles. But this is, in Bloch, we now know, as in religion, a hope without reason" (p. 231).

4. An interesting counterpoint to Bloch's political hope is that of Raymond Williams. Terry Eagleton, in an interview with Williams toward the end of his life, asked whether socialism were "anything more than wishful thinking which runs against the historical grain? . . . How far is your own trust in human creative capacities in part the product of an unusually warm and affectionate working-class childhood, of which it's in some sense the nostalgic memory?" In his reply, Williams recounts some important aspects of his life: being from Wales; his father being a socialist and a railway worker; and so on. It's the story of a very outstanding man who achieved a great deal against great odds. "That is why I say we must speak for hope. I don't think my socialism is simply the prolongation of an earlier existence. When I see that childhood coming at the end of millennia of much more brutal and thoroughgoing exploitation, I can see it as a fortunate time: an ingrained and indestructible yet also changing embodiment of the possibilities of common life" (Williams and Eagleton, 1989, pp. 182-183). Here, Williams demonstrates the hollowness of hope. Challenged, he tries to describe hope's future-content, but all he can produce is the past. When it has any content at all, hope is

filled with nothing but nostalgia: personal yearnings for what is always already known, tame, and simple.

5. The dualistic coding of hope/hopeless is, on our account, a semantic trap. In our scheme based on functional equivalents, a person could "give up hope" without, as a consequence, becoming "hopeless." She could, for example, trade hope for social trust. And social trust, with its positive affect, would be preferred by most persons to the negative affect of hopelessness.

6. The study referred to by Sethi and Seligman is the famous post-World War II work by Theodor Adorno and colleagues, *The Authoritarian Personality* (1950). This was a landmark study, and in its time it was very influential. Since that time, it has been subject to periodic re-examination and criticism. Though it can no longer be considered to be in fashion, it was recently described by Owen Flanagan as "still one of the chief works in the history of [moral psychology]" (Flanagan, 1991, p. 182).

7. The notion that hope and optimism, particularly *unrealistic* hope and optimism, are positively related to mental health has some strong supporters among psychologists. Shelley Taylor and Jonathan Brown, for example, argue that unrealistically positive judgments about oneself, one's control of events, and one's future are normal ways of thinking and lead to greater happiness and productivity and to higher levels of care for others (1988). Owen Flanagan (1991, Chapter 15) closely examines the arguments of Taylor and Brown and questions some of their conclusions.

8. The basis for John Dewey's interpretation of optimism and hope is his concern about the traditional depreciation of action relative to mental processes. Dewey was a man of action and would accept a notion of hope that was related somehow to action (see, for example, Dewey, 1929, p. 33).

9. We are relying on Richard Lattimore's translation of *Works and Days* (Hesiod, 1959), reprinted in Ronald Knox's anthology, *The Norton Book of Classical Literature* (1993).

10. On this matter, Michael Grant points out that "Evil things were collected in a casket or box—familiar to the psychologists as a symbol for the mother's womb—which Pandora opened. After that only Hope or Foreboding (Elpis) remained in the box, since this, for good or harm, remains within our own control" (1962, p. 109).

11. In addition to Pandora in Hesiod's *Works and Days*, Moses Hadas also appeals to Aeschylus' related *Prometheus*, in which the title character "lists his benefactions to mankind—fire, tools, housing, clothing, which made human life more comfortable; agriculture, navigation, and other arts, which enriched life; drugs which enabled man to survive sickness; and finally hope, which apparently is the ultimate drug for situations which are otherwise intolerable" (1965, p. 115).

12. Moses Hadas recognizes, of course, that good societies are able to accommodate both rationalist and sentimentalist accounts: "A significant aspect of the Greek experience is that outlooks so disparate could exist amicably side by side; the devout did not call the wrath of the heaven down upon the worldlings, and the rationalists could acknowledge the claims of sentiment. Because neither claimed sole and exclusive possession of truth each could both learn from and fructify the other" (1965, p. 116).

13. Day (1991) makes many distinctions—for example, between hope and hopefulness and between unreasoned and unreasonable hopefulness—that, while important to his argument, are too fine-grained for inclusion our very brief discussion of his work.

14. By "rationalist" we mean a reliance on abstract analysis and on rules of reason and justification. Opposed to this, for example, would be an interpretation based mainly on an account of the human experience of hope. The second interpretation would have the advantage of greater psychological realism.

15. The curative *education* that Day refers to is primarily in the workings of probability. But this is a vain hope. Evidence from a large body of psychological research indicates that the concepts of mathematical probability and statistics, at best, are difficult to learn and, more significantly, difficult to use in everyday life outside the psychological laboratory (see, for example, Kahneman, Slovic, and Tversky, 1982).

16. This is contained in the essay, "Method, Social Science, and Social Hope," published as Chapter 11 in *Consequences of Pragmatism (Essays: 1972-1980)* (Rorty, 1982).

17. Even a philosopher as concerned with rationality as Owen Flanagan is makes room for unjustified hope: "[W]e make certain complex allowances for a kind of hopefulness and optimistic expectancy about the future which may or may not be very clearly warranted by application of a straight inductive rule based on the past. It is important to emphasize, however, that this optimism and hopefulness about the future is not patently irrational. There exist other inductive generalizations which correctly lead us to judge that there is a relation between hope and optimism and making things better down the road—between hope and effort and making a difference" (1991, p. 320).

18. Hope, as Ludwig Wittgenstein insisted, "refers to a phenomenon of *human* life" (1968, p. 153e; emphasis added). Wittgenstein asked, "Can only those hope who can talk? Only those who have mastered the use of a language. That is to say, the phenomena of hope are modes of this complicated form of life" (p. 174e). Can we tell from a person's behavior that he never hopes? "The first answer is: I don't know. It would be easier for me to say how a human being would have to act who never yearns for anything, who is never happy about anything, or who is never startled or afraid of anything" (1980, p. 5e). For Wittgenstein, as for John Dewey, words don't matter; practice does. Similarly, for Erik Erikson, "hope is a very basic human strength without which we couldn't stay alive, and not something invented by theologians or philosophers" (Evans, 1967).

19. The contemporary term "multiple personality disorder" is the successor to the traditional psychiatric term "dissociation," which remains in use in some contexts. Histories of the use of these terms can be found in Ernest Hilgard's *Divided Consciousness* (1977) and in Jacques Quen's edited volume *Split Minds/Split Brains* (1986).

20. See, for example, *Childhood Antecedents of Multiple Personality* (Kluft, 1985).

21. Elster's account here, by conflating selves, persons, and homunculi, seems designed to make "multiple selves" seem silly. Which makes sense, since the notion of multiple selves makes the precepts of rational decision making seem silly. On the one hand, Elster acknowledges the enormous intuitive appeal of concepts referring to multiplicity; on the other, he does what he can to construct unitary interpretations for those concepts (1987, p. 31).

22. Harry Triandis and his colleagues, among others, have also demonstrated the effects of culture-based self-construal on various cognitive processes (Trafimow, Triandis, and Goto, 1991).

23. Not only does the Western conceptual self not fit Eastern cultures, Markus and Kitayama note, in many cases it doesn't fit the West: "Most people are still much less self-reliant, self-contained, or self-sufficient than the prevailing cultural ideology suggests that they should be. Perhaps Western models of the self are quite at odds with actual individual social behavior and should by reformulated to reflect the substantial interdependence that characterizes even Western individualists" (1991, p. 247). This point has obvious connections to the gender-related issues discussed by, among others, Carol Gilligan (1982).

24. Fiske has demonstrated the usefulness of his system in many areas of study. A striking example is altruism. For Western social scientists, altruism has always been problematic, in need of explanation given our Western conception of the self. Fiske points out, however, that the primacy of selfish individualism is contradicted by a wide variety of evidence. "Furthermore," Fiske argues, "the ethnographic evidence suggests that if altruism means a genuine concern for some good beyond the self, motivated by a deep sense of personal connection or moral obligation to others, then altruism is inherent in human nature" (Fiske, 1991b, 177).

25. J. Donald Moon's *Constructing Community* is an excellent explication of this position. Moon describes what he calls *discourse* theories of liberalism that "attempt to avoid the problems of contractarian approaches by focusing on the process of argumentation, rather than positing a particular conception of the self—that is, a particular conception of rationality and motivation—that can be used to ground specific normative principles" (1993, p. 74).

26. The liberal self is, of course, a joint project of both individual and social construction processes. Liberals tends to highlight the individual side of things, while communitarians stress the social.

27. Contrast this account with the public selves that opinion pollsters attribute to their respondents. For pollsters, the dominant attributes of the respondent self are its unity and stability, enduring over time. Interpreted as a narrative construction, however, the respondent is a context-specific subself, with generally unknown relations to other subselves. In brief, when a person responds to a pollster's questions, he is making up a story for a specific purpose. And since, in this case, the purpose is so different from the other purposes in his life, the context so odd, the relations between this story and the others he has constructed are problematic.

28. Risk plays a different role in a positive form of retreat described by Richard Rorty in his very helpful discussion of feminism and semantic authority (1991b, p. 247). The risk here is not that of dialogue with a different other; it is the parallel but seldom noted risk of monologue, dialogue with a similar other.

CHAPTER 7

1. In his book *Structures of Social Life* (1991a), a major contribution to our understanding of human sociality, Alan Page Fiske describes the four elementary forms of human relations in clear and generous detail, and he supports his construction with a wide variety of evidence. In an empirical study of social relationships, Fiske and his colleague Nick Haslam provide brief descriptions of their four models: "Communal

sharing relationships are based on equivalence and collectivity membership in which individual distinctiveness is ignored (e.g., relationships among close family members). Equality matching refers to an egalitarian relationship marked by in-kind reciprocity and balanced exchange (e.g., relationships between nonintimate roommates). Authority ranking relationships are asymmetrical, based on precedence, hierarchy, status, command, and deference (e.g., relationships within military organizations). Market pricing relationships, in turn, are based on proportionality, with interactions organized with reference to a common scale of ratio values, such as money; relational calculations of personal cost and benefit determine social transactions (e.g., commercial relationships)" (Haslam and Fiske, 1992, pp. 446-447).

2.   An evolutionary account of the relations between human sociality and human cultural variability is given by Michael Carrithers (1990).

3.   In a sense, a person *is* culture. Culture becomes a complexity-reducing strategy when a person interprets it as something *necessary, revelatory of reality*, and *correct*. Culture becomes a strategy, that is, when a person understands it as an *endpoint* rather than as one of many contingent products of an endless creative process.

4.   Cognitive-developmental theory is discussed in the work of Jean Piaget (1965) and Lawrence Kohlberg (1984). Alan Page Fiske points out similarities between the stages of Piaget and Kohlberg and his own fundamental forms of human relations (1991a, pp. 121, 122).

5.   A concise description of these competing positions is given by Richard Shweder and Jonathan Haidt (1993). Owen Flanagan provides an extended, thoughtful discussion of Lawrence Kohlberg's work as well as that of Carol Gilligan (Flanagan, 1991, Part III).

6.   Karl Dake (1992) provides full descriptions of these five worldviews, or cultural patterns, which are based on Douglas's "grid/group" or "social prescription/group identity" taxonomy. The following brief excerpt from Dake's article gives some sense of what is meant by culture theory's worldviews: "*Hierarchically* arranged groups (i.e., those stemming from high levels of stratified prescriptions—high grid—and strong group boundaries—high group) are hypothesized to foster the myth that nature is 'perverse or tolerant.' Nature, this myth holds, is robust, but only up to a point. . . . *Egalitarian* groups (i.e., those with strong ingroup/outgroup boundaries—high group—but with prescriptions that do not vary by rank and station—low grid) are thought to espouse the myth that nature is 'fragile.' . . . *Individualists* [low-grid/low-group] are hypothesized to hold the myth of nature as 'benign,' so that if people are released from artificial constraints (like excessive environmental regulations and enforcement sanctions) there will be few limits to the abundance for all, and this will more than compensate for any hazards that are created in the process. . . . Cultures of *fatalism* (i.e., those with high levels of prescription and with minimal collective participation) are hypothesized to hold the myth of nature as 'capricious.' Fatalists may be those who have been excluded from the other ways of organizing social life: those who cannot compete successfully in markets, who cannot meet the minimum social standards of bounded and stratified groups, and who cannot muster the time, energy, or resources required for political participation. . . . The fifth cultural pattern is *autonomy*—a largely asocial way of life" (pp. 28-30).

7.   The basic notion of culture theory, that preferences are guided by worldviews (as opposed, for example, to being guided by nature or reason or God), has been expressed in various ways in recent years by a wide variety of authors having no connection with Emile Durkheim or Mary Douglas. Commenting on the lack of attention writers on human nature had paid to culture, John Dewey, for example, noted that, "the views held regarding human nature were those appropriate to the purposes and policies a given group wanted to carry through. Those who wished to justify the exercise of authority over others took a pessimistic view of the constitution of human nature; those who wanted relief from something oppressive discovered qualities of great promise in its native makeup. There is here a field which has hardly been entered by intellectual explorers:—the story of the way in which ideas put forth about the makeup of human nature, ideas supposed to be the results of psychological inquiry, have been in fact only reflections of practical measures that different groups, classes, factions wished to see continued in existence or newly adopted, so that what passed as psychology was a branch of political doctrine" (Dewey, [1939] 1963, p. 29).

8.   The effects of cultural variations on human judgment have been an important focus of recent work in risk management (e.g., Douglas and Calvez, 1990) and political science (Eckstein, 1988; Wildavsky, 1987). A common complaint against such culture-based studies is that they are static, unable to deal with cultural change. Some recent work has begun to address this problem (Eckstein, 1988; Inglehart, 1988, 1990).

9.   Our discussion of cosmopolitanism is set primarily within an American cultural context. That is, we are primarily concerned with cosmopolitanism within a multicultural America. This sets us somewhat apart from the European discourse on cosmopolitanism, which is multi-national as well as multicultural. See, for example, Pascal Bruckner's *Le Vertige de Babel: Cosmopolitisme ou Mondialisme* (1994).

10.   Philosophy, in the Hellenistic period at least, was interpreted by many people as a practical, problem-solving tool. Pierre Grimal argues that at no other time "have historical conditions exerted a greater influence on the thought of philosophers. . . . Neither reason nor nature is dependent on fortune: on the contrary, they offer that fixed point to which everyone aspires and without which all life becomes intolerable" (1968, p. 192).

11.   This selection is from *The Discourses of Epictetus*, translated by George Long (Epictetus, 1920).

12.   For information on the life of Randolph Bourne, Bruce Clayton's *Forgotten Prophet* (1984) is a careful, detailed account.

13.   Robert W. Westbrook has given us a very useful interpretation of Dewey's life and work in his recent book, *John Dewey and American Democracy* (1991). George Dykhuizen's *The Life and Mind of John Dewey* (1973) deals more with the details of Dewey's life than with his work. Both books discuss Dewey's relations with Randolph Bourne. For an anti-Bourne, conservative, Sidney Hook-inspired account of these events, see *The Politics of John Dewey* (Bullert, 1983).

14.   The term "force" was central to the Dewey/Bourne disagreement. In attacking pacifists who argued against the use of force, Dewey pointed out, somewhat sophistically, that there are good and bad uses of force; force is simply part of the world. Force is good (power) when its use is controlled; force is bad (violence) when it is out of control. Bourne, of course, had simply to point out that Dewey was deluding himself if he

believed for a minute that war could be controlled. We use "force" here in the same, everyday way as the pacifists.

15. John Dewey outlived Randolph Bourne by thirty-four years. During that enormously productive final third of his life, Dewey indicated in many ways, including in his response to the Second World War, how much he had learned from his former student.

16. By "rationally" Rorty means "that one can give a retrospective account of why one changed—how one invoked old beliefs or desires in justification of the new ones— rather than having to say, helplessly, 'it just happened; somehow I got converted'" (1991a, p. 212).

17. In his discussion of European cosmopolitanism, Pascal Bruckner uses the related term *poreux* (porous): "Since the state of the world does not allow a society to withdraw permanently into itself, we should be porous, locating the propitious space between hiding and seeking—a space open to creative shocks and edifying dissonances" (1994, p. 59, our translation). The space—the shore?

18. Loose weaving is particularly important to Rorty with regard to integrating one's *personal* passions with one's ideas about society. In this, Rorty is restating the traditional liberal private/public distinction, the emergence of which we mentioned in our chapter on the history of social trust. Rorty warns that no strong attempt should be made to integrate the personal and the public. To do so is to "attempt to see yourself as an incarnation of something larger than yourself (the Movement, Reason, the Good, the Holy) rather than accepting your finitude. The latter means, among other things, accept-ing that what matters most to you may well be something that may never matter much to most people" (1992a, p. 148). Just as an individual (with his multiple selves) may be-long to several (at times) conflicting communities, his private and public selves may also pull in different directions. But there is no need for consistency in the loosely woven cosmopolitan life. With imagination, one muddles through.

19. William Shakespeare decried (and celebrated), through Juliet (Act II, Scene ii), the tragic contingency of language:

> "'Tis but thy name that is my enemy;
> Thou art thyself though, not a Montague.
> What's Montague? it is nor hand, nor foot,
> Nor arm, nor face, nor any other part
> Belonging to a man. O! be some other name:
> What's in a name? That which we call a rose
> By any other name would smell as sweet;
> So Romeo would, were he not Romeo call'd,
> Retain that dear perfection which he owes
> Without that title. Romeo, doff they name;
> And for that name, which is no part of thee,
> Take all myself.

Too familiar, perhaps. But not too well learned.

20. Rorty here is echoing John Dewey, though Dewey at times did speak of "the native constituents of human nature." Nonetheless, Dewey's primary emphasis was on social conditions. We should, he said, "get rid of the ideas that lead us to believe that democratic conditions automatically maintain themselves, or that they can be identified with fulfillment of prescriptions laid down in a constitution. Beliefs of this sort merely divert attention from what is going on . . . For what is actually going on may be the formation of conditions that are hostile to any kind of democratic liberties. This would be too trite to repeat were it not that so many persons in the high places of business talk as if they believed or could get others to believe that the observance of formulae that have become ritualistic are effective safeguards of our democratic heritage. The same principle warns us to beware of supposing that totalitarian states are brought about by factors so foreign to us that 'It can't happen here';—to beware especially of the belief that these states rest only upon unmitigated coercion and intimidation." Referring primarily to Germany, Dewey claimed that "no regime can endure long in a country where a scientific spirit has once existed unless it has the support of so-called idealistic elements in the human constitution" ([1939] 1963, pp. 34-35).

21. Pascal Bruckner (1994, p. 62) describes cosmopolitans as *"[les] hommes passerelles"*—"bridgers." The contrast between islets and clouds can serve, therefore, as a sign of the difference between our strong brand of cosmopolitanism and Bruckner's weaker version.

22. Of course, lots of cultural change has resulted (and will continue to result) from force and from mixtures of persuasion and force. The world is not yet cosmopolitan. Nonetheless, the murky, fluid cosmopolitan interpretation is always available. Richard Rodriguez, a strong interpreter of contemporary American cosmopolitanism, has beautifully described the mixture of force and persuasion in the history of Mexico: " Postcolonial Europe expresses pity or guilt behind its sleeve, pities the Indian the loss of her gods or her tongue. But let the Indian speak for herself. Spanish is now an Indian language. . . . The Indian stands in the same relationship to modernity as she did to Spain—willing to marry, to breed, to disappear in order to ensure her inclusion in time; refusing to absent herself from the future. The Indian has chosen to survive, to consort with the living. . . . I take it as an Indian achievement that I am alive, that I am Catholic, that I speak English, that I am an American. My life began, it did not end, in the sixteenth century" (1992, pp. 23-24).

23. In a valuable and sympathetic commentary on Rorty's cosmopolitan philosophy, Alexander Nehamas neatly connects multiple selves with multiple cultures. "Foreignness," Nehamas reminds us, "starts within the skin itself. Persons, as Rorty writes, are networks of beliefs, attitudes, and desires. But these form various clusters which need not all be consistent with one another; and each one of these clusters connects the same person to a variety of different groups whose identity cannot easily be separated from that of the individual in question. One can be Greek born, American educated, a Spanish citizen, a philosopher who spends more time with literature than science but admires science nonetheless, a late twentieth-century male, a reluctant bourgeois, and much more besides. We can be, and we are, foreign to ourselves" (1990, p. 114).

24. This is the position of Pascal Bruckner relative to cosmopolitanism in Europe. After describing the suffering that "superior beings" such as Élias Canetti, George Ste-

iner, and Vladimir Nabokov had to endure to achieve "true cosmopolitanism," Bruckner proclaims that "it is impossible, unthinkable, therefore, that cosmopolitanism could be 'democratized,' be made a right on the order of health and housing; even if it exists in a thousand forms, a thousand degrees and a thousand nuances, it will always remain the privilege of the few" (1994, p. 32, our translation). In contrast to Bruckner, we believe that our stronger—yet more modest—American brand of cosmopolitanism, less encumbered perhaps by cultures past than its European counterpart, can be a cultural option for large numbers of people, though never, of course, a right due anyone.

25. The context of the production of this work, as well as that of Wittgenstein's earlier life, is brilliantly presented in Ray Monk's biography (1990).

26. On this period, Ray Monk comments: "During the two months left of his life Wittgenstein wrote over half (numbered paragraphs 300-676) of the remarks which now constitute *On Certainty*, and in doing so produced what many people regard as the most lucid writing to be found in any of his work" (1990, pp. 577-578).

27. For a contemporary interpretation of Wittgenstein, see the various works of Richard Rorty; for example, his "Wittgenstein, Heidegger, and the Reification of Language" (1991b).

28. Richard Rorty, a leading contemporary Wittgensteinian, echos this interpretation of trust, linking interpersonal with social: "We should see allegiance to social institutions as no more matters for justification by reference to familiar, commonly accepted premises—but also as no more arbitrary—than choices of friends or heroes. Such choices are not made by reference to criteria. They cannot be preceded by presuppositionless critical reflection, conducted in no particular language and outside of any particular historical context" (Rorty, 1989, p. 54).

29. We use "person" here for simplicity. We could use the more cumbersome "person or institution" to indicate that both interpersonal and social trust are being discussed. On this interpretation, interpersonal and social trust are located at the opposite ends of a continuum, with the middle position consisting of person-institution mixtures. This description emphasizes the social nature of all forms of trust.

30. Hertzberg qualifies this formulation by noting that we can trust persons whom we judge in some ways to be unreliable. That is, a person may not "be himself" in all circumstances. Trust, therefore, is not as cut-and-dried as it may at first appear to be.

31. Other useful commentaries on Wittgenstein's trust are given by John Shotter (1991) and Peter Winch (1991), the former within the context of psychology and the latter within the context of political philosophy.

32. Paul Feyerabend (1993) comments trenchantly on the general point of the separation of intellectuals from the facts of life.

33. An interesting demonstration of this connection is provided by David Bloor in his book, *Wittgenstein: A Social Theory of Knowledge* (1983). Though he doesn't discuss social trust, Bloor uses the culture theory of Mary Douglas, a pluralistic construction, to elucidate Wittgenstein's related remarks on language and culture.

CHAPTER 8

1.   For an excellent discussion of what we call "standard rationality," see Robert Nozick's *The Nature of Rationality* (1993).

2.   We have identified, thus far, two forms of risk associated with social trust. One form, discussed in the present chapter, involves the trusted entity acting as expected. In Chapter 3, we described another form of risk—the risk of stasis. In this second form—which, unlike the first, is not a conscious judgment—a critical distinction is made between *pluralistic* and *cosmopolitan* social trust. The risk of stasis is inherent only in *pluralistic* social trust. The first form of risk—that which involves the trusted entity—applies to both types of social trust.

3.   Niklas Luhmann's interpretations of trust and the related concept, confidence, appear to have evolved over the years. Our interpretations are based primarily on his 1979 book *Trust and Power*. Luhmann's more recent formulations, in which he tends to talk more of confidence and less of trust, can be found in his essay, "Familiarity, Confidence, Trust" (1988) and in his books *Ecological Communication* (1989), *Essays on Self-Reference* (1990), and *Risk: A Sociological Theory* (1993).

4.   By "practical reason," Nussbaum is referring to the Aristotelian ethical procedure. She provides a very useful discussion of that process in her book *Love's Knowledge* (1990).

5.   Accounts of these recent studies are not yet available as journal articles. They are available, however, as technical reports published by the Western Institute for Social and Organizational Research, Western Washington University, Bellingham, Washington.

6.   This general newspaper story procedure derives from our work on risk communication (Earle, Cvetkovich, and Slovic, 1990). Our risk communication model is called IRA; it consists of three "message evaluation factors" (Involvement, Relevance, and Ability) and three "message effects factors" (Desire for Information, Capacity to Act, and Intention to Act). Each of these constructs is measured by three items, and the entire model has been validated using standard procedures. In the generic version of the model, Involvement is affected by Ability and Relevance. In turn, paths lead from Involvement to Desire for Information to Capacity to Act to Intention to Act. In any specific case, the general relations among the factors remains the same, but certain paths (for example, from Relevance to Intention to Act) may appear or not. The adequacy of the model is tested using structural equations techniques (Jöreskog and Sörbom, 1989).

7.   At this stage of our work, our method of measuring cultural orientations, although effective for our purposes, is still rather crude. We are currently working on new methods based on Alan Page Fiske's four forms of social relations (1991a).

8.   The relevant statistical tests, analyses of variance, produced these results for the story by subject cultural orientation interaction: For trust values ($F_{4,393} = 5.61$; $p < .001$); for trust judgments ($F_{4,393} = 8.39$; $p < .001$).

9.   It must be kept in mind when considering these results that each individual subject (classified after the fact as, for example, an Egalitarian) read only one form of the nuclear waste story, either Egalitarian, Individualistic, or Hierarchical. Comparisons are between subjects, not within subjects.

10. On a technical note, these elements are treated somewhat differently here than in our previous discussion. The cultural orientation of the story is represented by a single variable, indicating Egalitarian, Individualist, or Hierarchical. Trust values has three indicators—i.e., three of the six items previously described. Social trust, as before, has a single indicator.

11. Story credibility is measured by three indicators.

12. The model was evaluated using structural equation techniques (Jöreskog and Sörbom, 1989). All of the paths in the model are statistically significant, and the model fits the data very well (Chi Square with 15 degrees of freedom = 11.01, p. = .752; Adjusted Goodness of Fit Index = .980).

13. The reduced model, evaluated in the same manner as the full model, fits the data very poorly (Chi Square with 19 degrees of freedom = 157.75, p = .000; Adjusted Goodness of Fit Index = .821).

14. The general topic of similarity judgments is the topic of a very interesting article by Douglas Medin, Robert Goldstone, and Dedre Gentner (1993).

15. Perhaps the ultimate expressions of group cooperation and pluralistic social trust are the ethnic and nationalistic conflicts described, for example, in Michael Ignatieff's book *Blood and Belonging* (1993).

16. Any extended discussion of pluralism and liberalism, their various forms and alternatives, etc., is beyond our present intentions. We want only to make simple points about the pluralism/cosmopolitanism distinction that seem to us to be useful. An excellent discussion of liberal pluralism is given by J. Donald Moon in his book *Constructing Community: Moral Pluralism and Tragic Conflicts* (1993).

17. J. Donald Moon, another eloquent describer of liberalism, describes the contingencies of liberal life in somewhat less dramatic terms: "Learning to live with ambivalence, to recognize the contingencies of one's own identities, to abandon the quest for self-certainty, to recognize that even one's most cherished principles may be experienced as unjustly repressive—in many ways political liberalism may strike one as a philosophy of middle age, one that can appeal only to those who have lost the will and the imagination to pursue a purer and brighter vision" (1993, p. 220).

18. This is a caricature, but even the most persuasive defenders of pluralism don't seem to escape it. J. Donald Moon, for example, says that "having accepted plurality, we can go beyond a narrowly circumscribed toleration of difference to become enriched by the wonderful plenitude of human possibilities and projects, free of the need to grade, to rank, to enclose each culture or way of life in a grid defined by our own need for 'truth'" (1993, p. 221). This seems to us to be a description of multiple solitudes, each stuck in a static world, having in common only an appreciation of pure, pointless plurality. How does one become "enriched" without judging, without changing?

19. Some of Mikhail Bakhtin's cosmopolitan spirit can be found in the risk management work of Mary Douglas and Aaron Wildavsky. In their description of knowledge as a social process, for example: "Instead of the old recurrent imagery of knowledge as a solid thing, bounded or mapped out, we prefer the idea of knowledge as the changing product of social activity. It is not so much like a building, eventually to be finished, but more like an airport, always under construction. It has been compared to an open-ended communal enterprise, to a ship voyaging to an unknown destination but never arriving and never dropping anchor. It is like a many-sided conversation in

which being ultimately right or wrong is not at issue. What matters is that the conversation continue with new definitions and solutions and terms made deep enough to hold the meanings being tried" (1982, pp. 192-193).

20. In his various writings, Michel Serres uses many arresting metaphors in his discussions of the singular and the multiple. War is often used for the singular. At one point in *Rome*, Serres compares the singular *war* with the multiple *plague*. In war, everything is ordered, homogeneous, monotonic, classified, vitrified, standardized. Plague has none of these characteristics. One's ability to individuate, discriminate is gone. Society's leaders are spared war, but the plague can get them. "The leader saves himself from the plague via war; the state of plague is the one feared by the great, the state of war is the one in which they take refuge" (1991, p. 201). Serres' distinction between war and plague is similar to Niklas Luhmann's distinction between *risk* and *danger*. In brief, a risk involves a potential loss that is attributed to a decision involving alternative actions. In contrast, one is exposed to dangers. Whether and how a potential loss is constructed as a risk or a danger varies across individuals and groups, often leading to significant risk management problems (see Luhmann, 1993, Chapter 1).

21. Our concept of *relevance* is described in Earle, Cvetkovich, and Slovic (1990) and is derived from the work of Sperber and Wilson (1986). Our interpretation of relevance in risk communication is this: relevance is a judgment made by the recipient about the similarity between his currently salient values and those of the affected persons in the message. For example, if the affected persons are described as members of a certain group who engage in a specific behavior, then the message will be judged relevant to the extent that the receiver considers himself similar to the members of that group. Other factors aside, the greater the relevance of a message, the greater its effects.

22. On "Religion as Conversation-Stopper," see Richard Rorty (1994).

23. This idea—that our cultures are wrong (along with its companion idea that we, as individuals, are wrong)—seems to be the most difficult aspect of cosmopolitanism to accept because of its insistence on doubt. Without doubt, you have some kind of god, a religion and the end of conversation. Edward Said discusses these matters in the special case of intellectuals: "Those gods that always fail demand from the intellectual in the end a kind of absolute certainty and a total, seamless view of reality that recognizes only disciples or enemies." Better to doubt, Said says, "to keep a space in the mind open for doubt and for the play of an alert, skeptical irony (preferably also self-irony). Yes, you have convictions and you make judgments, but they are arrived at by work, and by a sense of association with others, other intellectuals, a grassroots movement, a continuing history, a set of lived lives. As for abstractions or orthodoxies, the trouble with them is that they are patrons who need placating and stroking all the time. The morality and principles of an intellectual should not constitute a sort of sealed gearbox that drives thought and action in one direction, and is powered by an engine with only one fuel source. The intellectual has to walk around, has to have the space in which to stand and talk back to authority" (1994, p. 13). Cosmopolitanism is demanding for intellectuals as for everyone else. That is why cosmopolitan leadership, such as that of Edward Said, is vital in every sector of society.

CHAPTER 9

1. Readers may be reminded of Paul Slovic's comments on the events at Three Mile Island, noted in Chapter 1.

2. But of course the contents of the narratives and how they are expressed vary widely among groups. Shoshana Blum-Kulka (1993) demonstrates this variety in her comparison between the dinner-time narratives expressed in Jewish American families and those expressed in Israeli families. Jewish-Americans favor a monologic mode of telling, for example, while the Israelis favor polyphony.

3. As Marianne DeKoven (1992) demonstrates, Gertrude Stein—in her repudiation of chronological time and her insistence on the "continuous present"—is a paradigmatic case of refusal followed by exclusion. Stein's refusal to follow the rules of narrative form led to her rejection by the reading public.

4. In her book, *Narrating Our Pasts: The Social Construction of Oral History* (1992), Elizabeth Tonkin gives us a very interesting and useful discussion of time and narrative in oral cultures.

5. Niklas Luhmann offers extended discussions of meaning as complexity reduction and selection in his collection *Essays on Self-Reference* (1990).

6. A classic account of the role of narrative in the construction of communities is given by Benedict Anderson in his book *Imagined Communities: Reflections on the Origin and Spread of Nationalism* (1991).

7. This process is manifested plainly in our smallest communities, our families. Calvin Trillin describes the process: "It seem to me that upbringings have themes. The parents set the theme, either explicitly or implicitly, and the children pick it up, sometimes accurately and sometimes not so accurately. When you hear people talking about their childhoods, you can often detect a theme. The theme may be 'Our family has a distinguished heritage that you must live up to' or 'We are suffering because your father deserted us' or 'No matter what happens, we are fortunate to be together in this lovely corner of the earth' or 'There are simply too damn many of us to make this thing work.' Sometimes there is more than one theme. It's possible, for instance, for an upbringing to reflect at the same time 'We are suffering because your father deserted us' and 'There are simply too damn many of us to make this thing work'" (1994, p. 66).

8. The idea of belonging to several communities and maintaining multiple selves is associated with individuals in modern, literate societies. The idea that communities make us and we make communities can be applied to all societies, oral, literate, and mixed. Discussing oral societies, Elizabeth Tonkin uses the phrase "memory makes us, we make memory." She points out the importance of this dynamic interpretation of narrative: "The notion that we make ourselves and others, cumulatively, and build a directive consciousness as part of the socialisation which humans have to experience if they are to become cultural beings . . . makes many classical conundrums secondary. The dualisms of body and mind, individual and society, cease to be fundamental as do those paradoxically co-existent oppositions which mean, for instance, that one has to explain how individuals participate in a society superordinate to them, and can't comfortably relate the two terms in a single theory" (1992, p. 117).

9. Among the classic work in this area is that of Erving Goffman (1959) and Theodore Sarbin (1954).

10. In a social drama, unlike a stage drama, individuals need not be aware of a script or its directions in order to be guided by it. Awareness can be produced by alterations in normal circumstances (see, for example, Garfinkle, 1967).

11. Roy Baumeister and colleagues (1993) describe the intriguing social context of *unrequited love*. One of the interesting aspects of this situation is that the rejector's role appears to be largely unscripted. "The rejector is abruptly (and not by choice) cast in an unscripted role of interpersonal villain, and so one may predict that the rejector would find considerable uncertainty and ambiguity about how to act. Rejectors may also be likely to look back with regret on the episode, to feel that they reacted incorrectly, or to wish that they had done something differently."

12. Baruch Fischhoff was an early and effective critic of the use of "values" in studies of decision making (see, for example, Fischhoff, 1991). A useful general critique is provided by Michael Hector (1992).

13. For discussions of the implications of the notion of cognitive limitations on the interpretation of moral judgments (requiring, in brief, that they be simple to make) see Alvin Goldman (1993) and Owen Flanagan and Amélie Oksenberg Rorty (1990).

14. A broad-ranging discussion of social psychology as rhetoric is provided by Michael Billig in *Arguing and Thinking* (1987).

15. Suddenly we have entered the world of the economist. For progressive discussions of the use of "values" by economists in studies of environmental risk management, see the work of Robin Gregory (for example, Gregory, Lichtenstein, and Slovic, 1993).

16. Paul Veyne (1988), reflecting on the function of narrative in ancient Greece and Rome—and today—concludes that "It would be better to admit that no knowledge is disinterested and that truths and interests are two different terms for the same thing; for practice thinks what it does. It was desirable to make a distinction between truth and interest only in order to explain the limitations of the former; it was thought that the truth was bounded by the influence of interests. This is to forget that interests themselves are limited (in every age they fall within historical limits; they are arbitrary in their fierce interestedness) and that they have the same boundaries as the corresponding truths. They are inscribed within the horizons that the accidents of history assign to different programs" (p. 85).

17. At this point, unfortunately, Stanley Fish slips into the pluralist stance that we discuss in our chapter on culture.

18. Narrative can be used to encourage change or to discourage it. Paul Veyne (1988) demonstrates the latter in his discussion of panegyrics in ancient Greece. "[T]hese panegyrics," Veyne points out, "aimed less at exalting one city above all others than at recognizing its dignity as a person. And these words of praise were addressed less to the group than to the individuals within it. In the panegyrics spoken before the assembled city, it was not the group that worshipped itself, as was the case in Nuremberg. The praises of the city made each citizen feel, not that he was carried by a collective force, but rather that, in addition to his other merits, he had another personal dignity, the quality of citizen. The glorification of the group was the glorification of individuals, as if one had praised nobility in front of a group of nobles. It was not patriotic pride; the individual was proud, not to belong to that city rather than another one, but to be a citizen instead of not being one" (p. 82). Veyne notes that the reactions of

Athenians, were complex, ranging from unalloyed exaltation to a derisive skepticism based on a keen awareness of rhetorical techniques. There were many contradictions in the stories, but the ancients seemed quite at home with the multiple.

19. The notion of "free spaces" was developed by Sara Evans and Harry Boyte in their book *Free Spaces: The Sources of Democratic Change in America* (1986). In a narrative context, advocacy of "free spaces" is consistent with Richard Rorty's advice to feminists regarding semantic authority. "To get such authority," Rorty says, "you have to hear your own statements as part of a shared practice. Otherwise you yourself will never know whether they are more than just ravings, never know whether you are a heroine or a maniac. People in search of such authority need to band together and form clubs, exclusive clubs. For if you want to work out a story about who you are—put together a moral identity—which decreases the importance of your relationships to one set of people and increases the importance of your relationships to another set, the physical absence of the first set of people may be just what you need" (1991b, 247).

20. George Howard (1991) gives us a useful roundup of recent narrative-based approaches to thinking, cross-cultural psychology, and psychotherapy.

21. Jerome Bruner gives his most detailed discussion of narrative thinking in his article, "The Narrative Construction of Reality" (1991). Bruner usefully explicates ten characteristics of narrative: narrative diachronicity, particularity, intentionality state entailment, hermeneutic composability, canonicity and breach, referentiality, genericness, normativeness, context sensitivity and negotiability, and narrative accrual. Bruner's discussion of these factors seems to us to offer the best available basis for constructing empirical studies of narrative thinking.

22. Joseph Rouse's book *Knowledge and Power* (1987) is a very useful guide to understanding science as practice, a social activity, as opposed as science as representation of reality. In his more recent work, Rouse describes the activity of science, scientists' understanding of it, as narrative.

23. Joseph Rouse makes this fine point about narrative in science and how it differs from narrative in some other fields of activity: "The advance of scientific research seems centrifugal rather than centripetal. New fields continually spin off with their own interests, methods, and interpretations. Their practitioners show little concern for how *retrospectively* to reconcile their interests and results with those of their progenitor disciplines. They will more typically consolidate their own results toward a new advance, perhaps in a still more divergent direction, than look back and try to see how it fits together with its origins" (1990, p. 192). Here, as in many ways, scientists are a model. While many communities are shackled by searches for global meaning rooted in their pasts, narrative coherence for scientists is local, practical, and future-oriented.

24. Bruno Latour provides useful descriptions of the construction of persuasion in science in his book *Science in Action* (1987).

CHAPTER 10

1. Even on their own terms, the designers of the DOE plan recognize that they are involved, somehow, in the generation of across-group social distrust. The task force says, for example, that it "understands that adopting many of these measures runs the

risk of *increasing* the trust and confidence of one segment of the public at the price of *decreasing* the trust and confidence of another" (U.S. Department of Energy, 1993, p. 59). Among the three suggestions the task force offers for dealing with this problem is this: "Make certain that no single stakeholder or group of stakeholders has its trust and confidence weakened consistently" (p. 59). Unfortunately, this seems to contradict the task force's earlier conclusion that, "regardless of what DOE does, some segments of the public will never accord it much trust and confidence. They are opposed as a matter of principle or tactics to the missions the Department of Energy has either been charged to undertake by Congress or has undertaken on its own discretion" (p. 57). In any case, the DOE plan seems mired in a muddle of trust and distrust.

2.   It seems that a moment's reflection would dispel this myth. We are all familiar, for example, with cases of unrelenting, bulletproof social trust that no amount of evidence could cause to be lost. The myth's persistence seems most likely due to its easy compatibility with the traditional interpretation of social trust—its support for the *status quo*.

3.   Benjamin Barber's (1984) vision is brilliant, positive, and inspiring. But unfortunately it is flawed by its rejection of representation and the psychologically unrealistic demands it makes of individuals. A concise and cogent critique of Barber's democracy is given by Joel Wolfe (1988).

4.   Although the empirical evaluation of traditional public participation efforts is complex, difficult, and rarely done, the consensus among researchers seems to be negative: it doesn't get the job (as defined in the particular case) done (Gittell, 1980; Kathlene and Martin, 1991). It is perhaps in the field of risk management that the need for effective public participation is felt the most and its failures are most evident. The paradigm case of radioactive waste management is discussed by Kraft and Clary (1991) and Kraft (1988).

5.   When a narrative becomes ritualized, it is like a dead metaphor. It no longer has the capacity to generate meaning. The difference between narrative and strategy disappears.

6.   The traditional public participation narrative played a prominent role in Hillary Rodham Clinton's attempted selling of her husband's health care plan. Commenting on this aspect of Mrs. Clinton's activities, Connie Bruck concluded that "Hillary's self-regard seems to cause her at times to see others as fungible—as so many pawns in a grand design. For, just as the seventy-five 'fact-finding' hearings in relation to education reform in Arkansas were said to be largely a way of building support for what had already been decided, so here, in health-care reform—on an exponentially larger scale, involving vast expenditures of time, energy, and money—a similar maneuver appeared to have taken place" (1994, p. 84). In fairness to Mrs. Clinton, we would argue that her actions in this case were based less on self-regard (some self-narrative) than on the role she was playing in the traditional public participation narrative. It was a role that could have been played by most of us, no matter how we regard ourselves. It was a role in a story of American failure.

7.   A great deal of valuable work on public participation has been completed in recent years, much of it attempting to describe free and open processes of public communication. Prominent among the contributors to this work are Jürgen Habermas (1984, 1985, 1987) and Richard Bernstein (1983, 1985, 1992).

8.   To some critics of science, and particularly to some critics of technology, our nomination of science as a model of cosmopolitanism may seem strange. Our selection is based on the cosmopolitan narrative of science. But there is another obvious point that should be mentioned. Because of its cosmopolitan narrative, science works. And because it works, it must be the basis for any hopes of positive change in the world. Richard Rorty (1992a) says it plainly when it comes to improving the lives of the poor: "Money remains the independent variable." And money, in this sense, comes from science and technology. Rorty tries to explain antitechnology talk: "I think that the sudden popularity of anti-technological talk among us Northern liberals, our turn over the last twenty years from planning to dreaming, and from science to philosophy, has been a nervous, self-deceptive reaction to the realization that technology may not work. Maybe the problems our predecessors assumed it could solve are, in fact, too tough. Maybe technology and centralized planning will not work. But they are all we have got. We should not try to pull the blanket over our heads by saying that technology was a big mistake, and that planning, top-down initiatives, and 'Western ways of thinking' must be abandoned. That is just another, much less honest, way of saying what Forster said: that the very poor are unthinkable" (pp. 15-16). The relations between science and technology are, of course, problematical—they can be interpreted as two of a kind or as opposites. Nonetheless, Rorty's point is telling. And since there are no alternatives to technology, it is vital that technology be guided by cosmopolitan science.

9.   Parts of this section are based on material that originally appeared in Earle and Cvetkovich (1994).

10. The domination of public discussion by paradigmatic formulations, the sidelining of art and literature, is a central concern for Michel Serres. "We must imagine a way," he says, "to teach, with the same gesture, both the poem and the theorem, without wronging either and with mutual enrichment: experimentation and experience, the new world of science and the storytelling of time immemorial, the immortal world of scientific laws and the new age of the arts. Those taught the third approach to knowledge, born from this mixed school, will have chucked the death wish that make us cut ourselves off, that puts our world in danger" (1989a, p. 34). The third approach, the mixed school—the cosmopolitan!

11. In her recent book *Love's Knowledge* (1990), Martha Nussbaum her process of public discussion—her Aristotelian procedure—in useful detail. For a thoughtful critique of Nussbaum's procedure, see J. Donald Moon's *Constructing Community* (1993). Moon's is a liberal critique, centering on Nussbaum's apparent essentialism: "If the point of a policy is to cultivate the qualities that conduce to human flourishing, as the Aristotelian strategy holds, and if there are different views of what constitutes human flourishing, then politics becomes a contest among those different views. Either the differences must be overcome through the participants coming to a deeper understanding of the human good, or one side must lose" (pp. 34-35). Nussbaum believes that agreement is possible; Moon is doubtful. Both have good arguments. In the end, Nussbaum is more social, more cosmopolitan—facing forward, taking risks, embracing change; Moon is more individualistic, more pluralistic—looking over his shoulder, hedging bets, wary of surprises.

12. The cosmopolitanism of Martha Nussbaum and that of Pascal Bruckner are most different here. For Bruckner, ethics and aesthetics are separate realms, mixed at

one's perile. Also, since Bruckner makes no distinction between good and bad literature, he can cite as exemplars both nationalists, such as Rodovan Karadijic, and
cosmopolitans such as Milan Kundera. Bruckner separates where Nussbaum unites and
unites where she separates. And he concludes that, "No matter how moving a books of
poems, nor how soothing a piece of music, one cannot deduce from them what one
should do, what behavior is just and unjust. Truth, beauty and goodness have long been
separated from one another" (1994, p. 18, our translation).

13. *De-individualization* and *de-centering* may seem like strange, new ideas, but
they shouldn't. An equivalent idea, usually called *unfreezing*, was central to the group-
dynamics theory of Kurt Lewin, one of the great social psychologists of the twentieth
century. Lewin applied *unfreezing* in the small and in the large. "The 'unfreezing' of
the present level may involve quite different problems in different cases," Lewin said,
referring to small groups, "To break open the shell of complacency and self-
righteousness it is sometimes necessary to bring about deliberately an emotional stir-up"
(1951, p. 229). And toward the end of World War II, Lewin, a German Jew exiled in
America, wrote that, "to bring about any change, the balance between the forces which
maintain the social self-regulation at a given level has to be upset. This implies for
Germany that certain deep-seated powers have to be uprooted" (1948, p. 47).

14. The narrative of Michel Foucault is brilliantly retold by James Miller in *The
Passion of Michel Foucault* (1994).

15. Pascal Bruckner (1994) concurs.

16. Describing the Aztecs, describing us, Michel Serres (1989) says that we must
free ourselves from our destructive pasts. "Give up sacrifices," he demands, "soon you
will see the sun nevertheless pursuing its course. Stop plundering, destroying, killing,
history will go on quietly without a bloodbath. And later, your great-grand nephews
will remember you with disgust. Forget the time, they would say to their sons, when
our barbarous forefathers called history their insurmountable taste for corpses. What
would happen if we did not assist death in its task? What could death do without us?
What if death's necessity resulted only from our whims? What if what we believe to be
nature's law was only a bad habit? What if death were to let go of its hold as soon as
we stopped helping it?" (p. 53). We have to try to imagine it.

References

Adorno, T. W., E. Frenkel-Brunswik, D. J. Levinson, and R. N. Sanford. 1950. *The Authoritarian Personality*. New York: Harper & Row.

Anderson, B. 1991. *Imagined Communities: Reflections on the Origin and Spread of Nationalism*. Revised and extended edition. London: Verso.

Aronson, R. 1991. Review of *The Principle of Hope* by E. Bloch. *History and Theory* 30:220-232.

Aronsson, K., and C. Nilholm. 1990. On memory and the collaborative construction and deconstruction of custody case arguments. *Human Communication Research* 17:289-314.

Asch, S. E. 1940. Studies in the principles of judgments and attitudes: II. Determination of judgments by group and ego standards. *Journal of Social Psychology* 12:433-465.

_____. 1952. *Social Psychology*. New York: Prentice-Hall.

Axelrod, R. 1984. *The Evolution of Cooperation*. New York: Basic Books.

Baier, A. 1986. Trust and antitrust. *Ethics* 96:231-260.

Bailey, F. G. 1991. *The Prevalence of Deceit*. Ithaca, NY: Cornell University Press.

Bakhtin, M. M. 1984. Toward a reworking of the Dostoevsky book. Appendix 2 in *Problems of Dostoevsky's Poetics*. Edited and translated by C. Emerson. Minneapolis: University of Minnesota Press.

_____. 1986. *Speech Genres and Other Late Essays*. Translated by V. W. McGee. Edited by C. Emerson and M. Holquist. Austin, TX: University of Texas Press.

Barber, B. 1983. *The Logic and Limits of Trust*. New Brunswick: Rutgers University Press.

Barber, B. R. 1984. *Strong Democracy*. Berkeley: University of California Press.

Barthes, R. 1982. *A Barthes Reader*. Edited by S. Sontag. Selection translated by S. Heath. New York: Hill and Wang.

Baumeister, R. F., S. R. Wotman, and A. M. Stillwell. 1993. Unrequited love: On heartbreak, anger, guilt, scriptlessness, and humiliation. *Journal of Personality and Social Psychology* 64:377-394.

Bellah, R. N., R. Madsen, W. M. Sullivan, A. Swidler, and S. M. Tipton. 1985. *Habits of the Heart*. Berkeley: University of California Press.

Bennett, W. L. 1978. Storytelling in criminal trials: A model of social judgment. *Quarterly Journal of Speech* 64:1-22.

Berlin, I. 1991. *The Crooked Timber of Humanity*. New York: Alfred A. Knopf.

Bernstein, R. J. 1983. *Beyond Objectivism and Relativism: Science, Hermeneutics and Praxis*. Philadelphia: University of Pennsylvania Press.

_____. 1985. From hermeneutics to praxis. In R. Hollinger, ed., *Hermeneutics and Praxis*. Notre Dame, Indiana: University of Notre Dame Press.

_____. 1992. *The New Constellation: The Ethical-Political Horizons of Modernity/Postmodernity*. Cambridge, MA: MIT Press.

Biafora, F. A., Jr., G. J. Warheit, R. S. Zimmerman, A. G. Gil, E. Apospori, and D. Taylor. 1993. Racial mistrust and deviant behaviors among ethnically diverse black adolescent boys. *Journal of Applied Social Psychology* 23:891-910.

Bianco, W. T., and R. H. Bates. 1990. Cooperation by design: Leadership, structure and collective dilemmas. *American Political Science Review* 84:133-147.

Billig, M. 1987. *Arguing and Thinking: A Rhetorical Approach to Social Psychology*. Cambridge: Cambridge University Press.

Bloch, E. 1986. *The Principle of Hope*. Translated by N. Plaice, S. Plaice, and P. Knight. 3 vols. Oxford: Basil Blackwell.

Bloch, J. R. 1988. How can we understand the bends in the upright gait? Translated by C. Rubin. *New German Critique* 45(fall):9-39.

Bloor, D. 1983. *Wittgenstein: A Social Theory of Knowledge*. London: Macmillan.

Blum-Kulka, S. 1993. "You gotta know how to tell a story": Telling, tales, and teller in American and Israeli narrative events at dinner. *Language in Society* 22:361-402.

Bohman, F. F. 1990. Communication, ideology and democratic theory. *American Political Science Review* 84:93-109.

Bok, S. 1979. *Lying: Moral Choice in Public and Private Life*. New York: Vintage Books.

Bourdieu, P. 1988. Vive la Crise!: For heterodoxy in social science. *Theory and Society* 17:773-787.

Bourne, R. S. 1964. *War and the Intellectuals: Essays by Randolph S. Bourne, 1915-1919*. Edited with an introduction by C. Resek. New York: Harper & Row, Harper Torchbooks.

Brewer, M. B. 1991. The social self: On being the same and different at the same time. *Personality and Social Psychology Bulletin* 17:475-482.

Brewer, S. 1990. Pragmatism, oppression and the flight to substance. *Southern California Law Review* 63:1753-1762.

Bruck, C. 1994. Hillary the pol. *The New Yorker*, 30 May, 58-96.

Bruckner, P. 1994. *Le Vertige de Babel*. Paris: Arléa.

Bruner, J. S. 1986. *Actual Minds, Possible Worlds*. Cambridge, MA: Harvard University Press.

_____. 1990. *Acts of Meaning*. Cambridge, MA: Harvard University Press.

_____. 1991. The narrative construction of reality. *Critical Inquiry* 18:1-21.

Brunvand, J. H. 1981. *The Vanishing Hitchhiker: American Urban Legends and Their Meanings.* New York: W. W. Norton & Company.

Bullert, G. 1983. *The Politics of John Dewey.* Buffalo, NY: Prometheus Books.

Canfield, J. D. 1989. *Word as Bond in English Literature from the Middle Ages to the Restoration.* Philadelphia: University of Pennsylvania Press.

Carlson, A. C. 1991. The role of character in public moral argument: Henry Ward Beecher and the Brooklyn scandal. *Quarterly Journal of Speech* 77:38-52.

Carrithers, M. 1990. Why humans have cultures. *Man* 25:189-206.

Carroll, J. S., and J. W. Payne, eds. 1976. *Cognition and Social Behavior.* Hillsdale, NJ: Lawrence Erlbaum.

Chaiken, S., A. Liberman, and A. H. Eagly. 1989. Heuristic and systematic information processing within and beyond the persuasion context. In J. S. Uleman and J. A. Bargh, eds., *Unintended Thought.* New York: Guilford Press.

Clayton, B. 1984. *Forgotten Prophet: The Life of Randolph Bourne.* Baton Rouge, LA: Louisiana State University Press.

Colignon, R. A. 1989. Reification: The "holistic" and "individualistic" views of organizations. *Theory and Society* 18:83-123.

Corbin, A. 1994. *The Lure of the Sea.* Berkeley: University of California Press.

Couto, R. A. 1993. Narrative, free space, and political leadership in social movements. *Journal of Politics* 55:57-79.

Cvetkovich, G., and T. C. Earle. 1994. The construction of justice: A case study of public participation in land management. *Journal of Social Issues*, 50(3): 161-178.

_____. 1995. Forest summit convenes in Portland, Oregon. In *Great Events from History II: Ecology and the Environment.* Pasadena, CA: Salem Press.

Cvetkovich, G., and P. M. Wiedemann. 1988. Results of the working group "Trust and credibility in risk communication." In H. Jüngerman, R. E. Kasperson, and P. M. Wiedemann, eds., *Risk Communication: Proceedings of the International Workshop on Risk Communication.* Jülich, Germany: Kernforschungsanlage Jülich GmbH.

Dake, K. 1991. Orienting dispositions in the perception of risk: An analysis of contemporary worldviews and cultural biases. *Journal of Cross-Cultural Psychology* 22:61-82.

_____. 1992. Myths of nature: Culture and the social construction of risk. *Journal of Social Issues* 48(4):21-37.

Dasgupta, P. 1988. Trust as a commodity. In D. Gambetta, ed., *Trust: Making and Breaking Cooperative Relations.* Oxford: Basil Blackwell.

Dawes, R. M. 1988. *Rational Choice in an Uncertain World.* San Diego: Harcourt Brace Jovanovich.

_____. 1991. Social dilemmas, economic self-interest and evolutionary theory. In D. R. Brown and J. K. K. Smith, eds., *Frontiers of Mathematical Psychology.* New York: Springer-Verlag.

Dawes, R. M., A. J. C. van de Kragt, and J. M. Orbell. 1990. Cooperation for the benefit of us—not me, or my conscience. In J. Mansbridge, ed., *Beyond Self-Interest.* Chicago: University of Chicago Press.

Day, J. P. 1991. *Hope: A Philosophical Inquiry*. Helsinki: Philosophical Society of Finland.

DeKoven, M. 1992. "Why James Joyce was accepted and I was not": Modernist fiction and Gertrude Stein's narrative. *Studies in the Literary Imagination* 25(2):23-37.

De Munck, V. C. 1992. The fallacy of the misplaced self: Gender relations and the construction of multiple selves among Sri Lankan Muslims. *Ethos* 20:167-190.

Deutsch, M. 1973. *The Resolution of Conflict: Constructive and Destructive Processes*. New Haven: Yale University Press.

Dewey, J. 1929. *The Quest for Certainty: A Study of the Relation of Knowledge and Action*. New York: Minton, Balch & Company.

_____. [1920] 1948. *Reconstruction in Philosophy*. Enlarged edition. Boston: Beacon Press.

_____. [1939] 1963. *Freedom and Culture*. New York: Capricorn Books.

Dobbs, D. 1987. Reckless rationalism and heroic reverence in Homer's Odyssey. *American Political Science Review* 81:491-508.

Donohue, W. A. 1990. *The New Freedom*. New Brunswick, NJ: Transaction Publishers.

Douglas, M. 1975. *Implicit Meanings: Essays in Anthropology*. London: Routledge & Kegan Paul.

_____. 1982. Introduction to grid/group analysis. In M. Douglas, ed., *Essays in the Sociology of Perception*. London: Routledge & Kegan Paul.

_____. 1994. Anthropological approach to risk is fundamental. *Risk Newsletter*, 1st quarter.

Douglas, M., and M. Calvez. 1990. The self as risk taker: A cultural theory of contagion in relation to AIDS. *Social Research* 38:445-483.

Douglas, M., and A. Wildavsky. 1982. *Risk and Culture*. Berkeley: University of California Press.

Dryzek, J. S. 1987a. *Rational Ecology: Environment and Political Economy*. Oxford: Basil Blackwell.

_____. 1987b. Discursive designs: Critical theory and political institutions. *Journal of Political Science* 31:656-679.

Dunn, J. 1988. Trust and political agency. In D. Gambetta, ed., *Trust: Making and Breaking Cooperative Relations*. Oxford: Basil Blackwell.

Dykhuizen, G. 1973. *The Life and Mind of John Dewey*. Carbondale: Southern Illinois University Press.

Eagleton, T. 1991. *Ideology: An Introduction*. London: Verso.

Earle, T. C., and G. Cvetkovich. 1992a. Social trust based on cultural values. Report DM/RC 92-01. Bellingham, WA: Western Institute for Social and Organizational Research, Western Washington University.

_____. 1992b. The effects of problem context and complexity on social trust judgments. Report DM/RC 92-02. Bellingham, WA: Western Institute for Social and Organizational Research, Western Washington University.

_____. 1994. Risk communication: The social construction of meaning and trust. In N. Sahlin and B. Brehmer, eds., *Future Risks and Risk Management*. Amsterdam: Kluwer.

Earle, T. C., G. Cvetkovich, and P. Slovic. 1990. The effects of involvement, relevance and ability on risk communication effectiveness. In K. Borcherding, O. I. Larichev, and D. M. Messick, eds., *Contemporary Issues in Decision Making.* Amsterdam: Elsevier Science Publishers B. V. (North Holland).

Eckstein, H. 1988. A culturalist theory of political change. *American Political Science Review* 82:789-804.

Eisenstadt, S. N., and L. Roniger. 1984. *Patrons, Clients and Friends: Interpersonal Relations and the Structure of Trust in Society.* Cambridge: Cambridge University Press.

Elster, J. 1987. Introduction. In J. Elster, ed., *The Multiple Self.* New York: Cambridge University Press.

Ember, C. R., and M. Ember. 1992. Resource unpredictability, mistrust and war. *Journal of Conflict Resolution* 36:242-262.

Epictetus. 1920. *The Discourses of Epictetus; with the Encheiridion and Fragments.* Translated by G. Long. New York: Thomas Y. Crowell & Co.

Etzioni, A. 1968. Social-psychological aspects of international relations. In G. Lindzey and E. Aronson, eds., *The Handbook of Social Psychology: Second Edition.* Volume 1. Reading, MA: Addison-Wesley.

_____. 1989. Toward an I and we paradigm. *Contemporary Sociology* 18:171-176.

Evans, R. I. 1967. *Dialogue with Erik Erikson.* New York: Harper & Row.

Evans, S. M., and H. C. Boyte. 1986. *Free Spaces: The Sources of Democratic Change in America.* New York: Harper & Row.

Ewing, K. P. 1990. The illusion of wholeness: Culture, self, and the experience of inconsistency. *Ethos* 18:251-278.

Fenno, R. 1978. *Home Style: House Members in Their Districts.* Boston: Little, Brown.

Feyerabend, P. 1991. Atoms and consciousness. *Common Knowledge* 1(1):28-32.

_____. 1992. Nature as a work of art. *Common Knowledge* 1(3):3-9.

_____. 1993. Intellectuals and the facts of life. *Common Knowledge* 2(3):6-9.

Fiorino, D. J. 1990. Citizen participation and environmental risk: A survey of institutional mechanisms. *Science, Technology and Human Values* 15:226-243.

Fischhoff, B. 1991. Value elicitation: Is there anything there? *American Psychologist* 46:835-847.

Fischhoff, B., S. Lichtenstein, P. Slovic, S. Derby, and R. Keeney. 1981. *Acceptable Risk.* New York: Cambridge University Press.

Fish, S. 1980. *Is There a Text in This Class? The Authority of Interpretive Communities.* Cambridge, MA: Harvard University Press.

_____. 1994. *There's No Such Thing as Free Speech: And It's a Good Thing, Too.* New York: Oxford University Press.

Fisher, W. R. 1987. *Human Communication as Narration: Toward a Philosophy of Reason, Value, and Action.* Columbia, SC: University of South Carolina Press.

Fiske, A. P. 1991a. *Structures of Social Life: The Four Elementary Forms of Human Relations.* New York: Free Press.

_____. 1991b. The cultural relativity of selfish individualism: Anthropological evidence that humans are inherently sociable. In M. S. Clark, ed., *Prosocial Behavior*. Newbury Park, CA: Sage Publications.

_____. 1992. The four elementary forms of sociality: Framework for a unified theory of social relations. *Psychological Review* 99:689-723.

Fiske, S. T. 1993. Social cognition and social perception. *Annual Review of Psychology* 44:155-194.

Flanagan, O. 1991. *Varieties of Moral Personality: Ethics and Psychological Realism*. Cambridge, MA: Harvard University Press.

_____. 1992. *Consciousness Reconsidered*. Cambridge, MA: MIT Press, Bradford Books.

Flanagan, O., and A. O. Rorty, eds. 1990. *Identity, Character, and Morality: Essays in Moral Psychology*. Cambridge, MA: MIT Press, Bradford Books.

Flynn, J., W. Burns, C. K. Mertz, and P. Slovic. 1992. Trust as a determinant of opposition to a high-level radioactive waste repository: Analysis of a structural model. *Risk Analysis* 12:417-429.

Forester, J., ed. 1985. *Critical Theory and Public Life*. Cambridge, MA: MIT Press.

Foucault, M. 1983. Preface. In G. Deleuze and F. Guattari, *Anti-Oedipus: Capitalism and Schizophrenia*. Minneapolis: University of Minnesota Press.

_____. 1984. In P. Rabinow, ed., *The Foucault Reader*. New York: Pantheon Books.

Freud, S. 1930. *Civilization and Its Discontents*. New York: J. Cope and H. Smith.

Freudenburg, W. R. 1993. Risk and recreancy: Weber, the division of labor, and the rationality of risk perceptions. *Social Forces* 71:909-932.

Friedman, L. M. 1993. *Crime and Punishment in American History*. New York: Basic Books.

Galbraith, J. K. 1992. *The Culture of Contentment*. New York: Houghton Mifflin.

Gallant, T. W. 1991. *Risk and Survival in Ancient Greece: Reconstructing the Rural Domestic Economy*. Stanford, CA: Stanford University Press.

Gambetta, D. 1988. Mafia: The price of distrust; and Can we trust trust? In D. Gambetta, ed., *Trust: Making and Breaking Cooperative Relations*. Oxford: Basil Blackwell.

_____. 1993. *The Sicilian Mafia: The Business of Private Protection*. Cambridge, MA: Harvard University Press.

Garfinkel, H. 1967. *Studies in Ethnomethodology*. Englewood Cliffs, NJ: Prentice-Hall.

Geertz, C. 1993. "Ethnic conflict": Three alternative terms. *Common Knowledge* 2(3):54-65.

Gergen, K. J. 1989. Warranting voice and the elaboration of the self. In J. Shotter and K. J. Gergen, eds., *Texts of Identity*. London: Sage.

Gergen, K. J., and M. M. Gergen. 1986. Narrative form and the construction of psychological science. In T. R. Sarbin, ed., *Narrative Psychology: The Storied Nature of Human Conduct*. New York: Praeger.

_____. 1987. Narratives of relationship. In R. Burnett, P. McGhee, and D. Clarke, eds., *Accounting for Relationships: Explanation, Representation and Knowledge*. London: Methuen.

_____. 1988. Narrative and the self as relationship. In L. Berkowitz, ed., *Advances in Experimental Social Psychology* Volume 21. San Diego: Academic Press.

Giddens, A. 1990. *The Consequences of Modernity*. Stanford, CA: Stanford University Press.

Gigerenzer, G. 1991. From tools to theories: A heuristic of discovery in cognitive psychology. *Psychological Review* 98:254-267.

Gilligan, C. 1982. *In a Different Voice: Psychological Theory and Women's Development*. Cambridge, MA: Harvard University Press.

Gitlin, T., ed. 1986. *Watching Television*. New York: Pantheon.

Gittell, M. 1980. *Limits to Citizen Participation: The Decline of Community Organizations*. Beverly Hills, CA: Sage Publications.

Glendon, M. A. 1991. *Rights Talk: The Impoverishment of Political Discourse*. New York: Free Press.

Goffman, E. 1959. *The Presentation of Self in Everyday Life*. Garden City, NY: Doubleday.

Goldfarb, J. C. 1991. *The Cynical Society: The Culture of Politics and the Politics of Culture in American Life*. Chicago: University of Chicago Press.

Golding, D., S. Krimsky, and A. Plough. 1992. Evaluating risk communication: Narrative vs. technical presentation of information about radon. *Risk Analysis* 12(1):27-35.

Goldman, A. 1993. *Philosophical Applications of Cognitive Science*. Boulder, CO: Westview.

Grant, M. 1962. *Myths of the Greeks and Romans*. New York: New American Library.

Gregory, R., S. Lichtenstein, and P. Slovic. 1993. Valuing environmental resources: A constructive approach. *Journal of Risk and Uncertainty* 7:177-197.

Grimal, P. 1968. *Hellenism and the Rise of Rome*. New York: Delacorte Press.

Habermas, J. 1984. *Theory of Communicative Action*. Volume 1. Translated by Thomas McCarthy. Boston: Beacon.

_____. 1985. Questions and counterquestions. In R. J. Bernstein, ed., *Habermas and Modernity*. Cambridge, MA: MIT Press.

_____. 1987. *Theory of Communicative Action*. Volume 2. Translated by Thomas McCarthy. Boston: Beacon.

Hadas, M. 1965. Self-control: The Greek paradigm. In S. Z. Klausner, ed., *The Quest for Self-Control: Classical Philosophies and Scientific Research*. New York: Free Press.

Haidt, J., S. H. Koller, and M. G. Dias. 1993. Affect, culture, and morality, or Is it wrong to eat your dog? *Journal of Personality and Social Psychology* 65: 613-628.

Hammond, K. R. 1986. Generalization in operational contexts: What does it mean? Can it be done? *IEEE Transactions on Systems, Man, and Cybernetics* 16:428-433.

Hammond, K. R., R. Hamm, and J. Grassia. 1986. Generalizing over conditions by combining the multitrait-multimethod matrix and the representative design of experiments. *Psychological Bulletin* 100:257-269.

Hardin, R. 1992. The street-level epistemology of trust. *Politics and Society* 21:505-529.

Hardwig, J. 1991. The role of trust in knowledge. *Journal of Philosophy* 88:693-708.

Harré, R. 1990. Some narrative conventions of scientific discourse. In C. Nash, ed., *Narrative in Culture: The Uses of Storytelling in the Sciences, Philosophy, and Literature*. London: Routledge.

Hart, V. 1978. *Distrust and Democracy: Political Distrust in Britain and America*. Cambridge: Cambridge University Press.

Haslan, N., and A.P. Fiske. 1992. Implicit relationship prototypes: Investigating five theories of the cognitive organization of social relationships. *Journal of Experimental Social Psychology* 28: 441-474.

Hastorf, A., and H. Cantril. 1954. They saw a game: A case study. *Journal of Abnormal and Social Psychology* 49:129-134.

Hector, M. 1992. Should values be written out of the social science lexicon? *Sociological Theory* 10:214-230.

Heifetz, R. A., and R. M. Sinder. 1988. Political leadership: Managing the public's problem solving. In R. B. Reich, ed., *The Power of Public Ideas*. Cambridge, MA: Ballinger Publishing Company.

Held, V. 1984. *Rights and Goods: Justifying Social Action*. New York: Free Press.

Hermans, J. M., H. J. G. Kempen, and R. J. P. van Loon. 1992. The dialogical self: Beyond individualism and rationalism. *American Psychologist* 47:23-33.

Hertzberg, L. 1988. On the attitude of trust. *Inquiry* 31:307-322.

Hesiod. 1959. *Works and Days*. Translated by R. Lattimore. Ann Arbor: University of Michigan Press.

Hilgard, E. R. 1977. *Divided Consciousness: Multiple Controls in Human Thought and Action*. New York: John Wiley & Sons.

Hodder, I. 1993. The narrative and rhetoric of material culture sequences. *World Archaeology* 25:268-282.

Hollan, D. 1992. Cross-cultural differences in the self. *Journal of Anthropological Research* 48:283-300.

Hollinger, D. A. 1985. *In the American Province: Studies in the History and Historiography of Ideas*. Bloomington: Indiana University Press.

_____. 1992. Postethnic America. *Contention* 2(1):79-96.

Hollinger, R., ed. 1985. *Hermeneutics and Praxis*. Notre Dame, Indiana: University of Notre Dame Press.

Holub, R. C. 1991. *Jürgen Habermas: Critic in the Public Sphere*. London: Routledge.

Hovland, C. I., I. L. Janis, and H. H. Kelley. 1953. *Communication and Persuasion: Psychological Studies of Opinion Change*. New Haven: Yale University Press.

Howard, G. S. 1991. A narrative approach to thinking, cross-cultural psychology and psychotherapy. *American Psychologist* 46: 187-197.

Hudson, W. 1982. *The Marxist Philosophy of Ernst Bloch*. New York: St. Martin's Press.

Hughes, R. 1993. *Culture of Complaint: The Fraying of America*. New York: Oxford University Press, New York Public Library.

Hull, C. 1943. *Principles of Behavior*. New York: Appleton-Century.

Hume, D. [1740] 1969. *A Treatise of Human Nature.* Harmandsworth, Middlesex: Penguin Books.

Hurwitz, J., and M. Peffley. 1987. How are foreign policy attitudes structured? A hierarchical model. *American Political Science Review* 81:1099-1120.

Ignatieff, M. 1993. *Blood and Belonging.* New York: Farrar, Straus and Giroux.

Inglehart, R. 1988. The renaissance of political culture. *American Political Science Review* 82:1203-1230.

_____. 1990. *Culture Shift in Advanced Industrial Society.* Princeton: Princeton University Press.

Jackman, R. W. 1987. Political institutions and voter turnout in the industrial democracies. *American Political Science Review* 81:405-423.

Jasanoff, S. 1990. American exceptionalism and the political acknowledgment of risk. *Daedalus* 119(4):61-82.

_____. 1991. Acceptable evidence in a pluralistic society. In D. G. Mayo and R. D. Hollander, eds., *Acceptable Evidence: Science and Values in Risk Management.* New York: Oxford University Press.

Jöreskog, K. G., and D. Sörbom. 1989. *LISREL 7: A Guide to the Program and Applications.* 2nd. edition. Chicago: SPSS.

Kagan, R. A. 1991. Adversarial legalism and American government. *Journal of Policy Analysis and Management* 10:369-406.

Kahneman, D., P. Slovic, and A. Tversky, eds. 1982. *Judgment Under Uncertainty: Heuristics and Biases.* New York: Cambridge University Press.

Kasperson, R. E., D. Golding, and S. Tuler. 1992. Siting hazardous facilities and communicating risks under conditions of high social distrust. *Journal of Social Issues* 48(4):161-187.

Kathlene, L., and J. A. Martin. 1991. Enhancing citizen participation: Panel designs, perspectives and policy formation. *Journal of Policy Analysis and Management* 10:46-63.

Katz, J. 1988. *Seductions of Crime: Moral and Sensual Attractions in Doing Evil.* NewYork: Basic Books.

Kazin, A. 1942. *On Native Grounds: An Interpretation of Modern American Prose Literature.* New York: Harcourt, Brace & World.

Kelman, S. 1981. *Regulating America, Regulating Sweden: A Comparative Study of Occupational Safety and Health Policy.* Cambridge, MA: MIT Press.

_____. 1992. Adversary and cooperationist institutions for conflict resolution in public policymaking. *Journal of Policy Analysis and Management* 11:178-206.

Kirkwood, W. G. 1992. Narrative and the rhetoric of possibility. *Communication Monographs* 59 (March):30-47.

Kluft, R. P., ed. 1985. *Childhood Antecedents of Multiple Personality.* Washington, D.C.: American Psychiatric Press.

Knox, B., ed. 1993. *The Norton Book of Classical Literature.* New York: W. W. Norton & Company.

Kohlberg, L. 1984. *Essays on Moral Development.* Volume 2: *The Psychology of Moral Development.* New York: Harper & Row.

Kondo, T. 1990. Some notes on rational behavior, normative behavior, moral behavior and cooperation. *Journal of Conflict Resolution* 34:495-530.

Kraft, M. 1988. Analyzing technological risks in federal regulatory agencies. In M. E. Kraft and N. J. Vig, eds., *Technology and Politics*. Durham, NC: Duke University Press.

Kraft, M. and B. B. Clary. 1991. Citizen participation and the NIMBY syndrome: Public response to radioactive waste disposal. *Western Political Quarterly* 44:299-328.

Kuhlmann, A. 1986. *Introduction to Safety Science*. New York: Springer-Verlag.

Kuklinski, J. H., E. Riggle, V. Ottati, N. Schwarz, and R. S. Wyer, Jr. 1991. The cognitive and affective bases of political tolerance judgments. *American Journal of Political Science* 35:1-27.

Landy, M. K., M. J. Roberts, and S. R. Thomas. 1990. *The Environmental Protection Agency: Asking the Wrong Questions*. New York: Oxford University Press.

Langton, S., ed. 1978. *Citizen Participation in America*. Lexington, MA: Lexington Books.

Laski, H. J. [1936] 1962. *The Rise of European Liberalism: An Essay in Interpretation*. London: George Allen & Unwin Ltd, Unwin Books.

Latour, B. 1987. *Science in Action*. Cambridge, MA: Harvard University Press.

Latour, B., and S. Woolgar. 1979. *Laboratory Life*. Princeton, NJ: Princeton University Press.

Lazarus, R. J. 1991. The tragedy of distrust in the implementation of federal environmental law. *Law and Contemporary Problems* 54:311-374.

Leitch, T. M. 1986. *What Stories Are: Narrative Theory and Interpretation*. University Park, PA: Pennsylvania State University Press.

Lewin, K. 1948. *Resolving Social Conflicts: Selected Papers on Group Dynamics*. Edited by G. W. Lewin. New York: Harper & Brothers.

_____. 1951. *Field Theory in Social Science: Selected Theoretical Papers*. Edited by D. Cartwright. New York: Harper & Brothers.

Lewis, J. D., and A. Weigert. 1985. Trust as a social reality. *Social Forces* 63:967-985.

Lindblom, C. E. 1990. *Inquiry and Change: The Troubled Attempt to Understand and Shape Society*. New Haven: Yale University Press.

Lindblom, C. E., and D. K. Cohen. 1979. *Usable knowledge*. New Haven: Yale University Press.

Lipset, S. M., and W. Schneider. 1983. *The Confidence Gap: Business, Labor, and Government in the Public Mind*. New York: Free Press.

Luhmann, N. 1979. *Trust and Power*. Chichester: John Wiley & Sons.

_____. 1984. *Religious Dogmatics and the Evolution of Societies*. Translated by P. Beyer. Chicago: University of Chicago Press.

_____. 1988. Familiarity, confidence, trust: Problems and alternatives. In D. Gambetta, ed., *Trust: Making and Breaking Cooperative Relations*. Oxford: Basil Blackwell.

_____. 1989. *Ecological Communication*. Translated by J. Bednarz, Jr. Chicago: University of Chicago Press.

_____. 1990. *Essays on Self-Reference*. New York: Columbia University Press.

_____. 1993. *Risk: A Sociological Theory*. Translated by R. Barrett. New York: Aldine de Gruyter.

MacIntyre, A. 1981. *After Virtue*. Notre Dame, Indiana: University of Notre Dame Press.

_____. 1988. *Whose Justice? Which Rationality?* Notre Dame, IN: University of Notre Dame Press.

Maines, D. R. 1993. Narrative's moment and sociology's phenomena: Toward a narrative sociology. *Sociological Quarterly* 34:17-38.

Maines, D. R., and J. C. Bridger. 1992. Narratives, community and land use decisions. *Social Science Journal* 29:363-380.

Malcom, N. 1988. Wittgenstein's "scepticism" in *On Certainty*. *Inquiry* 31:277-293.

Mansbridge, J. J. 1980. *Beyond Adversary Democracy*. New York: Basic Books.

Markus, H. R., and S. Kitayama. 1991. Culture and the self: Implications for cognition, emotion and motivation. *Psychological Review* 98:224-253.

Massing, M. 1993. Sharing room 101. *The New Yorker*, 15 November, 118-126.

McGarity, T. O. 1986. Risk and trust: The role of regulatory agencies. *Environmental Law Reporter* 16:10198-10229.

McKibben, B. 1992. Reflections: What's on? *The New Yorker*, 9 March, 40-80.

Medin, D. L., R. L. Goldstone, and D. Gentner. 1993. Respects for similarity. *Psychological Review* 100:254-278.

Merelman, R. M. 1984. *Making Something of Ourselves: On Culture and Politics in the United States*. Berkeley: University of California Press.

Meyrowitz, J. 1985. *No Sense of Place: The Impact of Electronic Media on Social Behavior*. New York: Oxford University Press.

Michotte, A. [1946] 1963. *The Perception of Causality*. Translated by T. R. Miles and E. Miles. New York: Basic Books.

Miller, J. 1994. *The Passion of Michel Foucault*. New York: Doubleday, Anchor Books.

Minow, M., and E. V. Spelman. 1990. In context. *Southern California Law Review* 63:1597-1652.

Misra, G. and K.J. Gergen. 1993. On the place of culture in psychological science. *International Journal of Psychology* 28(2): 225-243.

Mitchell, J. V. 1992. Perception of risk and credibility at toxic sites. *Risk Analysis* 12:19-26.

Mitchell, T. R., and L. R. Beach. 1990. ". . . Do I love thee? Let me count . . ." Toward an understanding of intuitive and automatic decision making. *Organizational Behavior and Human Decision Processes* 47:1-20.

Monk, R. 1990. *Ludwig Wittgenstein: The Duty of Genius*. New York: Free Press.

Moon, J. D. 1993. *Constructing Community: Moral Pluralism and Tragic Conflicts*. Princeton, NJ: Princeton University Press.

Murray, D. W. 1993. What is the Western concept of the self? On forgetting David Hume. *Ethos* 21:3-23.

National Academy of Sciences. 1983. *Risk Assessment in the Federal Government: Managing the Process*. Washington, D. C.: National Academy Press.

Nehamas, A. 1990. A touch of the poet. *Raritan* 10:104-125.

Nelkin, D. 1977. *Technological Decisions and Democracy: European Experiments in Public Participation*. Beverly Hills, CA: Sage Publications.

Nelson, J. S., A. Megill, and D. N. McCloskey, eds. 1987. *The Rhetoric of the Human Sciences: Language and Argument in Scholarship and Public Affairs*. Madison, WI: University of Wisconsin Press.

Neuberg, S. L., and J. T. Newsom. 1993. Personal need for structure: Individual differences in the desire for simple structure. *Journal of Personality and Social Psychology* 65:113-131.

Nisbett, R. E., and L. Ross. 1980. *Human Inference: Strategies and Shortcomings of Social Judgment*. Englewood Cliffs, NJ: Prentice-Hall.

Nozick, R. 1993. *The Nature of Rationality*. Princeton, NJ: Princeton University Press.

Nussbaum, M. 1986. *The Fragility of Goodness: Luck and Ethics in Greek Tragedy and Philosophy*. Cambridge: Cambridge University Press.

_____. 1990. *Love's Knowledge: Essays on Philosophy and Literature*. New York: Oxford University Press.

_____. 1992. Human functioning and social justice: In defense of Aristotelian essentialism. *Political Theory* 20:202-246.

O'Riordan, T. 1991. Towards a vernacular science of environmental change. In L. Roberts and A. Weale, eds., *Innovation and Environmental Risk*. London: Belhaven Press.

Ottati, V. C., and R. S. Wyer, Jr. 1990. The cognitive mediators of political choice: Toward a comprehensive model of political information processing. In J. A. Ferejohn and J. H. Kuklinski, eds., *Information and Democratic Processes*. Urbana and Chicago: University of Illinois Press.

Pagden, A. 1988. The destruction of trust and its economic consequences in the case of eighteenth-century Naples. In D. Gambetta, ed., *Trust: Making and Breaking Cooperative Relations*. Oxford: Basil Blackwell.

Parker, S. L., and G. R. Parker. 1993. Why do we trust our congressman? *Journal of Politics* 55:442-453.

Parsons, T. 1970. Research with human subjects and the "professional complex." In P. Freund, ed., *Experimentation with Human Subjects*. New York: Braziller.

Payne, J. W., F. R. Bettman, and E. J. Johnson. 1992. Behavioral decision research: A constructive processing perspective. *Annual Review of Psychology* 43:87-131.

Pennington, N., and R. Hastie. 1986. Evidence evaluation in complex decision making. *Journal of Personality and Social Psychology* 51:242-258.

_____. 1988. Explanation-based decision making: Effects of memory structure on judgment. *Journal of Experimental Psychology: Learning, Memory, and Cognition* 14:521-533.

_____. 1990. Practical implications of psychological research on juror and jury decision making. *Personality and Social Psychology Bulletin* 16(1):90-105.

_____. 1992. Explaining the evidence: Tests of the story model for juror decision making. *Journal of Personality and Social Psychology* 62:189-206.

Perrow, C. 1984. *Normal Accidents: Living with High-Risk Technologies*. New York: Basic Books.

Petty, R. E., and J. T. Cacioppo. 1986. The elaboration likelihood model of persuasion. In L. Berkowitz, ed., *Advances in Experimental Social Psychology* Volume 19. New York: Academic Press.

Pfaff, W. 1992. Editorial column. *San Francisco Chronicle*, 16 April, A28.

Piaget, J. 1965. *The Moral Judgment of the Child*. Translated by M. Gabain. New York: Free Press.

Polkinghorne, D. E. 1988. *Narrative Knowing and the Human Sciences*. Albany, NY: State University of New York Press.

Pratt, D. D. 1991. Conceptions of self within China and the United States: Contrasting foundations for adult education. *International Journal of Intercultural Relations* 15:285-310.

Priest, G. 1990. The new legal structure of risk control. *Daedalus* 119(4):207-227.

Putnam, H. 1990. A reconsideration of Deweyan democracy. *Southern California Law Review* 63:1671-1697; 1914-1916.

Quen, J. M. 1986. *Split Minds/Split Brains: Historical and Current Perspectives*. New York: New York University Press.

Radin, M. J. 1990. The pragmatist and the feminist. *Southern California Law Review* 63:1699-1726.

Reason, J. 1990. *Human Error*. Cambridge: Cambridge University Press.

Reich, R. B. 1988. Introduction. In R. B. Reich, ed., *The Power of Public Ideas*. Cambridge, MA: Ballinger Publishing Company.

Renn, O., and D. Levine. 1991. Credibility and trust in risk communication. In R. E. Kasperson and P. M. Stallen, eds., *Communicating Risks to the Public: International Perspectives*. Amsterdam: Kluwer.

Ricoeur, P. 1984. *Time and Narrative*. Volume 1. Translated by K. McLaughlin and D. Pellauer. Chicago: University of Chicago Press.

Rodriguez, R. 1992. *Days of Obligation: An Argument with My Mexican Father*. New York: Viking.

Rorty, A. O. 1990. Varieties of pluralism in a polyphonic society. *Review of Metaphysics* 44:3-20.

Rorty, R. 1979. Philosophy and Mirror of Nature. Princeton, NJ: Princeton University Press.

_____. 1982. *Consequences of Pragmatism*. Minneapolis: University of Minnesota Press.

_____. 1985. Postmodernist bourgeois liberalism. In R. Hollinger, ed., *Hermeneutics and Praxis*. Notre Dame, Indiana: University of Notre Dame Press.

_____. 1989. *Contingency, Irony and Solidarity*. Cambridge: Cambridge University Press.

_____. 1991a. *Objectivity, Relativism and Truth: Philosophical Papers*, Volume 1. Cambridge: Cambridge University Press.

_____. 1991b. Feminism and pragmatism. *Michigan Quarterly Review* 30:231-258.

_____. 1991c. *Essays on Heidegger and Others: Philosophical Papers*, Volume 2. Cambridge: Cambridge University Press.

_____. 1992a. Trotsky and the wild orchids. *Common Knowledge* 1(3):140-153.

_____. 1992b. Love and money. *Common Knowledge* 1(1):12-16.

_____. 1994. Religion as conversation-stopper. *Common Knowledge* 3(1):1-6.

Rosenberg, S. W. 1988. The structure of political thinking. *American Journal of Political Science* 32:539-566.

Ross, L., and R. E. Nisbett. 1991. *The Person and the Situation: Perspectives of Social Psychology*. New York: McGraw-Hill, Inc.

Rouse, J. 1987. *Knowledge and Power: Toward a Political Philosophy of Science*. Ithaca, NY: Cornell University Press.

_____. 1990. The narrative reconstruction of science. *Inquiry* 33:179-196.

Sacks, O. 1993. An anthropologist on Mars. *The New Yorker*. 27 December, 106-125.

Said, E. W. 1994. Gods that always fail. *Raritan* 13(4):1-14.

Samson, E. E. 1993. Identity politics: Challenges to psychology's understanding. *American Psychologist* 48:1219-1230.

Sandel, M. J. 1982. *Liberalism and the Limits of Justice*. Cambridge: Cambridge University Press.

Sarbin, T.R. 1943. The concept of role taking. *Sociometry* 6: 273-284.

_____. 1954. Role theory. In G. Lindzey, ed., *Handbook of Social Psychology*. Cambridge, MA: Addison-Wesley.

_____. 1986. The narrative as a root metaphor for psychology. In T. R. Sarbin, ed., *Narrative Psychology: The Storied Nature of Human Conduct*. New York: Praeger.

Saxonhouse, A. W. 1988. The tyranny of reason in the world of the polis. *American Political Science Review* 82:1261-1275.

Schlesinger, A. M. 1992. *The Disuniting of America: Reflections on a Multicultural Society*. New York: Norton.

Schwartz, B. 1986. *The Battle for Human Nature: Science, Morality and Modern Life*. New York: Norton.

Sears, D. O., and C. L. Funk. 1991. The role of self-interest in social and political attitudes. In M. P. Zanna, ed., *Advances in Experimental Social Psychology* Volume 24. New York: Academic Press.

Seligman, M. E. P. 1991. *Learned Optimism*. New York: Knopf.

Serres, M. 1982. *The Parasite*. Translated by L. R. Schehr. Baltimore: Johns Hopkins University Press.

_____. 1989a. Literature and the exact sciences. Translated by R. Lapidus. *SubStance* 59:3-34.

_____. 1989b. *Detachment*. Translated by G. James and R. Federman. Athens, OH: Ohio University Press.

_____. 1991. *Rome: The Book of Foundations*. Translated by F. McCarren. Stanford, CA: Stanford University Press.

_____. 1992. The natural contract. Translated by F. McCarren. *Critical Inquiry* 19:1-21.

_____. 1993. Anaximander: A founding name in history. Translated by R. Lapidus. *SubStance* 71/72:266-273.

Sethi, S., and M. E. P. Seligman. 1993. Optimism and fundamentalism. *Psychological Science* 4:256-259.

Shapiro, S. P. 1987. The social control of impersonal trust. *American Journal of Sociology* 93:623-658.

Sherman, S. J., C. M. Judd, and B. Park. 1989. Social cognition. *Annual Review of Psychology* 40:281-326.

Shotter, J. 1991. Wittgenstein and psychology: On our "hook up" to reality. *Philosophy Supplement*. 28:193-208.

Shweder, R. A. 1991. *Thinking Through Cultures: Expeditions in Cultural Psychology*. Cambridge, MA: Harvard University Press.

Shweder, R. A., and J. Haidt. 1993. The future of moral psychology: Truth, intuition, and the pluralist way. *Psychological Science* 4:360-365.

Shweder, R. A., and R. A. LeVine, eds. 1984. *Culture Theory: Essays on Mind, Self, and Emotion*. Cambridge: Cambridge University Press.

Shweder, R. A., and M. A. Sullivan. 1993. Cultural psychology: Who needs it? *Annual Review of Psychology* 44:497-523.

Silver, A. 1985. "Trust" in social and political theory. In G. D. Suttles and M. N. Zald, eds., *The Challenge of Social Control: Citizenship and Institution Building in Modern Society*. Norwood, NJ: Ablex Publishing Corporation.

Simon, H. A. 1957. *Models of Man*. New York: Wiley.

Slovic, P. 1993. Perceived risk, trust, and democracy. *Risk Analysis* 13:675-682.

Slovic, P., B. Fischhoff, and S. Lichtenstein. 1982. Facts versus fears: Understanding perceived risk. In D. Kahneman, P. Slovic, and A. Tversky, eds., *Judgment Under Uncertainty: Heuristics and Biases*. Cambridge: Cambridge University Press.

Smith, J. A. 1980. *American Presidential Elections: Trust and the Rational Voter*. New York: Praeger.

Sperber, D., and D. Wilson. 1986. *Relevance: Communication and Cognition*. Cambridge, MA: Harvard University Press.

Spiro, M. E. 1993. Is the Western conception of the self "peculiar" within the context of the world cultures? *Ethos* 21:107-153.

Stick, J. 1986. Can nihilism be pragmatic? *Harvard Law Review* 100: 332-401.

Stigler, J. W., R. A. Shweder, and G. Herdt, eds. 1990. *Cultural Psychology: Essays on Comparative Human Development*. Cambridge: Cambridge University Press.

Stotland, E. 1969. *The Psychology of Hope*. San Francisco: Jossey-Bass.

Tappan, M. B., and L. M. Brown. 1989. Stories told and lessons learned: Toward a narrative approach to moral development and moral education. *Harvard Educational Review* 59:182-205.

Tappan, M. B., and M. J. Packer, eds. 1991. *Narrative and Storytelling: Implications for Understanding Moral Development*. New Directions for Child Development, no. 54. San Francisco: Jossey-Bass.

Taylor, C. 1991. The dialogical self. In D. R. Hiley, J. F. Bohman, and R. Shusterman, eds., *The Interpretive Turn: Philosophy, Science, Culture*. Ithaca, NY: Cornell University Press.

Taylor, S., and J. Brown. 1988. Illusion and well-being: A social psychological perspective on mental health. *Psychological Bulletin* 103:193-210.

Thompson M. 1988. Socially viable ideas of nature: a cultural hypothesis. In E. Baark and U. Svedin, eds., *Man, Nature and Technology: Essays on the Role of Ideological Perceptions*. New York: St. Martin's Press.

Tiger, L. 1979. *Optimism: The Biology of Hope*. New York: Simon and Schuster.

Tonkin, E. 1992. *Narrating Our Pasts: The Social Construction of Oral History*. Cambridge: Cambridge University Press.

Trafimow, D., H. C. Triandis, and S. G. Goto. 1991. Some tests of the distinction between the private self and the collective self. *Journal of Personality and Social Psychology* 60:649-655.

Triandis, H. C. 1990. Cross-cultural studies of individualism and collectivism. In J. Berman, ed., *Nebraska Symposium on Motivation, 1989*. Lincoln, University of Nebraska Press.

Trillin, C. 1994. Messages from my father. *The New Yorker*, 20 June, 56-78.

Tversky, A., and D. Kahneman. 1974. Judgment under uncertainty: Heuristics and biases. *Science* 85:1124-1131.

Tyler, T., and R. M. Dawes. 1991. Fairness in groups: Comparing the self-interest and social-identity perspectives. In B. Mellers, ed., *Distributive Justice*. Cambridge: Cambridge University Press.

Ungar, S. 1992. The rise and (relative) decline of global warming as a social problem. *Sociological Quarterly* 33:483-501.

U.S. Department of Energy. 1993. *Earning Public Trust and Confidence: Requisites for Managing Radioactive Waste*. Final report of the Secretary of Energy Advisory Board Task Force on Radioactive Waste Management. Washington, D.C.

Vanderford, M. L., D. H. Smith, and W. S. Harris. 1992. Value identification in narrative discourse: Evaluation of an HIV education demonstration project. *Journal of Applied Communication Research*, May, 123-160.

Verma, R. 1986. Winners and losers: A study of *Macbeth* and *Antony and Cleopatra*. *Modern Language Review* 81:838-852.

Veyne, P. 1988. *Did the Greeks Believe in Their Myths?* Translated by P. Wissing. Chicago: University of Chicago Press.

_____. 1990. *Bread and Circuses: Historical Sociology and Political Pluralism*. Translated by B. Pearce. London: Penguin Press, Allen Lane.

Voltaire. [1759] 1966. *Candide: Or Optimism*. Translated by R. M. Adams. New York: W. W. Norton.

Waldrop, M. M. 1992. *Complexity: The Emerging Science at the Edge of Order and Chaos*. New York: Simon and Schuster.

Walzer, M. 1990. The communitarian critique of liberalism. *Political Theory* 18(1):6-23.

Warren M. 1990. Ideology and the self. *Theory and Society* 19:599-634.

West, C. 1989. *The American Evasion of Philosophy: A Genealogy of Pragmatism*. Madison: University of Wisconsin Press, 1989.

Westbrook, R. B. 1991. *John Dewey and American Democracy*. Ithaca, NY: Cornell University Press.

White, H. 1973. *The Historical Imagination in Nineteenth-Century Europe*. Baltimore: Johns Hopkins University Press.

_____. 1978. *Tropics of Discourse: Essays in Cultural Criticism*. Baltimore: Johns Hopkins University Press.

_____. 1987. *The Content of the Form: Narrative Discourse and Historical Representation*. Baltimore: Johns Hopkins University Press.

Wildavsky, A. 1979. Speaking Truth to Power. Boston: Little, Brown.

_____. 1987. Choosing preferences by constructing institutions: A cultural theory of preference formation. *American Political Science Review* 81:3-21.

_____. 1988. *Searching for Safety*. New Brunswick, NJ: Transaction Books.

Will, F. L. 1985. Reason, social practice and scientific realism. In R. Hollinger, ed., *Hermeneutics and Praxis*. Notre Dame, Indiana: University of Notre Dame Press.

Williams, B. 1988. Formal structures and social reality. In D. Gambetta, ed., *Trust: Making and Breaking Cooperative Relations*. Oxford: Basil Blackwell.

Williams, R. N. 1992. The human context of agency. *American Psychologist* 47:752-760.

Williams, R., and T. Eagleton. 1989. The politics of hope: An interview. In T. Eagleton, ed., *Raymond Williams: Critical Perspectives*. Boston: Northeastern University Press.

Winch, P. 1991. Certainty and authority. *Philosophy Supplement* 28:223-237.

Witherell, C., and N. Noddings, eds. 1991. *Stories Lives Tell: Narrative and Dialogue in Education*. New York: Teachers College Press.

Wittgenstein, L. 1968. *Philosophical Investigations*. Translated by G. E. M. Anscombe. Oxford: Basil Blackwell.

_____. 1969. *On Certainty*. Edited by G. E. M. Anscombe and G. H. von Wright. Translated by D. Paul and G. E. M. Anscombe. New York: J. & J. Harper Editions.

_____. 1980. *Remarks on the Philosophy of Psychology*. Volume 2. Edited by G. H. von Wright and H. Nyman. Translated by C. G. Luckhardt and M. A. E. Aue. Chicago: University of Chicago Press.

Wolfe, J. D. 1988. Varieties of participatory democracy and democratic theory. *Political Science Reviewer* 16:1-38.

Wyer, R. S., and S. E. Gordon. 1984. The cognitive representation of social information. In R. S. Wyer and T. K. Srull, eds., *Handbook of Social Cognition*, Volume 2. Hillsdale, NJ: Lawrence Erlbaum

Wyer, R. S., and T. K. Srull. 1986. Human cognition in its social context. *Psychological Review* 93:322-359.

_____. 1989. *Memory and Cognition in its Social Context*. Hillsdale, NJ: Lawrence Erlbaum.

Zaller, J. R. 1992. *The Nature and Origins of Mass Opinion*. Cambridge: Cambridge University Press.

Index

About the Authors

TIMOTHY C. EARLE is research associate with the Western Institute for Social and Organizational Research in the Department of Psychology at Western Washington University in Bellingham.

GEORGE T. CVETKOVICH holds positions with the Department of Psychology and with the Western Institute for Social and Organizational Research at Western Washington University in Bellingham. He is the editor (with C. Vlek) of *Social Decision Methodology for Technological Projects* (1989).

ISBN 0-275-94845-5

9 780275 948450

HARDCOVER BAR CODE